Navy Board Ship Models

Navy Board Ship Models

Nick Ball and Simon Stephens

Naval Institute Press
Annapolis, Maryland

First published in Great Britain in 2018 by
Seaforth Publishing,
A division of Pen & Sword Books Ltd,
47 Church Street,
Barnsley S70 2AS

www.seaforthpublishing.com

Published and distributed in the
United States of America and Canada by the
Naval Institute Press,
291 Wood Road, Annapolis,
Maryland 21402-5034

www.nip.org

Library of Congress Control Number: 2018947661

ISBN 978 1 68247 374 0

Published in association with Royal Museums Greenwich, the group name for the National Maritime Museum, *Cutty Sark*, the Royal Observatory, and the Queen's House. www.rmg.co.uk

Typeset and designed by David Rose

Printed and bound in India

HALF TITLE PAGE
Yacht, 8 guns, see page 104.

TITLE PAGE
Equestrian figurehead, SLR0372.

Contents

Foreword

The ship model collection at Royal Museums Greenwich is the largest publicly owned one in the world, totalling over 4,500 models. Foremost amongst them is the highly prized collection of fifty-four 'Navy Board models' dating from the 1650s through to 1775. These rare and exquisite models have held a fascination for generations, with notable collectors including Samuel Pepys, Charles II and George III. Viewed with the Museum's outstanding collections of ship plans, plus the drawings and paintings by the Dutch marine artists, the Van de Veldes, the Museum's ship models provide unrivalled insight into many aspects of the seventeenth- and eighteenth-century British Navy. The Museum is indebted to our founding benefactor, Sir James Caird who, together with fellow Trustee and collector Dr R.C. Anderson, was instrumental in acquiring these models for the nation during the Museum's formative years. Even in today's digital age, these amazing objects still intrigue people of all ages; the detail and quality of the craftsmanship, considering the limited tools and materials to hand at the time they were made, hold a particular fascination.

I well remember venturing into the world of plastic kit models as a young boy and managed (very inexpertly) to produce the Airfix versions of the *Golden Hind*, *Endeavour* and the *Sovereign of the Seas*. For my fumbling fingers the painting stage was particularly challenging but I still found it a great way to understand the hull design and the complexities of the sailing rig. To this day, I have a small collection of models, amongst which I especially enjoy a splendid submarine made from Meccano, which sits on the windowsill in my office.

It was very pleasing for me that the Museum, in partnership with Chatham Historic Dockyard Trust and the Imperial War Museum, in 2010 succeeded in building a new state-of-the-art storage facility, ship model gallery and research room at the historic dockyard in Chatham. Known as No.1 Smithery, this facility provides a more public-facing approach to access our models off display. In addition, most of our models can be viewed online as well.

The Museum has possessed great expertise in the field of ship models for many years and I congratulate our curators Simon Stephens and Nick Ball for their vision and hard work in producing this illuminating study. I would also like to thank David Thomson, for his generosity in supporting Nick to further his career.

Dr Kevin Fewster AM
Director, Royal Museums Greenwich

Introduction

Ship models have been made in Britain since at least the sixteenth century. The oldest surviving model is likely to be the 'Tradescant' in the Ashmolean Museum, Oxford, thought to date from the early seventeenth century.[1] Ship models were made for a number of reasons, whether religious, commemorative or decorative. Simple 'votive' models, made to hang in churches, have been known across Europe since medieval times.

Votive model of an armed Dutch East Indiaman with 'Anno 1657' carved into the stern decoration. These 'votive' models were made to remind the congregation where their prosperity came from and of the dangers faced by seafarers. By comparison to Navy Board models, votive models are much less detailed and were not made to a specific scale. (SLR0365)

It was not until the mid-seventeenth century that the first truly accurate scale ship models appeared in Britain. Unlike the models of the previous century, which were crudely carved from a solid piece of wood, these new models were made with a hull constructed of individual frames that was left partly unplanked to show aspects of the internal construction. They are quite unlike the ship models of any other country. French and Spanish models can be equally as decorative, but do not have the same style of open frame. Danish models are larger, less decorative models that were directly related to shipbuilding. Dutch models have an idiosyncratic style that shares aspects of the votive model tradition.

Representing ships of the Royal Navy, British models from this period have since become known as 'Navy Board ship models' after the board that administered naval shipbuilding under the governing body of the Admiralty. They have also been known as 'Admiralty' models or 'Dockyard' models. The name for these open-framed models comes from the belief that they were made for the Navy Board, so that its members could scrutinise the design before they approved the building of the ship at full scale. This idea was popularised in John Seymour Lucas's nineteenth-century painting *A New Whip for the Dutch*, which shows an imagined scene at the seventeenth-century Navy Office.

Historians of the early twentieth century generally assumed that Navy Board models were used in this way, and they were defined in 1925 as 'models made by the people employed in the actual service of the Navy, whether at head-quarters or in the dockyards'.[2]

The earliest Navy Board model in the National Maritime Museum, thought to date from around 1650. (SLR0217)

However, this definition implies that they had some official status, whereas one of the questions surrounding the Navy Board ship models today is the extent to which they were actually associated with the Navy Board at all. The term 'Navy Board ship model' is a modern invention; no reference to the name has been found from the period. This lack of evidence for their original use has led modern research to define Navy Board models based on their style: the unplanked open-framed ship models of the seventeenth to eighteenth centuries.

In the introduction to the *Catalogue of Caird Collection of Old Ship Models* (published in 1930), Geoffrey Callender, the first Director of the National Maritime Museum, wrote:

> Once a model of this kind had received the seal of Royal approval, nothing more was necessary than to multiply every measurement by some such figure as 48 or 54, and the result was a *Royal Prince* or a *Sovereign of the Seas*.[3]

Models made by those associated with the ships themselves are among the best records of vessels from the period and are incredibly important sources for understanding technological development. However, the relationship of ship models to shipbuilding in the seventeenth and eighteenth centuries is more complex than might at first be assumed. Indeed, the significance of the Navy Board ship models goes beyond the history of shipbuilding. Aside from their technical accuracy, their distinctive open-framed hulls and partial planking, they established new standards in ship model making. Their extraordinarily lavish decoration and high level of detail set the Navy Board models apart from other styles of ship models and gave them a unique cultural significance.

Despite increasing interest in seventeenth- and eighteenth-century ship models, much of this research has been concerned with the history of the ships they represented. Consequently, little light has been shed on the story behind the production and use of ship models themselves. Following on from John Franklin's *Navy Board Models*, which made significant inroads into the understanding of Navy Board models, this book aims to place the models, rather than the ships, at the centre of the narrative.[4] The name 'Navy Board' has stuck, but today these models are defined by their unique construction style, rather than by where they were made or how they were used. The National Maritime Museum (NMM) holds the largest collection of surviving Navy Board models in the world, and with increasing understanding of the seventeenth- and eighteenth-century Admiralty and Navy Board, it is time for a reassessment of the Navy Board models' role in this period.

The book is broken down into three main sections: Historical Background, Construction, and the Catalogue. The Historical Background section investigates the social and cultural context of the Navy Board models by questioning their relationship to shipbuilding and the Navy Board itself. It also considers why some of the most famous personalities of the time, including Charles II, James II, and Samuel Pepys, collected Navy Board models, and why so little is known about the model makers. Finally, it discusses the relationship between ship models and art in this period. The Construction section outlines how a typical Navy Board model was made, including the materials, tools, and processes involved, and considers what makes the Navy Board models unique. In the Catalogue, each surviving Navy Board model in the National Maritime Museum collection is illustrated alongside detailed descriptions and measurements. For the first time, the complete NMM collection of Navy Board ship models is brought together in a single illustrated volume.

Bow
1 Figurehead
2 Cathead
3 Deadeye
4 Upper Cheek
5 Lower Cheek
6 Gun Port
7 Main Wale
8 Hull Planking
9 Second Futtock
10 First Futtock
11 Floor Timbers
12 Cutwater
13 Trailboard
14 Hawse Holes
15 Lower Head Rail
16 Upper Head Rail
17 Main Rail
18 Cathead Support Knee

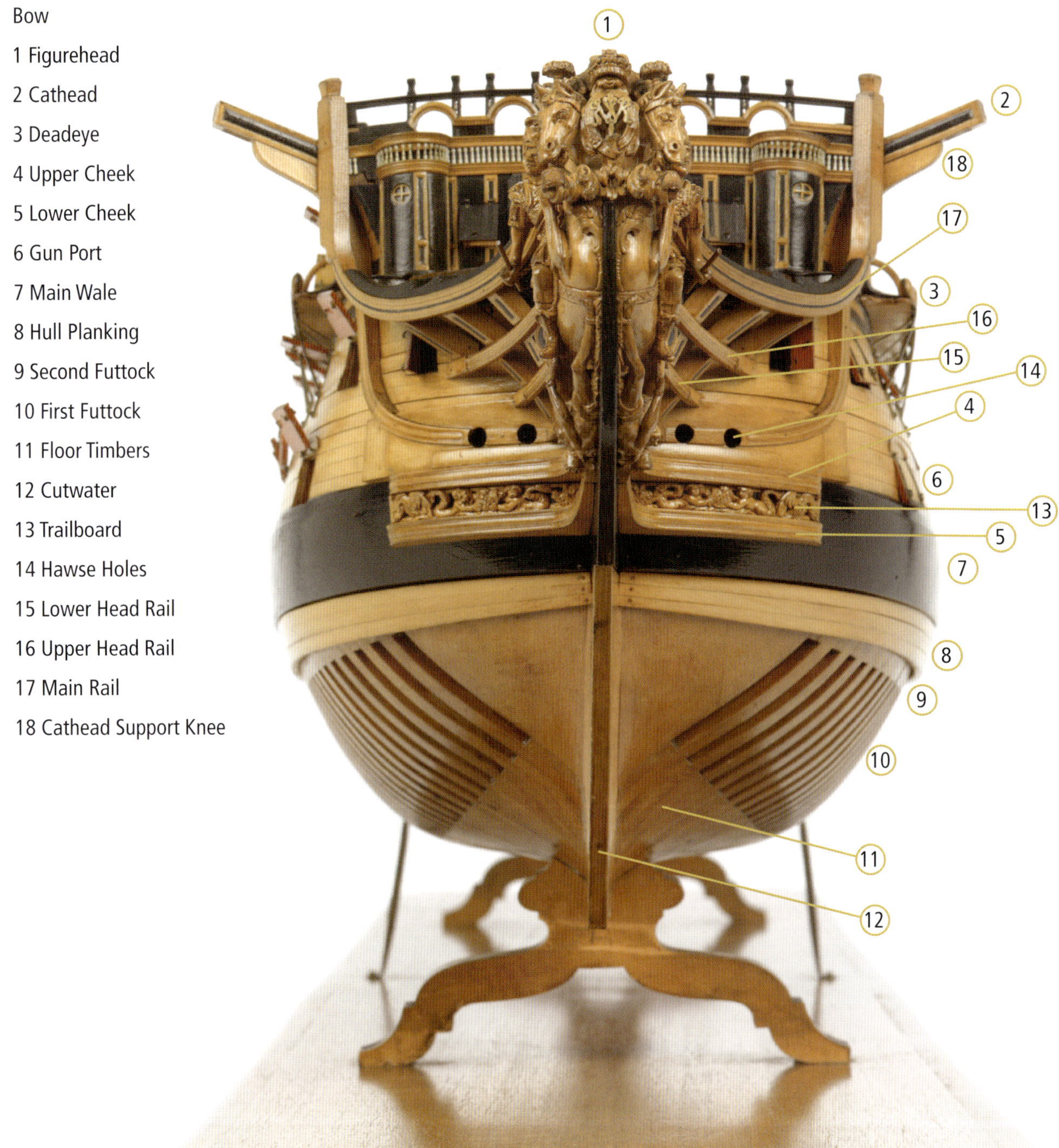

(SLR0409)

Stern
1 Taffrail
2 Quarter Figures
3 Lower Finishing
4 Stern Chase Port
5 Beading of the Rudder
6 Gudgeons and Pintles
7 Rudder
8 Planking
9 Lower Counter
10 Main Wale
11 Lower Gun Deck
12 Upper Counter
13 Middle Gun Deck
14 Baluster
15 Upper Gun Deck
16 Quarter Deck
17 Pilaster
18 Coach

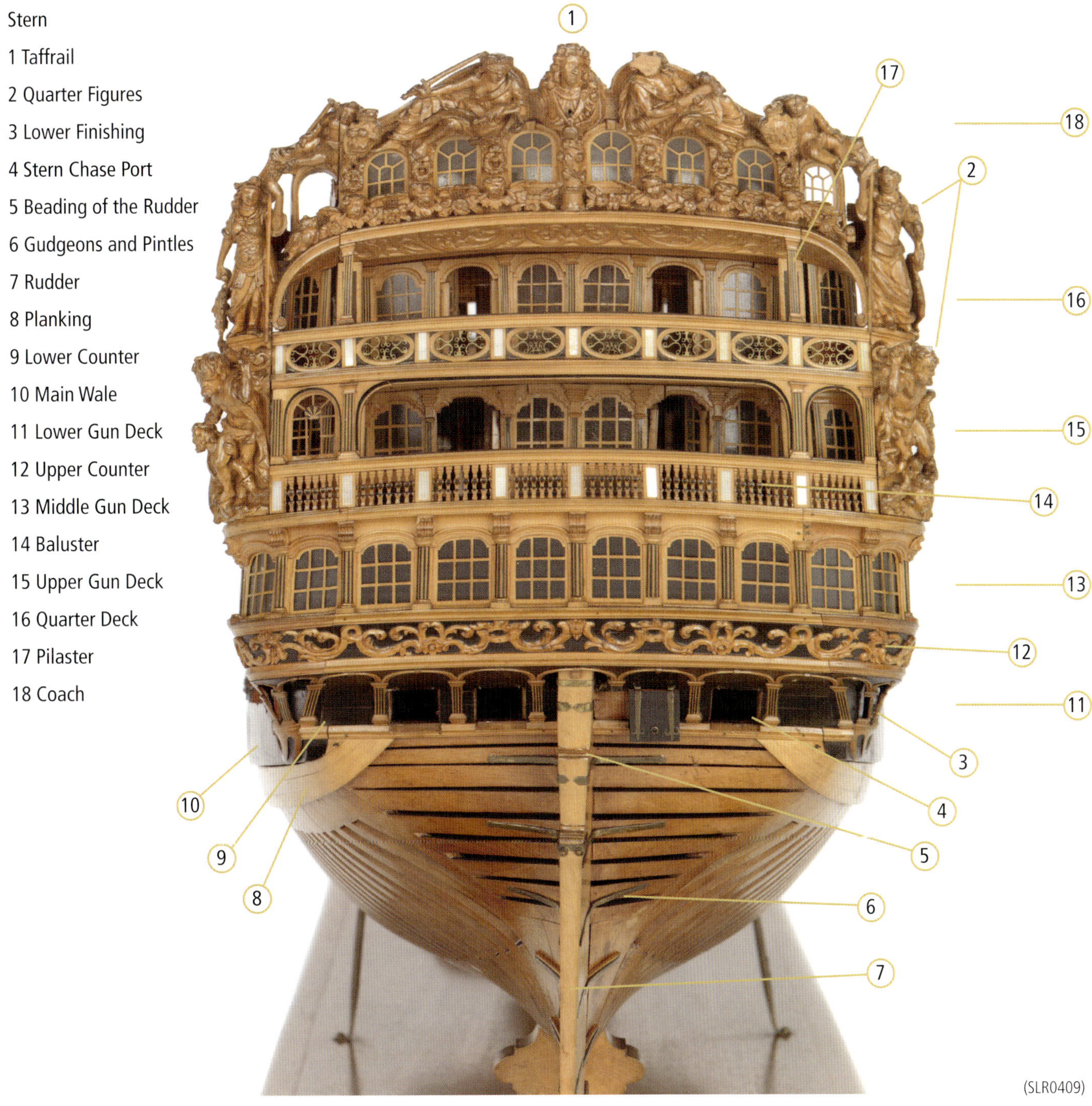

(SLR0409)

Broadside Split View

1 Exposed Stylised Framing
2 Rudder
3 Gudgeons and Pintles
4 Stern Post
5 Keel
6 Position of Mizzenmast
7 Position of Mainmast
8 Stempost
9 Cutwater
10 Carlings and Ledges
11 Riding Bitts
12 Deck Beam
13 Capstan Beds
14 Bilge Pumps
15 Coach
16 Deck Beam
17 Poop Deck
18 Quarter Deck
19 Upper Gun Deck
20 Middle Gun Deck
21 Gun Deck
22 Quarter Galleries
23 Lower Finishing Pieces
24 Gunport
25 Bulwark Screen
26 Channels
27 Entry Port
28 Skid Beams
29 Upper Wale
30 Hull Planking
31 Chain Plates
32 Main Wale
33 Deadeyes
34 Bulkhead Beakhead
35 Figurehead
36 Deck Planking
37 Position of Foremast
38 Stove Chimney
39 Belfry
40 Capstan
41 Deck Gratings
42 Waist Gangways

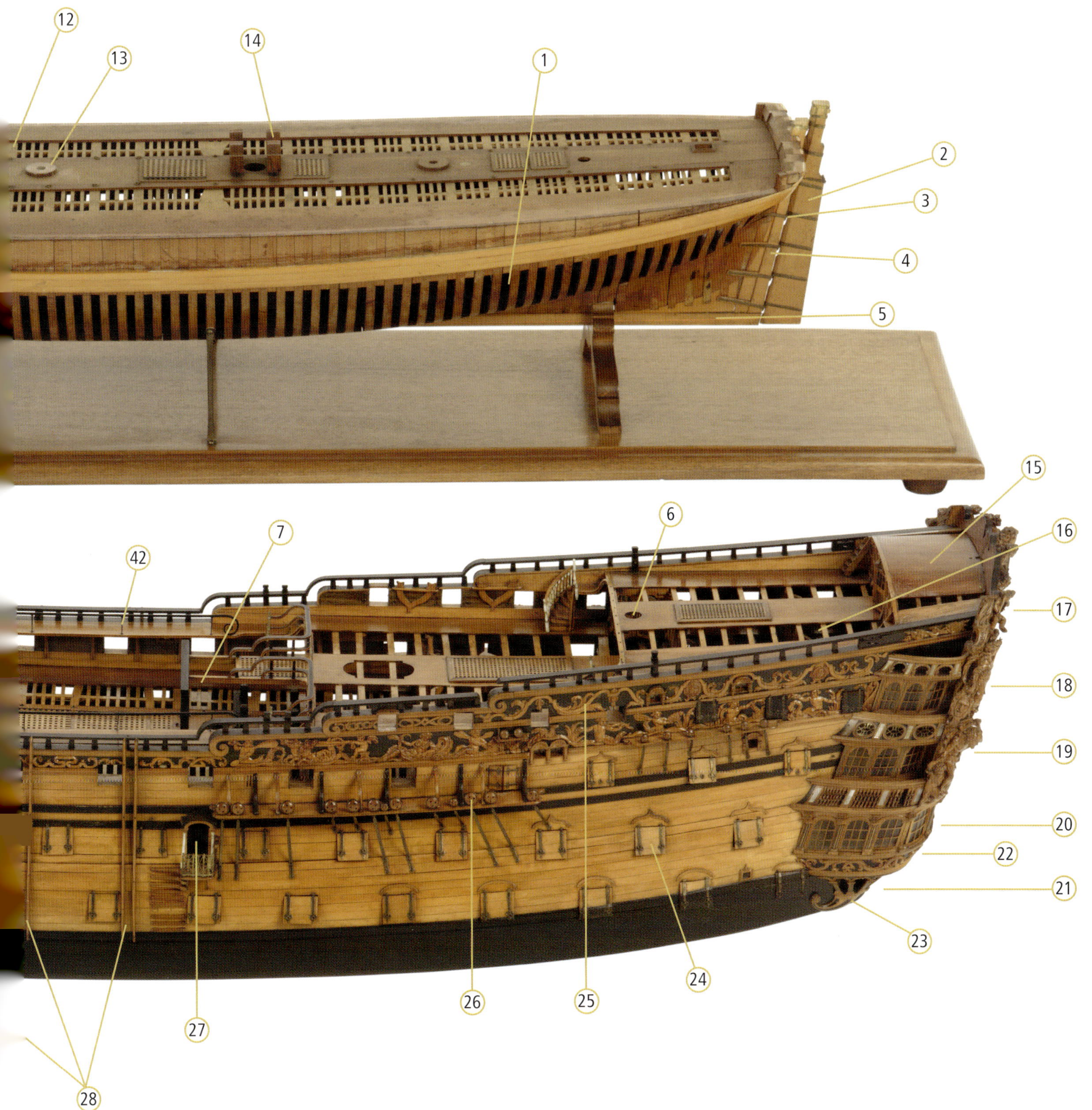
12
13
14
1
2
3
4
5
15
6
7
42
16
17
18
19
20
22
21
23
24
25
26
27
28

Historical Background

Ship Models and Naval Administration

In the seventeenth century, far greater resources were dedicated to shipbuilding for the Royal Navy than ever before. The establishment of colonies in the Americas, as well as maritime trade rivalries with other European powers, served to make naval shipbuilding the single biggest manufacturing enterprise in England. To manage the building, equipping, and maintaining of ships on this scale, the administrative structure needed to become more efficient. The small Navy Board, created by Henry VIII in 1546 to advise him on naval matters, was expanded and placed under the control of the Board of Admiralty, which was created by Charles I in 1628. It was at this time that the Navy Board-style models first appeared. However, the exact relationship of these models with shipbuilding and naval administration remains unclear.

The Navy Board was responsible for building, repairing, and fitting out ships, as well as managing the Royal Dockyards at Woolwich and Deptford on the Thames; Chatham and Sheerness on the Medway; and Portsmouth and Plymouth on the south coast. It was made up of Principal Officers and Commissioners, who generally met twice a week at the Navy Office on the corner of Crutched Friars and Seething Lane at Tower Hill, London. They in turn reported to the Admiralty at Whitehall once a week.

'A View of the Navy Office, London', 1698. (British Library, Kings 43, f.147)

The Admiralty was concerned with matters of naval strategy and putting the government's naval policy into effect. At its head was the Lord High Admiral appointed by the monarch. The Lord High Admiral was in charge of a group of officials known as Lords Commissioners of the Admiralty. Although it was not directly concerned with shipbuilding, strategic decisions often rested on the number and type of ships that could be fitted out for war.

It had long been assumed that ship models played an integral part in the design and commissioning of a ship. An early example, hinting at the role ship models had in securing royal patronage, was recorded by the shipbuilder Phineas Pett when he

'The True Portraicture of His Maties Royall Ship the *Soveraigne of the Seas*. Built in the Yeare 1637', by John Payne (*c.*1637). (PAJ2441)

presented a model to Charles I in 1634:

> His Highness, calling me aside, privately acquainted me with his princely resolution for the building of a great new ship, which he would have me to undertake, using these words to me: – 'You have made many requests to me, and now I will make it my request to you to build this ship' ... The 29th October, the model made for the great new ship was carried to Hampton Court and there placed in the Privy Gallery. Where, after his majesty had seen and thoroughly perused, he commanded us to carry it back to Whitehall ... [1]

This was a model to demonstrate the *Sovereign of the Seas*, an enormous 100-gun ship built by Phineas's son Peter Pett and launched in 1637. A visitor to Peter Pett's house the same year noted a model 'of admirable workmanship, curiously painted and gilt, with azure and gold, so contrived that every timber in her might be seen, and left open and unplanked for that purpose'.[2]

This model, which certainly followed the same unplanked style exposing the lower hull, has been cited as possibly being the first example of a Navy Board-style model.[3] However, the ship that the model depicted – the lavishly decorated *Sovereign of the Seas* – was more a statement of royal power than it was a typical warship. With a gun deck of 167ft 9in, 127ft on the keel, and an extreme breadth of 47ft 11in, the *Sovereign of the Seas* was larger than any ship that had been built before.

'A New Whip for the Dutch', John Seymour Lucas, 1883. (© Victoria and Albert Museum)

In this case, a model of this enormous ship was presented to the king, but there is little to suggest that this was a normal part of commissioning a ship.

Undoubtedly, ship models required a huge amount of time and dedication to construct, but they may have had a less important role in naval administration and shipbuilding than this single example suggests. Despite the survival of many ship models from the seventeenth and eighteenth centuries, there is very little written evidence to explain why ship models were made, or how long they took to make. It is not unreasonable to suggest that an intricate and ornate Navy Board model could have taken several years to make, so they would have been a rather inefficient and costly way of securing a commission.

It is hard to believe that such intricate models would have been needed simply to show the preliminary designs for a ship, particularly as this purpose could be fulfilled by paper draughts. We must ask if these ship models would have actually been useful to the Navy Board. Despite including remarkably detailed fixtures and fittings, the framing of the models is, in fact, a stylised simplification of the actual framing of a ship. This would have made the models of little use for demonstrating ship construction. Furthermore, the skill, time, and effort necessary to construct these intricate models would make them impractical for preliminary designs, particularly if a scheme was to be altered or simply rejected.

By seventeenth-century standards, the Navy Board was highly organised and kept detailed records. Much of its correspondence survives in the collections of the National Maritime Museum's Caird Library and The National Archives, Kew. The process of commissioning a ship is well documented, but few references to ship models have been found. Even less has been found that can be linked to what we now call the Navy Board ship models. While it is very hard to link surviving models to specific written references from the seventeenth century, it should be noted that in England in the second half of the century there was essentially only one style of ship model – the Navy Board style. Votive models, which were common in churches on the Continent, were uncommon in England and were not likely to have garnered much interest from those associated with shipbuilding or the Navy, who would have demanded greater detail.

When written references to ship models do occur, they stand out as anomalous within the context of the rest of the correspondence about shipbuilding. For example, in 1649 the Admiralty wrote to the Navy Commissioners requesting that 'five ships be built frigott fashion … but before the said builders proceed in building, this Committee desire you to order the builders to present models of the frigotts'.[4] It is possible that these models were paper draughts, rather than three-dimensional

One of the earliest in the Navy Board style, this model has similar dimensions to the frigates of the Commonwealth period. (SLR0217)

models. Confusingly, in the seventeenth century the word 'model' could also refer to a two-dimensional draught on paper. Samuel Johnson's *Dictionary* had no fewer than seven entries for the word 'model', including 'a representation in little of something made or done' and 'a copy to be imitated'.[5] Thomas Miller's *Complete Modellist*, published in 1667, is not about physical ship models, but instead explains how to draw a two-dimensional plan for rigging a ship.[6]

The Admiralty probably wanted to see the designs prior to building because at the time the frigate was a relatively new and innovative type of fast, lightly armed ship. It was often too small for the line of battle, but large enough to engage the enemy in independent action in all conditions. The order states that one of the frigates intended 'for the winter guard in the Irish Seas' was to be built by Peter Pett at Deptford. Whether these were models or not, the earliest surviving Navy Board model in the National Maritime Museum's collection (SLR0217) has very similar dimensions to the *Fairfax*, a 52-gun frigate launched at Deptford by Pett in 1650, which was put under the command of Captain William Penn as vice-admiral for the Irish coast.

To direct the business of shipbuilding, the Navy Board sent written warrants to the Royal Dockyard outlining the ships to be built and the other work that needed to be undertaken. Each Royal Dockyard had a Master Shipwright who was

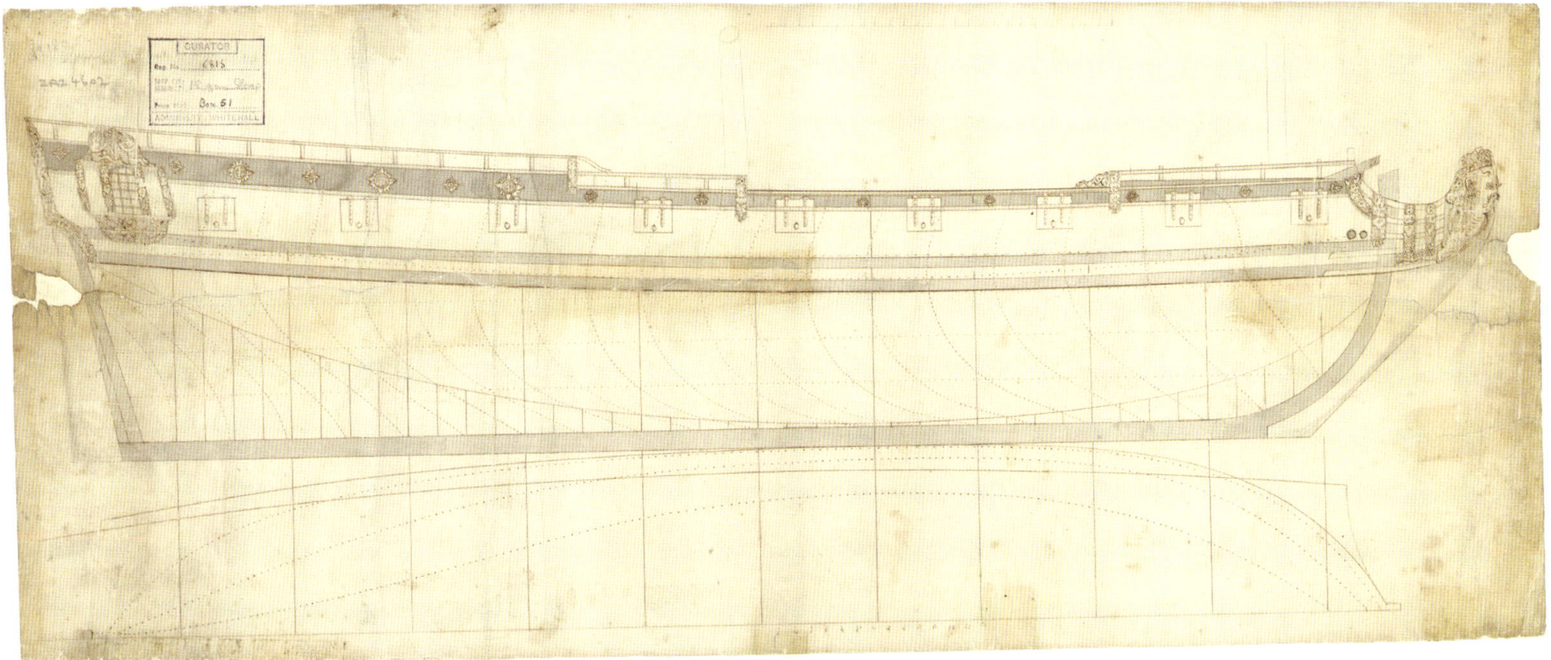

1:48-scale plan for an unknown 18-gun sloop from the late seventeenth century (ZAZ4602). To design a ship, a master shipwright would have first set out his design on paper in the form of a lines plan. The traditional lines plan includes three views of a ship: the body plan shows the ship's bow and stern, with lines to illustrate the shape of the hull along the body of the ship; the sheer plan shows the broadside of the ship in profile, illustrating the position of decks and gunports; and finally the half-breadth shows one half of the ship from above. In this plan the curved body sections have been placed along the sheer draught.

charged with designing and building ships, and with the exception of Woolwich and Deptford (which were closer to the Navy Office) each also had a Resident Commissioner – a member of the Navy Board who stayed at the dockyard to ensure that orders were put into effect.

Despite receiving orders from the Navy Board, in the seventeenth century the Master Shipwright had relative freedom in the design of ships, only having to conform to basic 'Establishments'. These regulations, first set out in 1677, later defined the dimensions for each Rate of Royal Navy vessel. First Rates were the largest ships with the most guns, followed by Second, Third, Fourth, Fifth, and Sixth Rates, each smaller than the rate above. It was hoped that the Establishments would increase efficiency through the standardisation of ship size and number of guns.

When further Establishments were issued in 1706, 1719, and 1745, with additional revisions in 1733 and 1741, they became increasingly detailed. It has been suggested that some of the Navy Board models do not represent specific ships, but demonstrate Establishment proposals.[7] However, improvement of ship design was incremental and it was hardly necessary to construct a model with highly detailed fixtures and fittings to show slight changes, such as increasing the breadth of a ship's hull by a fraction.

Alternatively, it has also been thought that some models were made to show advances in individual features on board ship.[8] For example, an unidentified model of a First Rate from about 1702 (SLR0386) shows the earliest known example of a steering system worked by rope. This was probably an experimental fitting prior to the introduction of the steering wheel in about 1703 (see SLR0218). For this

This First Rate of around 1702 has an early example of a steering mechanism worked by rope at the aft of the waist. (SLR0386)

purpose, a three-dimensional model would have been preferable since it allowed much greater detail to be shown than on a two-dimensional draught.

However, if the model was made to demonstrate this feature, it prompts the question as to why it includes so many other fittings and lavish decoration that are not relevant to the steering mechanism. Many of these features were of a standard design and would not need to be part of any demonstration. One answer could be that models were not used in the design process, but fulfilled some other, non-technical, function.

There is evidence of ship models produced at the Royal Dockyards, but outside official Navy Board business. In 1677, for example, Richard Beach, the Resident Commissioner at Chatham Dockyard, complained to the Navy Office about men employed in making ship models privately without an order. The letter, which provides a window into model making and its relationship to dockyard administration, is worth quoting at length:

> It having been made a common practice here by the Master Shipwright to keep several of our workmen, viz. three or four at a time, employed in making of models privately, either in his own house or elsewhere without any order procured for the doing thereof, or even acquainting me therewith, to the great hindrance of the service and charge to his Majesty – and missing of the said workmen, did ask the deputy Clerk of the Cheque if he knew what was become of them of where they wrought who told me the Shipwright kept them privately employed, and as he supposed upon models, whereupon I forthwith sent for the men and charged them to desist their further proceeding thereon, till the Shipwright produced an order either from his Majesty, his Highness or your Honours for the same – for I am confident his pretence with that they are either for his Majesty or his Highness … I have given an account thereof to the Secretary and withal desired the favour of him as, when it is his Majesty's or Royal Highness's pleasure to have any models made here that he would advise me thereof. Mr Lawrence, the Shipwright Assistant's son, entered in the workers here, informed me, how that his Majesty has lately ordered him, to make a model for another yacht, to which I can but give little credit, as having seen no order for it.[9]

It is highly likely that this letter refers to three-dimensional models because it talks of 'several workmen'. One of these men, Joseph Lawrence, the son of Joseph

Lawrence Senior, the Master Shipwright's Assistant, was making a model of a yacht for Charles II. It is likely that this was a private commission, because there is no record of the model being ordered through the official channels, and this was the main reason for Commissioner Beach's annoyance.

Charles II and his brother James, Duke of York, were known to have collected models of the yachts that they both owned and raced. They had picked up an interest in the sport during their exile in the Netherlands prior to the Restoration of the monarchy in 1660. In October 1660, the Duke of York sent instructions to Peter Pett (who was then Commissioner at Chatham) stating: 'Whereas the King my Sovereign Lord and Brother hath signified his pleasure that a Yacht be built in his Majesty's Yard at Chatham, and hath approved of the Model of a Yacht, by you presented unto him'.[10]

Charles II. A late copy based on a portrait type by Sir Peter Lely of around 1675. (BHC2608)

Not only did the royal brothers take a keen interest in the latest yacht designs, but they had a personal as well as professional interest in the Royal Navy. Charles regularly attended Navy Board meetings and the Duke of York was Lord High Admiral. For the shipwrights in this period, personal contacts were very important for securing positions and influence. Making a ship model for a wealthy patron, such as the king or the Duke of York, was one method by which a shipwright could gain favour and secure prestigious work such as building royal yachts.

1:32-scale Navy Board model of a Royal Yacht, *c.*1685. (SLR0375)

Standard lion figureheads, like this 7½-foot full-sized example dated to around 1720, were fitted to most Royal Navy ships. Normally only the larger First and Second Rates had unique figureheads. (FHD0088)

Commissioner Beach's concern in his 1677 letter was not so much that a ship model was being made, but that the model was being made without Navy Board approval, using Navy Board materials and in Navy Board time. The line between the public and private spheres was blurred, and some, such as the young Joseph Lawrence, may have used their professional position to make additional private income or gain favour.

There are several documented cases of shipwrights using models to secure the favour of a wealthy patron. On 24 December 1663, Samuel Pepys, diarist and Clerk of the Acts of the Navy Board, had called at Woolwich, 'where Mr. Christopher Pett having an opportunity of being alone did tell me his mind about several things he thought I was offended with him in, and told me of my kindness to his assistant. I did give him such an answer as I thought was fit and left him well satisfied, he offering to do me all the service, either by draughts or modells that I should desire'.[11]

In fact, in the same month, at the house of Sir William Coventry, Commissioner of the Navy, Pepys recorded in his diary seeing 'Mr. Christopher Pett bringing him a modell, and indeed it is a pretty one, for a New Year's gift; but I think the work not better done than mine'.[12] These examples certainly refer to three-dimensional models, rather than paper draughts.

Model making at the Royal Dockyards was not without its problems. In the 1670s, Fisher Harding, Master Shipwright at Deptford, was accused in an anonymous letter to the king, of being 'a great Encroacher upon your Majesties Naval Interests' and it was suggested that 'there be no Pictures, Schemes, or any sorts of Draughts or Moddels of Shipps Carved by your Majesties Carver, or Guilded by Your Majesties Painter insatiably exausting your Majesties Treasure'.[13]

It was common for shipwrights to be accused of being wasteful. Undoubtedly, highly decorative models, often with elaborate gilt and carved work, were always costly to produce. The fact that ship models were specifically cited as an example of this 'encroachment' upon Charles II's 'naval interests', suggests that they were indeed superfluous to the normal process of shipbuilding.

It is tempting to think that because of their detailed carving, the models were once used as designs for the carved work for the full-sized ships. It is unlikely that the carvings on the models were used as maquettes or *bozzetti*, the preliminary designs that were widely used in stone carving. The usefulness of a model in illustrating the standard Royal Navy lion figurehead, which appears on the majority of the Navy Board models, is questionable. The Royal Navy lion figurehead underwent only minor stylistic changes from the mid-seventeenth to late eighteenth century. In the same way that the hull of a Navy Board model was not simply a preliminary design for the construction of the ship, the carving on the models should not be considered a plan for the full-sized scheme on the ship.

Edmund Dummer, who became Surveyor of the Navy in August 1692, introduced exact standards for each new ship and argued for the use of scale ship models to test a ship's design.[14] Later he employed a model maker at the Navy Office, 'in making models of docks, ships and vessels which, being new inventions, could not be managed without such instructions to the artificers that were to perform them'.[15] It is clear that these particular ship models were intended to be used in the design process, but this was not standard practice and it is unlikely that a model was necessary for every ship that was built.

Dummer made little progress in extending the practice of using ship models to the rest of the shipwrights. When he lost his job as Surveyor in 1699, after a dispute with the Admiralty, Dummer left the office in a hurry, taking only 'some particular models of his own invention and not used'.[16] In the seventeenth century, model making did not form part of the official procedure, but the practicalities of ensuring the shipwrights' adherence to increasingly detailed Establishments introduced in the eighteenth century caused administrators to explore using models to help to standardise the shipbuilding process. However, these models were quite different from the Navy Board models. In 1708, a letter from Furzer and Lee, Surveyors of the Navy, to the Navy Board discussed using a demonstration model to show the sheathing of a ship's hull with copper.[17] And in the summer of 1716, the Surveyor of the Navy, Jacob Acworth, introduced a new style of ship model, called 'block models', which were specifically used for demonstrating the design of ships. Acworth's order effectively implemented the strategy that Dummer had not been able to, stating that each Master Shipwright now had to produce a scale block model detailing the hull form which would supposedly serve as a simple but accurate representation of their proposed design.[18]

1:48-scale block model of a 60-gun Third Rate of about 1730. (SLR0439)

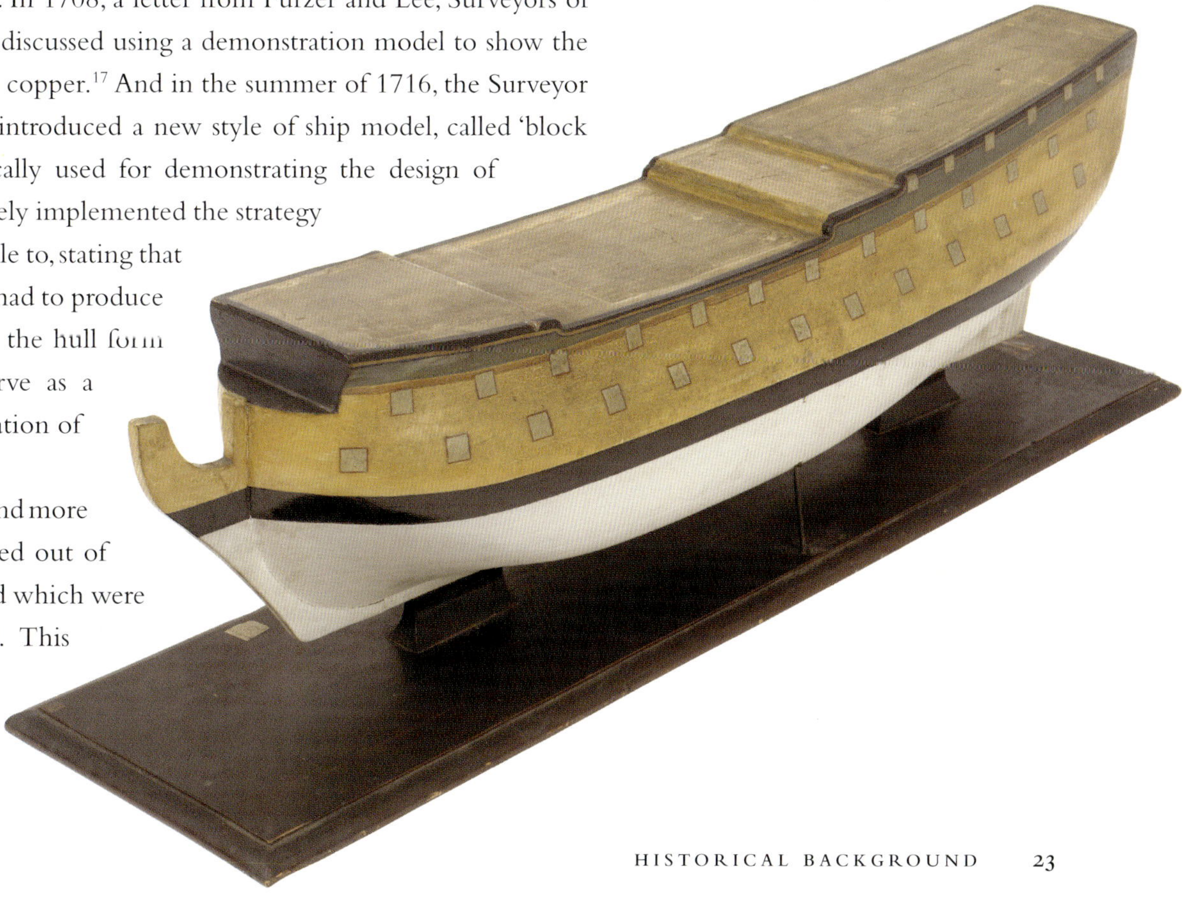

Block models were simple and more robust hull models, constructed out of horizontal layers of solid wood which were then carved and smoothed. This style of model making is known as 'bread-and-butter' because the layers are

1:48-scale model of a 50-gun two-decker, built entirely 'in frame', 1715. (SLR0405)

stuck together like a multi-layered sandwich. It was the normal practice to paint on various fittings such as gunports, channels, and in some cases elaborate decoration. Ordered to be made for every ship, they regularly appear in the written record as 'solids' – a name that indicates their solid construction, in contrast to the unplanked Navy Board style.

Block models illustrated the hull form and other details of ship construction with less demanding craftsmanship than the Navy Board models. It allowed models to be produced quickly and at relatively low cost. Furthermore, their robust form made them easy to transport. The delicate Navy Board models, on the other hand, would have been very difficult to move from the dockyards to the Navy Office.[19]

As well as block models, ship models showing a ship's construction 'in frame' were also made during this period. The earliest example of this type is thought to be a model of a Fourth Rate, dated to around 1715. In contrast to the stylised framing of the Navy Board models, this model shows the detailed construction of the ship's framing exactly how it was to be built at full scale.

Despite the introduction of block models and models in frame, the stylised and decorative Navy Board ship models continued to be made well into the eighteenth century. The last contemporary model of a known ship in the NMM's collection depicts the *Ajax* launched in 1767, and there is another unidentified Navy Board-style models thought to date from around 1775 (see SLR0313). The co-existence of practical block models and detailed frame models alongside the more ornate Navy Board models implies that they each fulfilled a different role.

In the seventeenth century it seems that ship models only appear in a few cases: in relation to vessels that were somehow out of the ordinary – either large or particularly ostentatious ships such as the *Sovereign of the Seas*; when the vessel was of

1:48-scale model of the 74-gun *Ajax*, 1767. (SLR0311)

relatively new design, such as the frigates of 1649; when the vessel was for the personal use of the king, such as royal yachts; or during the proposed introduction of copper sheathing in 1708.

Late seventeenth-century attempts to standardise Royal Navy shipbuilding sometimes involved the use of ship models, but this was never systematic. In the early eighteenth century, block models and models in frame were introduced and were used regularly in the design process by the end of that century. However, the Navy Board style of model continued to be made, which suggests it had an entirely different purpose. Moreover, the evidence of ship models being made outside of official dockyard work suggests that they were made for private individuals rather than for the Navy Board.

The Navy Board models are among the finest ship models ever made and their decorative nature may provide a clue to how the models were appreciated at the time. Overall, evidence that Navy Board ship models were directly used in shipbuilding is largely absent. Not only was it unlikely that they were made for the Navy Board at all, but it also prompts the question as to their original function. As accurate and decorative representations of Royal Navy ships, the Navy Board ship models illustrated the increasing cultural significance of ship models in a burgeoning maritime nation. It is much more probable that the Navy Board models were privately commissioned and collected by wealthy patrons with a connection to the Royal Navy, something which will be discussed in the next section.

Collectors

Ship models have long been regarded as highly collectable objects and can still be found in museums and private collections. The prices ship models now fetch at

Portrait of Samuel Pepys, by Godfrey Kneller, 1689. Pepys was initially Clerk of the Acts on the Navy Board, and from 1688 to 1686 he was Secretary of the Admiralty. (BHC2947)

James, Duke of York, 'by Henri Gascar, 1672–73'. (BHC2797)

auction illustrate their desirability – and there was little difference in the seventeenth and eighteenth centuries, when models often sold for high prices. In this respect, ship models can be considered on a par with the greatest works of fine art.

The ship models held in private hands include several major collectors, such as James, Duke of York; Samuel Pepys; the shipbuilder and Navy Board Commissioner Peter Pett; and naval administrator Charles Sergison. It is likely that there were many more models than those that have survived. Samuel Pepys mentions ship models no less than sixteen times in his famous diary, undoubtedly the best written source for this period. There are further examples of ship models being privately commissioned or advertised for sale in newspapers, which give an intriguing glimpse into the world of ship model collecting in the seventeenth and eighteenth centuries.

In this period, ship models were prized objects, commended for their beauty as well as their ingenuity, and would often be shown to important visitors. When the Grand Duke of Tuscany, Cosimo III de' Medici, visited the Duke of York's residence at St James's Palace in 1669, he was shown the ship model collection. His travelling companion Magalotti noted:

> the most remarkable objects, are to be seen, inclosed in glass cases, some miniature models of men of war, beautifully executed after the designs of his royal highness, who, from living the superintendence of the naval armaments, has a particular genius for the construction of vessels.[20]

Ship models should be considered part of the wider phenomenon of collecting in a period when displays of art and curiosities adorned the great houses of royals, aristocrats, merchants, administrators, and shipwrights. In the seventeenth century, it was common for the wealthy to have a small room called a 'cabinet', or 'closet', at home dedicated to housing the owner's prized possessions, which could be shown off to visitors.[21] Pepys recorded a visit to Commissioner Peter Pett's house at Chatham, where he 'saw his closet, which come short of what I expected, but there was fine modells of ships in it indeed, whose worth I could not judge of'.[22]

It was customary for a collector to show his ship models to distinguished guests, and no doubt discuss aspects of ship design with a learned guest. On a visit to Chatham in August 1663, the well-travelled gardener and diarist John Evelyn remarked that Commissioner Pett 'showed me his study and models, with other curiosities belonging to his art. He is esteemed for the most skilful shipbuilder in the world.'[23]

In 1697, when Peter the Great, the tsar of Russia, travelled to England to learn about shipbuilding and navigation to establish the first Russian Navy, he stayed

1:48 scale Navy Board model of a 44-gun two-decker (SLR0367). It represents a Fourth Rate of around 1660, and is likely to be similar in size to the model purchased by De Vauvré.

at a house belonging to Evelyn. It was close to the dockyards at Deptford, which suited Peter because he could easily visit ships being built. He was especially keen to study the drawing of ship plans. When Peter returned to Russia, he was given ship models to take back with him. He initially kept them in his own house before they were moved to the St Petersburg shipyard, where they can still be seen in the Maritime Museum of Russia.[24]

Charles II took a considerable interest in his navy, perhaps more so than any other monarch.[25] He regularly attended Navy Board meetings, when the fleet was expanded during wars with the Dutch in the late seventeenth century. However, he also enjoyed yachting and commissioned models of his own yachts. It seems that Charles was such an avid ship model collector that on 6 June 1662, when Pepys opened a chest that stood in his office and 'found a modell of a fine ship', he wondered whether it belonged to the king.[26]

Not surprisingly, ship models could command a considerable sum of money. Pepys recorded that 'Captain Wentworth did in the year [16]71 sell a model of a 4th rate ship to Monsieur De Vauvre for 55 guineas' (about £60).[27] The sale price was equivalent to over half of Wentworth's annual income, which was just over £8 per month at sea as captain of the 36-gun *Exchange*. The buyer was a high-ranking French naval administrator, Jean-Louis Girardin de Vauvré, who was made *commissaire général* in 1673 to oversee the French naval dockyard at Rochefort. For a man of his experience, involved in naval shipbuilding at the top level, to have bought it, it is likely that the model was of very high quality.

The high value of ship models was demonstrated during the Second Anglo-Dutch War, in which the English and Dutch fought to control important trade routes. In June 1667, the Dutch orchestrated a daring raid up the river Medway to

'Dutch Ships in the Medway, June 1667', by Willem Schellinks, late seventeenth century. (BHC0294)

launch a surprise attack on the English ships anchored just off the Royal Dockyard at Chatham. During this attack the Dutch captured the fort at Sheerness, forced their way past the defensive chain at Gillingham and then burnt the ships *Royal James*, *Loyal London*, and *Royal Oak* at Chatham. Many more ships were destroyed and the *Royal Charles* was towed off to the Netherlands (where its carved coat of arms from the stern can still be seen at the Rijksmuseum).

The audacious raid was an enormous shock. The Dutch seemed to strike at the heart of the Royal Navy. However, Peter Pett, Commissioner of Chatham Dockyard, was recorded by Pepys as having 'carried away things of great value, and these were his models of ships'.[28] The fact that Pett dedicated time to rescuing models in a time of great danger demonstrates their value. However, the models were more of personal value to Pett, rather than having any real technical value for the Dutch shipbuilders. Pepys noted that Pett's claim that 'the Dutch would have made more

1:48-scale model of the *Boyne*, 1692. (SLR0006)

advantage of the models than of the ships' was met with laughter during the subsequent inquiry.[29]

Pett's actions notwithstanding, it stands to reason that shipwrights were enthusiastic ship model collectors whose pride in their ships was reflected in these models. The model of the 80-gun *Boyne* (SLR0006), built in the Navy Board style, is thought to be unique in that it bears the name of both the vessel and her builder, carved in a scroll at the break of the poop deck. 'YE BOYNE Bt [built] BY MR HARDING DEP [Deptford] SA.' The inscription may refer to Fisher Harding, Master Shipwright at Deptford between 1686 and 1705, as the builder of the ship, which he launched in 1692; or as the maker of the model; or possibly both.

Harding collected ship models and when he died in 1705, his will left 'all Modells, Blocks and draughts' to his son Fisher Harding the younger.[30] It is uncertain whether the *Boyne* was part of his collection, although the model was subsequently part of the Royal Collection until William IV donated it to Greenwich Hospital in 1830.

Portrait of Fisher Harding, by Jonathan Richardson, *c.*1701. Harding's right hand rests on a wooden rule while he holds a pair of dividers over a draught plan for a ship, with a ruler beneath it. He gestures with his left hand towards the launch of the First Rate *Royal Sovereign* (1701) on the left. (BHC2743)

Sir Anthony Deane was another Master Shipwright associated with ship models. A model of a 90-gun First Rate (SLR0372) in the National Maritime Museum collection has been linked to Deane due to its similarity to a draught in his *Doctrine of Naval Architecture*, published in 1670. Deane was a friend of Pepys, who recorded that he gave a model to Christ's Hospital School on Newgate Street in London. In 1705, there were models of two fully rigged ships in the Mathematical School – one of which may have been Deane's gift.[31]

Former captains are thought to have commissioned ship models of the ships that they commanded. The model of the *St Michael* shows the ship as a Second Rate with provision for around eighty-four guns, although after 1672 it was re-classified

1:48 scale model of *St Michael* (1669), a three-decker ship of the line, made in the Navy Board style. (SLR0002)

as a First Rate 98-gun ship. At this time, Sir Robert Holmes was captain of the *St Michael* at the Battle of Solebay, when a seventy-five-strong Dutch fleet surprised a combined Anglo-French fleet of ninety-three ships. After the inconclusive battle, Holmes retired from the Royal Navy to become Governor of the Isle of Wight. He used his military experience, gained in the Royalist cavalry, to improve the fortifications of the island. Holmes also spent time improving his own house at Yarmouth. When he died in November 1692 his will listed 'Two Moddles of Shipps'.[32] The ownership of the *St Michael* model cannot be traced back to the seventeenth century, although it was possibly used to celebrate Holmes's service.

A model of a 40-gun two-decker (SLR0005) may have been owned by a wealthy gentleman, George Savile, 1st Marquess of Halifax. In 1938, the NMM acquired the model from the estate of his descendant, John Savile Lumley-Savile, 2nd Baron Savile (1853–1931).[33] As a Member of Parliament, George Savile published a pamphlet entitled *A Rough Draft of a New Model at Sea* in 1694. Rather than discuss physical models, the use of the word 'model' in this case refers to the 'ideal', what Dr Johnson defined as the 'standard; that by which anything is measured'.[34] The pamphlet discusses the comparative merits of appointing officers from the gentry or promoting them from the ranks of the experienced seamen of lower social status known as 'tarpaulins'.[35] Considering his interest in the Royal Navy, it would not be surprising if the model, which dates to the 1685, once belonged to George Savile. It is certainly tempting to assume that these ship models somehow served an official function, or that those linked to the Royal Navy collected ship models in a professional capacity, but in fact models were usually privately owned.

Even for Pepys, as a member of the Navy Board, it was personal curiosity that had led him to collect and study ship models. On 5 October 1661, he had spent the morning at home 'putting up my Lord's model of the *Royal James*,

1:48 scale model of a 40-gun two-decker thought to have been owned by George Savile, 1st Marquess of Halifax. (SLR0005)

which I borrowed of him long ago to hang up in my room'.[36] The following year Pepys eagerly wrote that Deane 'promises me also a modell of a ship, which will please me exceedingly, for I do want one of my own'.[37]

However, collecting and displaying ship models could be as much technical as it was aesthetic, and often took a didactic form. As early as 1625, Sir Henry Mainwaring expounded the use of both books and ship models as educational tools in the preface to his *Seaman's Dictionary*, writing:

In six months, he, who would let me read this book over with him,

> and be content to look sometimes at a model of a ship and see how things are done, shall (without any great study, but conversation) know more, be a better seaman, and speak more properly to any business of the sea, than another gentleman who shall go two or three years together to sea without this.[38]

As well as appreciating their beauty as decorative objects, it was normal for a collector to study ship models to learn about ships. On 26 July 1662, Pepys wrote 'to my office again, causing the model hanging in my chamber to be taken down and hung up in my office, for fear of being spoilt by the workmen, and for my own convenience of studying it'.[39] In the same year, former Master's Mate Richard Cooper, whom Pepys had met on board the *Royal Charles*, gave him a series of lectures about ships, using the model as an instructional tool. There is no doubt that an accurate high-quality model was a technical object and that this added to its importance.

In 1679, ship models were drawn into the Popish Plot, which saw widespread anti-Catholic hysteria when it was alleged that there was a conspiracy to assassinate Charles II. Pepys and his friend Sir Anthony Deane, the shipwright who by this point was Commissioner at Portsmouth, were accused by a Parliamentary Com-

Label attached to a model yacht (SLR0379), dated to around 1675.

mittee of carrying over to Catholic France 'certain Maps, Sea-Journals, Draughts of his Majesty's best-built Ships, Models of Ships, and fill'd 14 Sheets of Paper, closely written, with an Account of the Number, State and Economy of the Navy Royal … in order to carry on and support the Popish Plot against his Majesty'.[40] As a result, both Pepys and Deane were sent to the Tower of London. The charges, thought to be orchestrated by Pepys's political enemies, were almost entirely fabricated. Pepys did visit France with Deane in the summer of 1675, but strongly denied the charges of conspiracy. In fact, Pepys pointed out that since neither draughts or ship models 'are portable without being exposed to view, as being bulky', it would have been very difficult to take either to France unnoticed.[41]

Pepys went on to claim that Captain Fasby, in command of the yacht, and his servant were both ready 'to attest of the baggage he carried with him'.[42] Fasby, who commanded several of the royal yachts between 1666 and 1688, was a collector of models himself. A yacht model in the NMM's collection (SLR0379) is accompanied by a framed paper label, dated 1677, stating that the model was owned by Captain Fasby. He would no doubt have noticed and taken an interest if Pepys and Deane had been transporting models onboard his yacht.

Many understood that ship models included detailed technical features, but their practical use to the shipbuilder, whether English, Dutch or French, should not be overstated. The value of ship models was primarily symbolic, as representations of naval power and technology, rather than as practical objects. Pepys took a keen interest in any ship models that came up for sale. In the 1670s, Pepys made a note that 'Sir A. Deane speaks of a model of the *Royal Charles* shewn at a public house, viz. the Three Pigeons at Ratcliffe'.[43] In 1684, Pepys recorded:

> that two models of Mr Phineas Pett of Woolwich, one of the *Captain*, and the other he thinks of the *Grafton* … did stand at Garraway's to be sold three weeks for public sale and were sold, one to Mr Upton for £12 (which Mr Upton told Sir A. D. he would send to Leghorn [Livorno]) and the other to Mr H. Johnson 4 (Sir H. Johnson's son) for £20. They bought them of Mr Pett's kinsman that lives at the Anchor in Lombard Street.[44]

Garraway's was a famous coffeehouse in Change Alley in the City of London, a place famously frequented by those trading in shares and commodities. Coffeehouses and similar establishments were places where the well-to-do could meet to relax, conduct business, and discuss politics. This made them ideal locations to sell an expensive ship model. Some establishments had their own ship models, such as the popular Tory rendezvous, Ozinda's Chocolate House on St James's Street in Westminster. After the proprietor Dominico Ozinda died in 1722, a 'curious Model of a Ship in a Glass Case' was advertised for sale in *The Daily Post*.[45]

By the end of his life, Pepys himself had amassed a collection large enough for one of his friends to refer to the models, books, and paintings as 'an incomparable Museum'.[46] In 1702, bishop and antiquarian William Nicholson recorded a visit to William Hewer's house at Clapham, where Pepys was staying:

> In the House mighty plenty of China-ware and other Indian Goods, vessels of a sort of past[e]; harden'd into a Substance like polish'd Marble. Picture in full pains of wainscot; which (by haveing one moveable, painted on both sides) admits of three several Representations of the whole Room. Models of the Royal Sovereign & other Men of War, made by the most famous Master-Builders; very curious and exact, in glass Cases. Mr Pepys's Library in 9 Classes, finely gilded and sash-glass'd; so deep as to carry two Rows ... of Books on each footing.[47]

When Pepys died in 1703, he left his ship models to his friend Will Hewer, 'recommending it to him to consider how these also together with his own may be preserved for publick benefit'.[48] The ship models were last recorded in 1719 and the house at Clapham was closed to the public in 1723.[49] Pepys's books were bequeathed to Magdalene College, Cambridge, but, unfortunately, it is unclear

Pepys Library, York Buildings, by Sutton Nicholls (*c.*1693). (Pepys Library, Magdalene College, Cambridge)

what happened to the collection of models. It is possible that some were acquired by Charles Sergison, who took over Pepys's old job as Clerk of the Acts to the Navy Board in 1690. Sergison himself accumulated a substantial collection of ship models at his house at Cuckfield Park in Sussex. Fifteen of the best models were sold to the American Colonel Henry Huddleston Rogers around 1920, who later donated his collection to the US Naval Academy in Annapolis.[50]

By the eighteenth century, it was not uncommon for ship models to be advertised in newspapers, read by a burgeoning middle class. Some of the earliest adverts for the sale of ship models can be found in these gazettes. On 14 March 1709, London's *Evening Post* featured an advert for 'the Household Goods of the Hon. Col. Douglas, at his House in Arllington Street, St. James's' including 'a fine Model of a Ship'.[51] Another in *The Daily Advertiser*, 10 February 1778, hints at the sense of worldliness and grandeur associated with sales that included ship models:

> To be Sold by Auction by Mess. Clayton and Bertels, At their spacious Room, in King-Street, St. James's Square, in a few Days, The elegant neat Furniture of a Town Residence, recently quited by A PERSON of RANK, gone Abroad. Comprehensing fashionable Suites of Drawing-Room Furniture, Bed-Chamber and parlour Apparatus, in a Variety of general Articles, and Abandance of those domestick and useful Appendages to the Atticks and Offices; together with some Plate, Jewels, China, a Harpsichord, and accurate rigged Model of a Ship of Force, a Bird of Paradise, and various valuable Effects. Further Particulars and Notice of View and Sale will be soon given.[52]

The sailing ship was the machine behind the global power and trade of a growing British Empire. To those associated with the Royal Navy, trade, ship-owning or shipbuilding, this symbolism was likely to have been an attractive aspect of ship models. The First Lord of the Admiralty between 1681–84, Daniel Finch, owned a Navy Board model of a 90-gun Second Rate (dated 1706–30), which is now at the Science Museum, London. In 1742, Trinity House, the organisation founded to administer and regulate navigation, was said to have 'the exact Model of a Ship of great Size rigged, enclosed in a Frame glazed round; the Gift of Sir Jeremy Smith: Likewise two large Globes enclosed, as was the Model of the Ship; the Gift of Sir Thomas Allen; both Admirals of the Navy under King Charles II.'[53]

Around 1710, the earliest surviving models built in the so-called 'Georgian' style appeared, whereby the lower hull is fully planked. These superseded the Navy Board style as the most popular style of ship model by the late eighteenth century.

These portraits, both by Sir Peter Lely, were part of a series, known as the 'Flagmen of Lowestoft', commissioned by the Duke of York, after the Battle of Lowestoft in 1665, during the Second Anglo-Dutch War. Both Sir Jeremiah Smith (BHC3031) and Sir Thomas Allin (BHC2512) served in the First and Second Anglo-Dutch Wars and retired with the rank of admiral.

However, Navy Board-style models continued to be made, and collectors were still known to have owned or commissioned them for their collections. For example, a Navy Board model of a 50-gun Fourth Rate (SLR0396) is thought to have been owned by Samuel Barrington, who commanded the 50-gun *Norwich*, launched in 1745. The model represents a ship of a much earlier date than that which Barrington commanded. It would likely have been a valued object for the captain, who went on to become an admiral, and was kept in the Barrington family until it was acquired by the NMM in 1993. The model of the *Royal Oak* (SLR0230) is thought to have belonged to George II, who in turn gave it to the Duke of York. The model has been identified as the rebuilt *Royal Oak* of 1741, and the dimensions agree closely with the original plans held in the NMM's collection.

In this period, when commissioning a model, a collector may have stated whether he wanted the model to be planked in the style we now know as 'Georgian', or left unplanked below the wale – the style we now call 'Navy Board'. In 1747, George Anson, 1st Baron Anson, commissioned a Georgian model of *Centurion*, the ship in which he circumnavigated the globe in 1740–44. Writing from Plymouth, the model maker Benjamin Slade informed Anson that he had

> finished the hull of the model, spun the rigging, made and set the masts, cast and turned the brass guns, and are in hand with the carriages, when they are done shal only have the blocks to make and put the rigging overhead, which can't wel be done till next summer I am at present so poorly handed that it can't be done sooner. I hope for your Lordship's favor if any vacancy should happen at Chatham, Deptford, Portsmouth or even Woolwich.[54]

The model, which survives today in the NMM's collection, indicates that Anson evidently preferred the 'Georgian' style of ship model. However, although increasingly rare by this time, the Navy Board style survived, possibly catering for collectors who preferred the more traditional style. The model of the *Ajax* (1767) (SLR0311) is not only constructed in the Navy Board style, but also includes a number of old-fashioned features, such as the style of the stern and a lack of gangways in the waist. It is possible that this model was specially commissioned by a former captain with traditional tastes.[55]

It is clear that ship models spanned both the professional and the private spheres. The most expensive models, such as the Navy Board models, were probably not 'prototypes' used in shipbuilding, but highly decorative objects with a technical as well as cultural significance. Models were collected by individuals connected to

Navy Board model of a small 50-gun two-decker (*c.*1714), built plank-on-frame in the Navy Board style (SLR0396). It is known as the 'Barrington model' because of its provenance in the family.

the Royal Navy, and as such needed to be accurate and realistic. The style of model favoured by collectors meant that the accuracy required was based on appearance, proportions, and decorations. However, while they were occasionally used for the study of ships, the models' primary role was not technical, and they were not always used to illustrate specific construction methods. Instead, ship models served as a prestigious celebration of service at sea or in the dockyard.

Georgian-style model of *Centurion* made for Lord Anson, 1747. (SLR0442)

Model Makers

Remarkably little has been written about the people who built the Navy Board models. Like so many artisans, the story of these great model makers has drifted into obscurity, despite the survival of their extraordinary work. Considering that most ship models were not officially commissioned, it is understandable that model makers are almost unknown in the voluminous official records of the Navy Board. It is probable that they were employed in other positions in the dockyard, and so do not appear in the pay books as model makers.

One of the earliest known references to ship model making comes from the shipwright Phineas Pett, who recorded making a model for the Surveyor of the Queen's Ships, John Trevor:

> In December this year, 1599, I began a small model, which being perfected and very exquisitely set out and rigged, I presented it to my good friend Mr. John Trevor, who very kindly accepted the same of me.[56]

Boyne (SLR0006) with inscription on the break of the poop deck.

However, it is difficult to link Navy Board models to specific makers, although some left enigmatic clues such as carved initials on model cradles or sterns. Master Shipwright Benjamin Rosewell's initials can be found on the Navy Board model of the *Rose* (SLR0393), and the model of the *Boyne* of 1692 (SLR0006) is inscribed 'Ye Boyne Bt [built] by Mr Harding Dep'.

A Navy Board model of a Third Rate of 1706, now in the Pitt Rivers Museum, Oxford, is recorded in the *Book of Benefactors* as being made by William Lee, who was Master Shipwright of Woolwich before becoming Joint Surveyor of the Navy with Daniel Furzer between 1699 and 1706.[57] Nevertheless, these references to the Master Shipwrights fail to give an indication of the many individuals who must have been involved in model making. In 1607, when Phineas Pett 'began a curious model for the Prince' he proudly stated that the 'most part where of I wrought with my own hands; which being most fairly garnished with carving and painting', which suggests that model making could also be a collaborative process.[58] It is possible that a Master Shipwright, who had designed the ship, supervised a team of model makers. When the model was finished, it was the Master Shipwright who was credited when it was presented to the king or influential patron.

The carved initials 'BR' on the cradle of the model of the *Rose* (1712) are those of Benjamin Rosewell, Master Shipwright at Chatham Royal Dockyard between 1705 and 1732. (SLR0393)

Unlike today, where information is readily available to model makers from museums, archives, and well-researched publications, in the seventeenth and eighteenth centuries only a privileged few would be allowed to see ship plans or enter the Royal Dockyards. Shipwrights would have been among the few people with

Robert Seppings's model (1783) depicts the starboard bow of a ship with twelve separate vertical frames, mounted to an oak backboard, with the later inscription 'Made by Sir Robt Seppings in the 3rd Year of his Appren'p.' (SLR2179)

the necessary skills and specialist knowledge needed to make a Navy Board model. The layout of a ship's fixtures and fittings – including the position of capstans, channels, deadeyes, gun ports, belfries, and rigging – can all be seen replicated in detail on the Navy Board models.

Much like a shipwright, a model maker needed to understand the mathematical principles of naval architecture that define the shape of a ship's hull. A shipwright would have started as an apprentice, normally around the age of sixteen, and would learn the trade by working under the supervision and instruction of an experienced shipwright. With few books on the subject, in the seventeenth century shipwrights generally learnt through practical application, rather than theoretical study.

In the late eighteenth century, model making formed an important part of this apprenticeship. In 1783, the young Robert Seppings, who went on to become Surveyor of the Navy, made a simple half-bow model constructed in frame and mounted on a back board, during the third year of his apprenticeship. Even though it is possible that apprentices were put to work on Navy Board models as part of their work, the models are much too complex and decorative to be considered as a practical exercise for an apprentice.

The Master Shipwright Sir Anthony Deane, who wrote one of the earliest books on the subject, *Deane's Doctrine of Naval Architecture*, made a model for Pepys. On 9 August 1662 Pepys wrote in his diary:

> Up by four o'clock or a little after, and to my office, whither by and by comes Cooper, to whom I told my getting for him the Reserve, for which he was very thankful, and fell to work upon our modell, and did a good morning's work upon the rigging, and am very sorry that I must lose him so soon.[59]

Pepys was given a series of lectures about the workings of a ship by experienced Ship Master Richard Cooper. Most of the Navy Board models are thought to have originally been left unrigged, but it is possible Cooper was also engaged in rigging the model.

Joseph Lawrence, son of the Master Shipwright's Assistant at Chatham (also called Joseph Lawrence), was actually employed as a shipwright himself and would have earned around 2s 1d per day.[60] In 1677, he built the sloop *Experiment*; however, in the same year he was also recorded making a model yacht for Charles II.[61] Therefore, it is possible that Lawrence the younger supplemented his income, or gained favour, by making ship models for wealthy patrons.

But Lawrence did not work alone. It is likely that other shipwrights joined Lawrence as part of a team of model makers. In July 1677, Commissioner Beach sent a note to the Navy Board explaining: 'With regard to the workmen who are marked absent on the enclosed list, John Ward and Edward Scott, shipwrights have gone to work with Mr. Lawrence's son.'[62]

While the position of shipwright was undoubtedly highly skilled, shipbuilding relied on numerous different craftsmen. Each had their own skills and duties, and all were necessary to complete a ship. Caulkers waterproofed the ships by tightly hammering strands of old rope called 'oakum' between the seams of the planks, which were then sealed with tar. Carpenters were responsible for building the workshops and wooden buildings in the dockyard. Joiners made furniture and carried out the finer aspects of woodwork. To rig a ship properly required mastmakers, ropemakers, sailmakers, block makers, and riggers. Blacksmiths and nailsmiths made all the nails, anchors, and iron fittings. Carvers were responsible for the figurehead and ornate decoration on the ship. Painters carried out both the decorative and preservative painting of the ship. Colourmakers dyed cloth to make the flags. The scavelmen carried out any necessary groundwork such as digging the docks.

Likewise, the diverse skills required to make a model means that the Navy Board ship models were probably the work of many different specialist craftsmen, each selected for a particular aspect of the work – in contrast to today, where model makers often work alone. Model making also required additional skills to those

The elegant decoration along the stern of this model of an unidentified 100-gun ship of around 1725, which includes fine veneers, gold-painted frieze work, and delicately carved bone, shows the variety of skilled craftsmanship exhibited on the Navy Board models. (SLR0422)

normally expected of a shipwright. Model makers needed knowledge of joinery and cabinet making, including working with fine veneers and decorative carving. An understanding of rigging was another essential skill.

Little evidence can be found about model makers' workplaces or working conditions. Commissioner Beach wrote that the Master Shipwright of Chatham employed model makers 'either in his own house or elsewhere' in 1677.[63] Later, the Surveyor of the Navy Edmund Dummer reputedly employed a model maker named Boneland to work in his own house in the 1690s.[64]

A model advertised for sale as 'a curious Model Ship rigged after the nicest manner by Mr David Hartley, late Boatswain of his Majesty's Ship the *Royal George*' was possibly made and kept at Hartley's family home in Broad Street in Brompton, near Chatham Dockyard. The advert, posted by his widow in the *London Journal* on 27 November 1725, went on to describe the model thus:

> It is wrought by a Scale of one quarter Inch to a Foot, stands in a Glass Frame; the Blocks belonging to the Rigging are mostly Ivory, and the small Rigging all Silk with all other Things requisite for such a Machine.[65]

However, because the naval architectural skills and information required to make a model's hull were closely linked to those of the shipwrights, it is most likely that model makers occupied the same space in the Royal Dockyards. A lot of the shipwrights' work would naturally have taken place where the ship was being constructed in the dockyard, either in dry-dock or on a slipway. Master shipwrights even personally travelled to the forest to select suitable trees. However, much of the design work would take place in the mould loft, which was a large room used for chalking out the shape of the frames on the floor from measurements that were scaled up from plans. For model makers, working in the mould loft would not only have allowed access to the ship plans that they needed, but exposed them to discussion among shipwrights about the construction and the hull shape.

By the mid-eighteenth century, references to model makers became more frequent, possibly due to better record-keeping. Most of these are connected to the more frequent use of block or frame models for ship design. The working conditions of model makers in the mid-eighteenth century give an indication of model-making practice in the preceding decades, despite the fact that by this time the Navy Board-style model had begun to decline in favour of the fully planked Georgian style. It is possible that many of these model makers learned their trade from working in the traditional Navy Board style.

In May 1727, the Navy Board approved Samuel Bastard 'now employed in the Model Loft at Portsmouth … to be made Foreman on Float'.[66] The explicit reference to a 'model loft' is significant because it is known that during the nineteenth century, ship models were made in small workshops located in the roofs of dockyard buildings.[67] However, it is possible that the author simply mistakenly wrote 'model loft' instead of 'mould loft', as both words have the same etymology. The

Georgian-style 1:34.3 scale model of the First Rate *Victory* (1737), commissioned for the Admiralty boardroom in 1740. The main wale is japanned. (SLR0449)

English word 'model' is derived from the Middle French *modelle* and the Italian *modello*, meaning 'a model or mould', which came from the Romance *modellus*, which in turn came from Latin *modulus*, meaning 'a small measure or standard'. 'Mould' is derived from the Old French *modle*, which also comes from the Latin *modulus*.[68] Both the words and objects are intertwined, but their relationships have changed and adapted to suit the context.

The Admiralty commissioned a Georgian-style model of a First Rate to stand in the boardroom in 1749 but complained that it had still not been finished four years later. They requested to 'have the assistance of the three persons from Deptford who have experience in making models', presumably to speed up construction.[69] Three shipwrights from Deptford – James Edwards, John Mitchell, and Adam Cooper – were promptly sent to Woolwich 'to assist in completing the ship model for the Admiralty Boardroom'.[70] Once the model was made, the Admiralty hired a specialist London 'Japanner', George Elphick, to work on the model. Japanning was a technique that involved coating in a dark lacquer and polishing.[71] This highly decorative Georgian model is now in the NMM collection (SLR0449).[72]

When making ship models, it is likely that specialists were brought in to work on them rather than risk moving the delicate objects. In 1752, the carved work on a model at the Naval Academy in Portsmouth was deemed too fragile to be moved 'without running the risk of breaking some part thereof, as it is so curiously cut'.[73] The complex and multifaceted nature of model making meant that it was a collaborative process involving highly specialised skills. The exquisite carved work on the Navy Board ship models, for example, not only required the model maker to have the practical skill of carving in miniature, but also a knowledge of the symbolism and historical background that lend force to that art.

Models and Art

Navy Board models are a curious blend of technical skill and artistic endeavour: they are both accurately proportioned representations of a ship and furnished with delicate and intricate decoration. Their function spans the same divide, evident, for instance, in Pepys's use of ship models both as objects to display proudly and as an educational tool. This part discusses the artistic and stylistic influences on the decoration of Navy Board models, much of it taken from architectural styles over the period. It then looks at the relationship between the ship model and marine painting in the seventeenth and eighteenth centuries, including the use of models as a source of study by artists. Finally, it investigates the ship model as a subject for painting in its own right, blending even further the realms of art and science.

Ship Models and Ship Decoration

While navy ships always had some form of decorative detail, the ornate style common during the seventeenth and early eighteenth centuries became popular under Charles I. The most elaborate example was the *Sovereign of the Seas*, the largest and most expensive warship of its type when launched in 1637 at Chatham Dockyard. The total cost was £65,586 (equivalent to nearly £10 million today), of which the decoration accounted for some £6,691. As a patron of the arts, Charles I took a particular interest in the finished detail of the ship's design, and he employed the services of the court painter Anthony van Dyck (1599–1641) and the famous playwright Thomas Heywood (*c.*1570–1641) to submit designs for the carved decoration. Charles issued an order on 23 March 1636, stating:

> The head with all the carved work thereof, and the rails to be all gilt, and no other colour used thereupon but black. The stern and galleries to be gilt with gold and black in the same manner, with the rails on them to be likewise gilt with gold. The sides to be all carved

'Peter Pett and the *Sovereign of the Seas*', by Sir Peter Lely, *c.*1645–50. (BHC2949).

> work according to the draught which was presented to his majesty and that carved work to be all gilt with gold, and all the rails of the sides to be likewise gilt with gold and no other colour to be used on the sides but black. Also the figures in the upper strake to be altered into badges of carved work answerable to the other strake, that runs fair with it, and to be gilt answerable to the rest.[74]

This detailed royal guidance on the warship's decoration provides clear evidence for the influence of classical iconography and baroque art and architecture on the subjects depicted and their style of representation. Heywood's published description of the decoration of the *Sovereign of the Seas* reveals how heavily he drew on his knowledge of Latin plays and the characters and iconography from the classical period. This was combined with the baroque style's theatricality, projection of power, triumph and control to create the visual narrative that Charles demanded for his most powerful statement of English naval power.[75]

Despite the austerity of the Commonwealth period (1649–60), the models made during this time do not show any significant change in decoration. It seems that the lavishly carved royal iconography was simply replaced with Commonwealth imagery, such as the *Naseby*'s figurehead depicting Cromwell. In fact, at the Restoration of Charles II in 1660, the royal symbols, such as coats of arms, were restored to the suitably renamed ships. For example, the *Naseby* became the *Royal Charles* and a new royal coat of arms was added to the stern. The ship model went through a similar transformation, as illustrated by SLR0217, where a royal coat of arms has been added to a model from the Commonwealth era. After, endorsing the political position of the king seems to have set the trend for decoration in the rest of the seventeenth century.

This model of a frigate (SLR0217), which fits the dimensions of those built in the Commonwealth period, has a Stuart royal coat of arms on the stern.

During the Restoration period the influence of delicate carvings made of wafer-thin limewood by carvers like Grinling Gibbons can clearly be seen in the Navy Board models of the late seventeenth century. Described by Horace Walpole as a 'citizen of nature',[76] Gibbons's style was characterised by ornate festoons, foliage, birds, and fish. Elements on the models that were otherwise purely structural were formed into decorative figures, and the carvings on the stern and quarter galleries that included mythological figures and putti were given a lifelike quality.[77] This delicate skill can also be seen in the Continental cabinet-makers who came over to Britain after the Restoration of Charles II and there may have been some crossover in skills and subject matter between furniture and model makers.

By the beginning of the eighteenth century, the cost of decorating warships was considered by the Admiralty to be getting out of hand. In 1700, the carved decoration for a First Rate could cost up to £900.[78] On 16 June 1703, the Admiralty issued an order limiting the amount of decoration allowed on the ships:

> That the carved workes be reduced to only a Lyon and Trayl board for the Head, with Mouldings Instead of Bracketts placed against the Timbers. That the Stern have only a Taffarell & Two Quarter Pieces, & in lieu of Bracketts between the Lights of the Stern, Galleryes & Bulkheads, to have Mouldings fixed against the Timbers; That the Joyners workes of the sides of the great Cabbins, Coach, Wardroom, & Round-house, of each ship be fixed only with Slit Deales glewed, & plained, without any sort of Moulding or Cornish, & the painting be onely plain Colour ...[79]

This change is reflected in many of the Navy Board models after this date. This includes the substantial replacement of carved work with lighter, more elegant carvings and the omission of wreathed gun ports and the gold paint of previous decades. While the standard figurehead for the period was the lion rampant, this was not the case for the First or Second Rates, whose figureheads would sometimes be a symbolic representation of the ship's name.

In the early eighteenth century, Classical and Palladian architectural styles increasingly influenced decorative and structural details – notably from architects like Inigo Jones (1573–1652) who pioneered the classical style in his designs for the Banqueting House in Whitehall and the Queen's House in Greenwich. These influences are reflected in the decoration of ship models, most noticeable in features surrounding the lights (windows); on the stern and quarter galleries, the earlier carved caryatids made way for pilasters and mullions.

BELOW LEFT
Banqueting House, designed by Inigo Jones, completed 1622.

BELOW RIGHT
Stern of the *Royal William.* (SLR0409)

The figurehead of the *Royal William*. (SLR0409)

The classical influence during the seventeenth and eighteenth centuries can be seen in carved decoration depicting monarchs in classical attire as a Greek or Roman hero, together with other associated figures and trophies of war. For example, the *Royal William* (1719) (SLR0408) has a double mounted equestrian figurehead depicting William III as a Roman general or legate carrying a marshal's baton in his hand. The figurehead is comparable to a depiction of William III on a medal commemorating the bombardment of the French coast during the Nine Years War. The obverse shows William with laureate, dressed as a Roman general, the symbolic lightning bolt known as a fulmen in his right hand. Representations such as these were part of a wider visual vocabulary that was expressed in ship decoration as much as it was in the rest of the arts.

The classical influence can also be seen in the tradition of naming warships after classical figures. For example, the figurehead on a model of the 74-gun *Ajax* (1767) (SLR0311) shows a full-length warrior in stylised classical armour and plumed helmet. When a ship was named after a town or city, it often included a reference to this in some form or another, typically in the coat of arms on the taffrail. This can be seen on the model of the *Yarmouth* (SLR0454), which includes the town's coat of arms of three lions, each with the tail of a herring. As many of the models do not have their names painted on the stern counter, this can be the only way to identify which ship the model represents – further confirmed by the plans, if they have survived.

Stern of *Yarmouth* (1748) showing the coat of arms of the town of Great Yarmouth in the middle of the taffrail. (SLR0454)

The importance of Greek and Roman iconography as the basis for a visual narrative is readily illustrated on the friezes along the bulwarks. These often consist of a series of interacting figures and trophies of war, together with foliage and animals. On the models they are either painted directly onto the wood or painted onto paper and then attached to the planking. Occasionally, depending upon the importance of the ship portrayed or the quality of the model, the interiors were also decorated. This could be in the form of painted cabins and bulkheads with inlaid woods of different colours (see SLR0012 in the Catalogue). The way these cabins were fitted out to some extent reflected domestic influences from wealthy homes on land, albeit with the inherent restrictions of a ship. The decks in the large cabins at the stern could be decorated either with an inlaid compass rose or with diamond designs mimicking the painted canvas floor covering of the actual ship, but this may actually follow the style of marble flooring in large houses. These too were both features painted directly onto the model's deck, or onto paper and glued on.

Medal commemorating the bombardment of the French coast. On the obverse, the Latin legend translates as 'To Jove, the Thunderer' with the exergue below as: 'William by the Grace of God King of Great Britain'. The reverse shows ships bombarding coast towns, buildings in flames; the sun in glory above and the legend translates as: 'He beholds the cities in flames, and cannot bear so great a heat' and the exergue as: 'Thunder hurled against the maritime towns of France'. (MEC0343, 1694, F. Kleinert)

Ship Models and Marine Art

English marine painting developed in the seventeenth century as a result of England's expanding mercantile and imperial power. Many early marine paintings were produced by non-specialists with little knowledge of seafaring or ships.[80] However, the increasing political and cultural significance of ships meant that depicting them accurately was important. From the middle of the seventeenth century there was an influx of Dutch artists who were familiar with the maritime genre, especially seascapes and ships. It was at this time that the Navy Board models first appeared, but the extent to which ship models were used by marine artists is still unclear, as the sources are limited.

Most classically trained artists used maquettes or models as aids to help achieve the correct proportions and structure within the composition of a picture. This was certainly the case with the famous Dutch father-and-son partnership of Willem van de Velde the Elder and Younger. Their reputation was well established in the Netherlands and they were brought to the attention of Charles II during his exile from Commonwealth Britain. Later, in about 1672, as a consequence of the Dutch economic collapse brought about by the French invasion, the family was forced to move abroad and settled in England. They were soon employed again in the drawing and painting business and within a year were working by Royal Appointment. On 12 January 1673, Charles II issued an order to the Board of Admiralty:

> for paying ye summe of 100£ during his Majesty's pleasure unto William Vande Velde the Elder for taking and making draughts of sea

fights and also for paying the like sum to William Vande Velde the younger, for putting the draughts of sea fights into colours.[81]

The south facade of the Queen's House with the van de Veldes' studio located in the bottom left.

They were also offered space for their studio in the Queen's House, the royal palace in Greenwich designed by Inigo Jones for James I's wife Anne of Denmark in 1616. An order dated 26 May 1674 to the Keeper of Her Majesties' Lodgings offers them 'working space in the Queen's House for the painting of a large Shuite of designes for tapestry hangings', where they set up studio in the southwest parlour.[82] It has been noted that after the death of Willem van de Velde the Elder, the residue of the estate that remained unsold from the public auction on 24 January 1694 included a ship model.[83] Furthermore, in 1705, Bainbrigg Buckeridge mentioned him in his *Essay towards an English school of painting* :

> He gave an easy freedom to his Sails and Tackle, as also to every part of a ship due proportion with infinite neatness. For his better information in this way of Painting, he had a Model of the masts and tackle of a Ship always before him, to that nicety and exactness, that nothing was wanting in it, nor nothing unproportionable.[84]

Miniature of Willem van de Velde the Younger, by an unknown artist, *c.*1675. (MNT0131)

Buckeridge finally mentions that this model was now in the hands of van de Velde's son, whom he describes as 'a living master, whom no age has equalled in Ship painting'.[84] Accuracy was highly prized in marine art and the van de Veldes were even known to have taken to the sea in order to sketch the detail of events as they happened. However, they did not always have the opportunity to study ships at sea, so back in their studio they would use their numerous sketches, notes, and ship models to produce what are now considered among the best maritime masterpieces. Their paintings were commissioned by patrons who were probably serving or retired senior officers, or wealthy individuals with a maritime background. Therefore it was important for their reputation that they were able to portray the complex curves, proportions, and layout of the ship and its rigging accurately. The use of a three-dimensional model, which could be physically articulated at various angles and lines of sight, must have proved invaluable.

Apart from the van de Veldes, there is nothing similar recorded about other high-profile artists who painted portraits and maritime scenes. For instance, Peter Lely's portrait of Peter Pett and the *Sovereign of the Seas* (BHC2949) includes a highly detailed and well-proportioned illustration of the ship. There is no evidence that Lely either painted that part of the composition or had access to a model, although whoever completed the portrait of the ship must have had detailed knowledge to

OPPOSITE PAGE
'The English Ship *Royal Sovereign* With a Royal Yacht in a Light Air', by Willem van de Velde the Younger, 1703. (BHC3514)

get it right. The Dutch artist Isaac Sailmaker (*c.*1633–1721) was perhaps the first marine artist working in England, but again there is no surviving evidence for his using models when painting the many warships, yachts, and portraits that appear in his works.

Further references to the use of models by artists during the eighteenth century are very rare. However, from the nineteenth century onwards, a number of well-known marine artists such as E.W. Cooke, J.M.W. Turner, Clarkson Stanfield, and William Lionel Wylie are all known to have used and owned ship models, some of which survive in public collections today.[86] More recently, art has been used to identify ship models. In the early twentieth century, nautical scholar and founding NMM trustee Dr R.C. Anderson was able to establish the identity of a model (SLR0002) as the *St Michael* after comparing it to two drawings of *St Michael* by the van de Veldes, one showing the figurehead (PAF6608) and another the broadside (PAI7579). The similarities between the drawings and the model, which also matched the dimensions of the original ship, confirmed it was *St Michael*, making it the oldest English model to be identified as a specific ship.

An unsigned pencil drawing by Willem van de Velde the Younger shows a figurehead labelled 'd Mighal', possibly depicting the Greek myth of Ganymede, shown in a chariot being drawn by an eagle to be Zeus's cup bearer. (PAF6608)

The gunport arrangement and decoration of this 1:48 scale model of the *St Michael* (SLR0002) dated to *c.*1669 matches closely with the van de Velde drawings.

Ship Models in Art

In seventeenth-century England, ship models were not only tools for artists' studies to capture the hull shape accurately, but the models themselves showcased the carved and painted decoration of the ships with all its cultural and political significance. The wealthy men who commissioned these models were usually professionally connected to the sea, and so ornate ship models were not only complex works of art, but became important symbols of social status. Models were certainly considered valuable enough to have appeared in the wills and inventories of the wealthy, either to be sold at auction or passed down to family members. This led to models being depicted as prominent 'furniture' within depictions of house interiors, and later as the subject of artistic depiction in their own right. An early example is an engraving by Bernard Lens (1659–1725) entitled 'The Representation of a First Rate Ship in the Manner they are Moddelled'. It is clear from this work that it represents a scale ship model built in the Navy Board style, and as the title suggests, it illustrates the modelling style then in favour.

Another early example of a picture of a ship model is an undated drawing in the NMM's Admiralty ship plans collection. This depicts the First Rate *Royal William*, launched in 1719, and clearly shows a Navy Board-style model mounted within

The *St Michael* by Willem van de Velde the Elder dated to *c*.1676, illustrating the arrangement of the gun ports, channels, double wale and entry port amidships on the middle gun deck. (PAI7579)

FOLLOWING PAGES
'The Representation of a First Rate Shipp in the Manner they are usually Moddelled', by Bernard Lens (*c*.1702). (PAI5059)

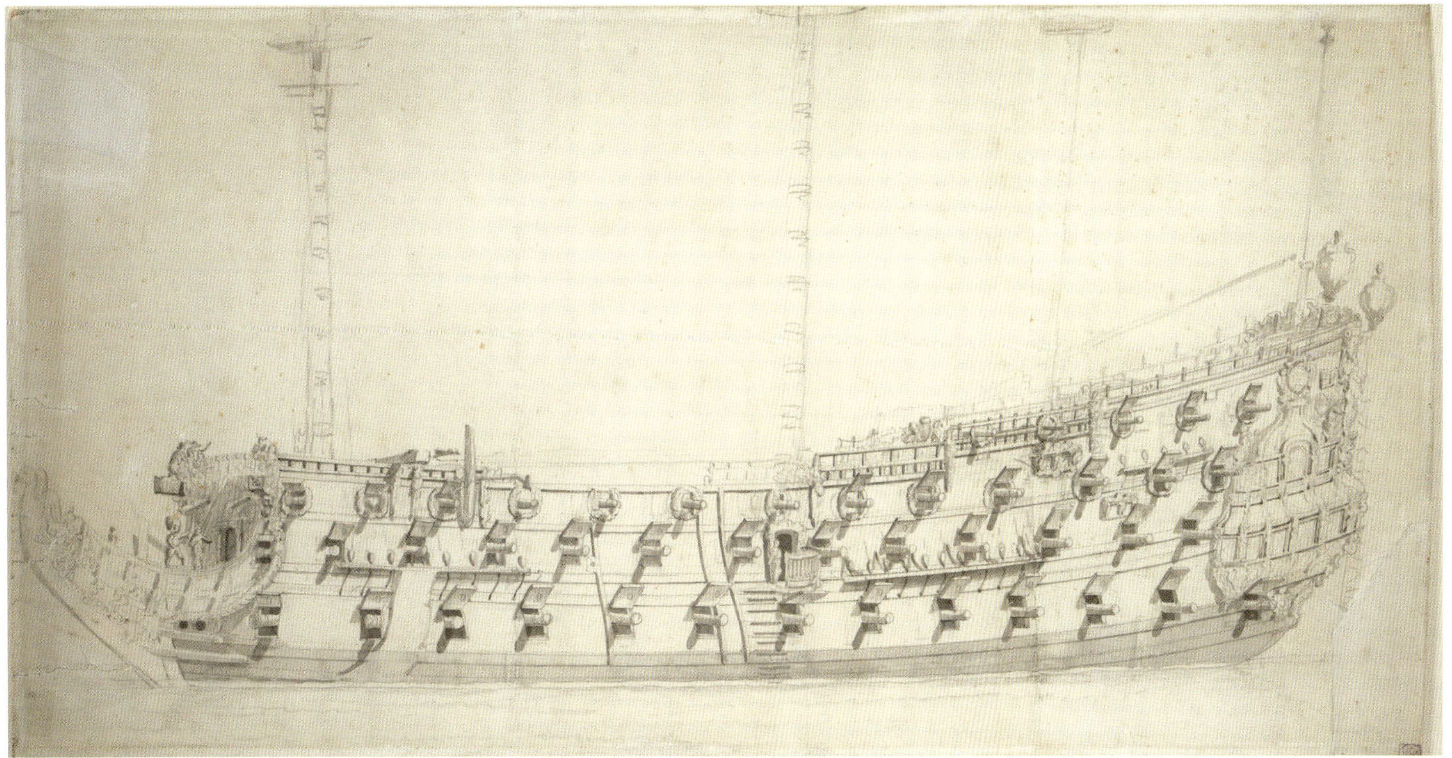

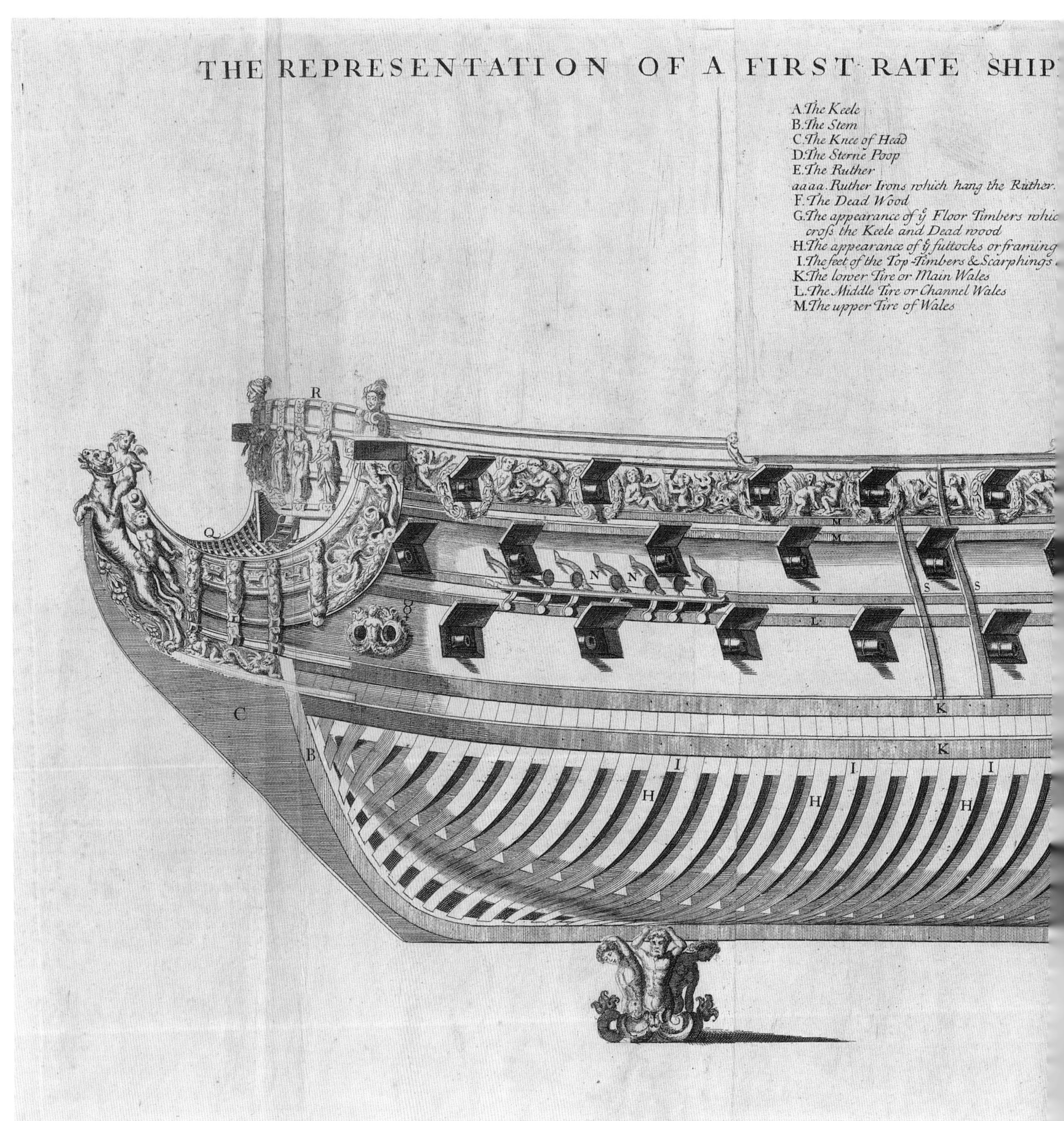
THE REPRESENTATION OF A FIRST RATE SHIP
A. The Keele
B. The Stem
C. The Knee of Head
D. The Sterne Poop
E. The Ruther
aaaa. Ruther Irons which hang the Ruther.
F. The Dead Wood
G. The appearance of ye Floor Timbers whic
cross the Keele and Dead wood
H. The appearance of ye futtocks or framing
I. The feet of the Top-Timbers & Scarphings
K. The lower Tire or Main Wales
L. The Middle Tire or Channel Wales
M. The upper Tire of Wales

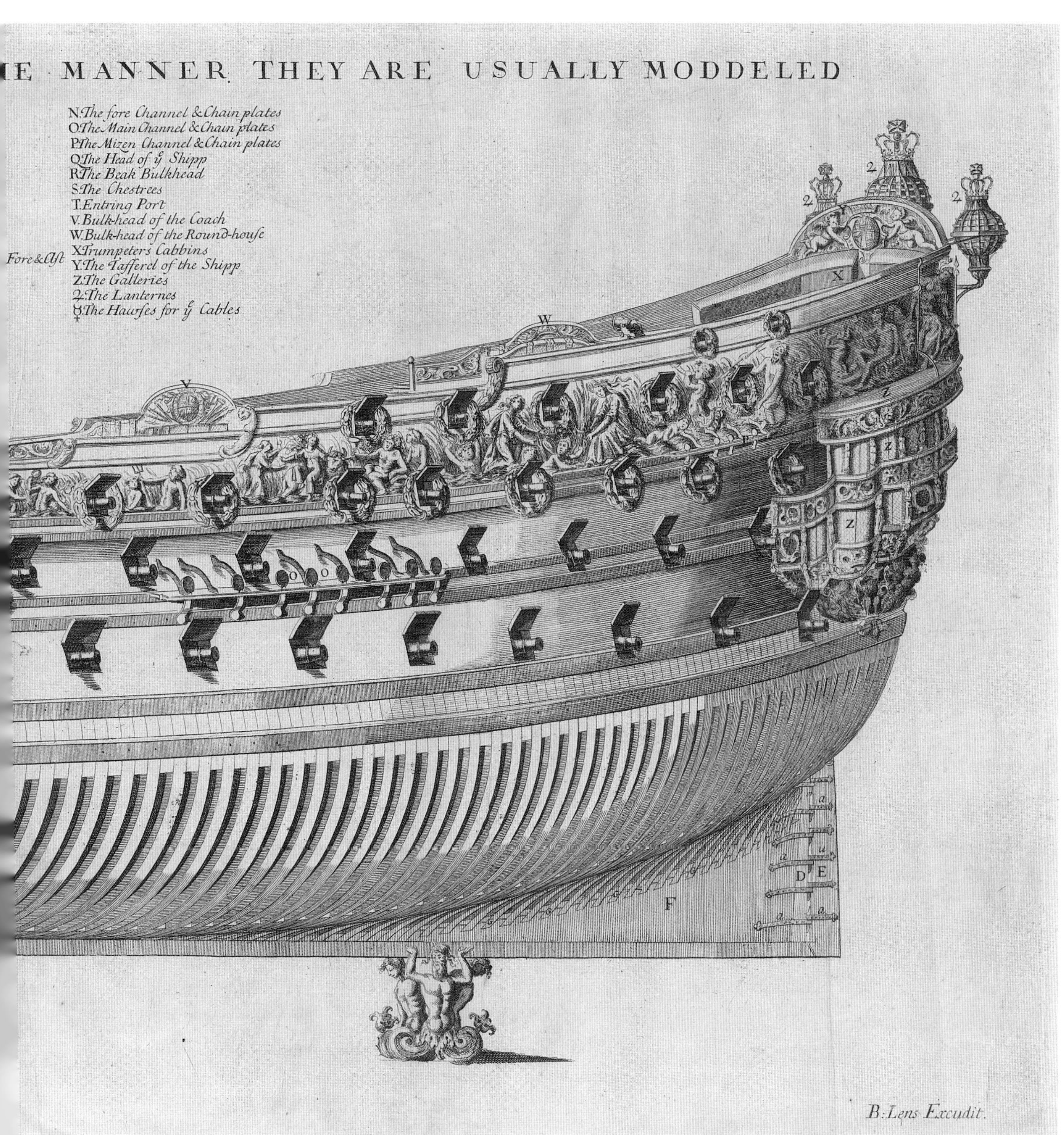
E MANNER THEY ARE USUALLY MODDELED
N. The fore Channel & Chain plates
O. The Main Channel & Chain plates
P. The Mizen Channel & Chain plates
Q. The Head of ye Shipp
R. The Beak Bulkhead
S. The Chestrees
T. Entring Port
V. Bulk-head of the Coach
W. Bulk-head of the Round-house
Fore & Aft X. Trumpeters Cabbins
Y. The Tafferel of the Shipp
Z. The Galleries
2. The Lanternes
☿. The Hawses for ye Cables
B: Lens Excudit.

a display case, complete with the baseboard and case columns. While it looks very similar to a draught of a ship plan, the perspective and detailed depiction of the decoration work suggest that it is more likely to be a study in preparation for a later painting. There are at least four contemporary models of the *Royal William* (1719), but it bears a striking resemblance to a model in the NMM's collection (SLR0409), with some minor differences at the bow, such as the lack of

BELOW
Perspective drawing of the starboard outboard profile of a Navy Board model of the *Royal William* (1719). (ZAZ0143)

BOTTOM
1:60 scale model of the *Royal William* (1719). (SLR0409)

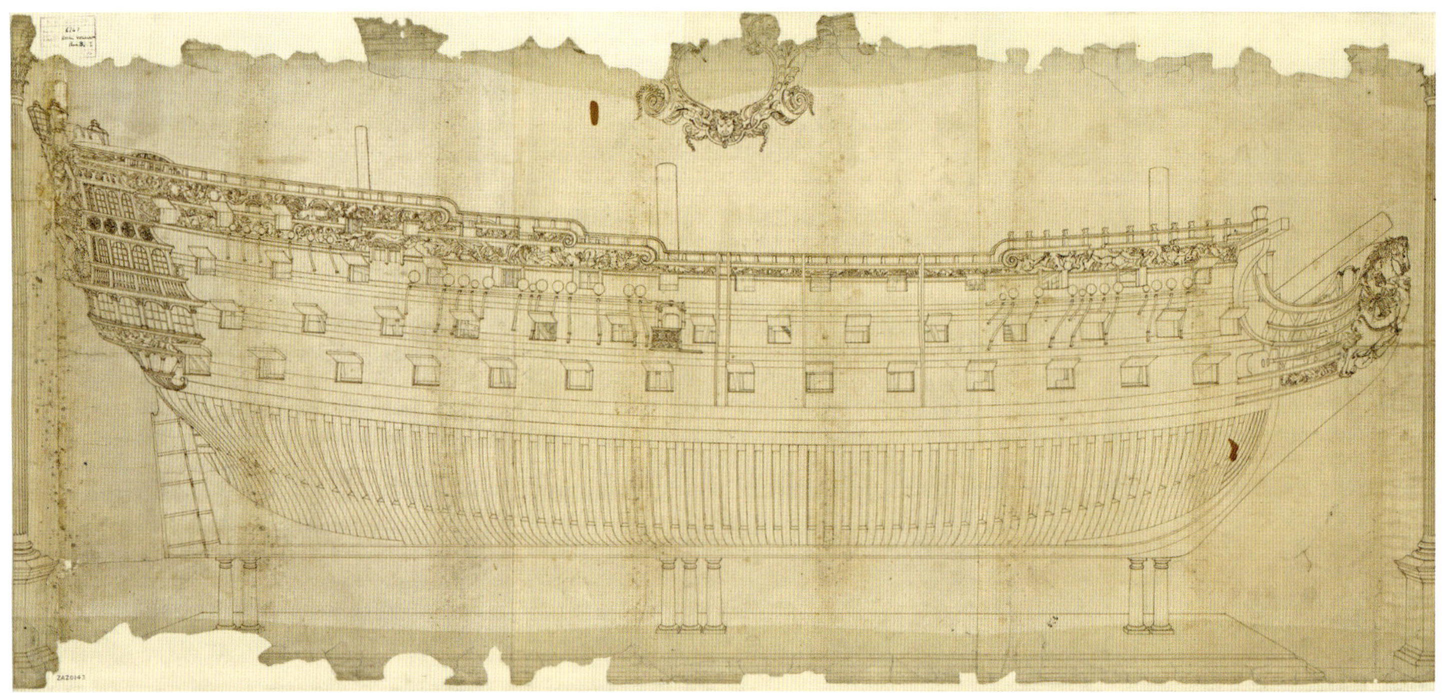

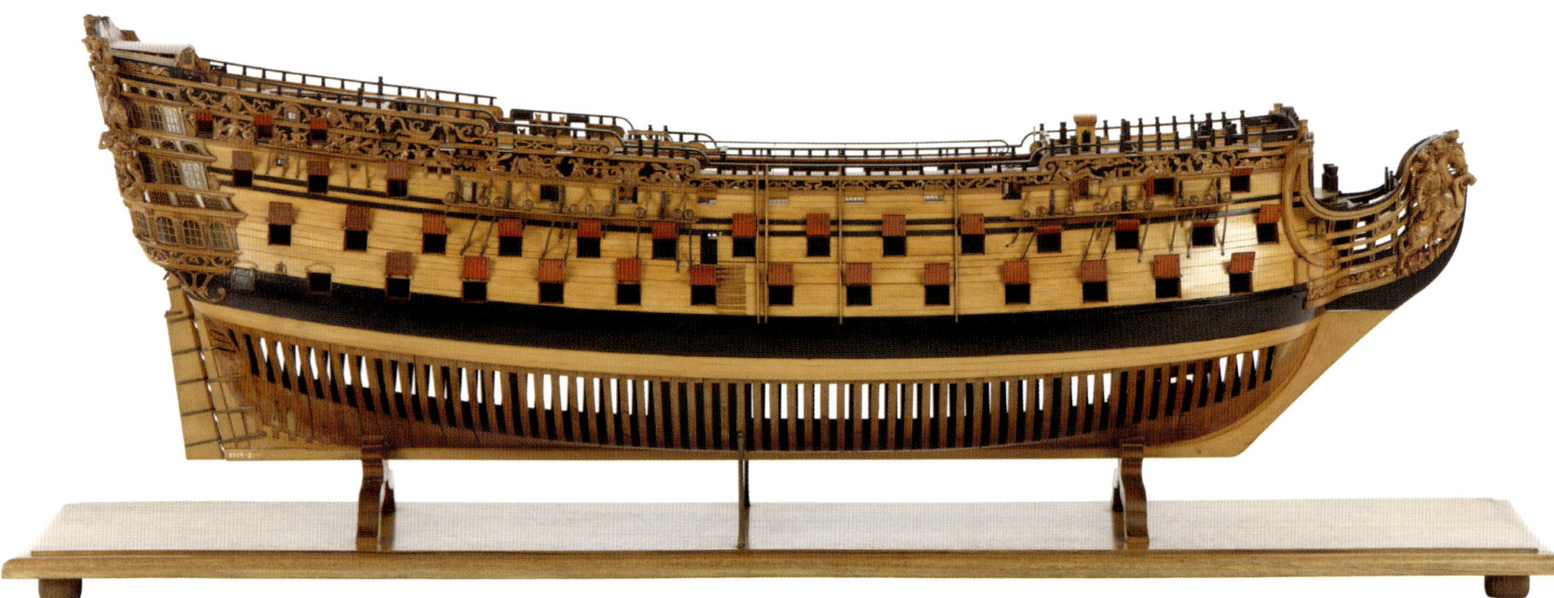

cant frames and the inclusion of a bow chase-port on the model. There is also a slightly later unsigned painting of this ship on paper, laid on board, complete with a cartouche dated 1729.[87]

Another example of this unique genre is a series of oil paintings commissioned by Lord Sandwich, First Lord of the Admiralty, for George III as part of a wider scheme to stimulate his interest in the Navy. This was in response to a royal request to Sandwich in August 1773, 'to have a Book containing the plans of the most capital Ship of each Rate to be made. This I think would thoroughly compleat the Naval Collection'.[88] Sandwich consulted with Sir John Williams, the Surveyor of the Navy, and they looked at two possibilities. First was a conventional scale plan with the outboard works marked in black and the inboard detail in red. The second option was a pair of paintings showing a bow and stern view of a model of the

'A Model of HMS *Enterprise*', by Joseph Marshall, 1777. One of two in the original series, now held at the National Maritime Museum. (BHC3323)

Berwick, launched in 1743, painted by Williams in 1747. The latter style was chosen and paintings of twelve ships were commissioned, ranging from a First Rate ship of the line down to a fireship.

The draughtsman, Joseph Williams, was ordered to assist the painter, Joseph Marshall, to produce a bow and stern view of each ship. The last six paintings were delivered in August 1775. It is interesting to note here that the artist, Joseph Marshall, needed to be assisted by the draughtsmen Joseph Williams and John Binmer, suggesting that Marshall was unfamiliar with the technical nature of naval architecture. This solution to fulfilling the king's request was a better use of time and cost less. The paintings could be hung on walls, thus taking up less space.

The paintings clearly show the models in the earlier Navy Board style, with their open frames, despite the fact that by the 1770s this type of model construction was superseded by the more realistic and 'clinically finished' Georgian style. However, the open frames, with the light colour of the wooden frames and their dark shadows, portray the hull shape in a more interpretive way, enabling the eye to better understand the complex shapes of the underwater hull.

This section has illustrated how the Navy Board models were influenced, like the full-scale warships, by the art and architecture of the period. They reflect changes in taste and style, as well as the different Admiralty Orders to try to make building and fitting of warships cheaper. The models were also muses for early marine artists who appreciated their accuracy when creating correctly proportioned ships in their marine paintings, and ultimately the models became the subject of paintings themselves, even when their style was effectively obsolete. The Navy Board models' blend of technical and artistic qualities makes them all the more precious and fascinating for those who own them, work with them, make modern replicas, or paint them.

'A Model of the *Royal George*', by Joseph Marshall, 1779. (BHC3603)

ROYAL GEORGE
1st Rate 100 Guns
850 Men

Construction and Materials

Ship plans can tell us a great deal about seventeenth- and eighteenth-century shipbuilding but the earlier designs give little indication of materials, framing patterns, and planking structures. Maritime archaeology has also contributed enormously to our understanding, but rarely is an archaeologist presented with the level of preservation seen on the *Mary Rose* or the *Vasa*.[1] It was once assumed that there was little difference between a Navy Board model's construction and that of a full-sized ship.[2] However, in more recent times, previous assumptions about the Navy Board models have been questioned. In fact, building on research by Dr R.C. Anderson in the early twentieth century, John Franklin illustrated that many of the models' construction features differed from those of full-sized ships.[3]

Despite the fact that there is variation between the construction of a full-sized ship and the models that represent them, ship models remain an invaluable source for understanding seventeenth- and eighteenth-century shipbuilding practices. It is important to understand that taking the construction of the Navy Board models at face value can pose problems for their interpretation. Almost all ship models, no matter how faithful, will differ from the full-sized vessel in some aspect of their construction. For this reason, it is important that models are treated as objects of material culture in their own right, somewhat separate from that of their full-sized counterparts.

Every model maker must strike a balance between realism and practicality when making a reduced-scale model. Not only will the availability of materials and tools have a direct impact on a ship model's construction, but so will the model's intended purpose. Consequently, the chosen method of construction needs to best suit the purpose of the model, rather than simply being a recreation of the process of shipbuilding at a small scale. A ship model must not be judged solely against how accurately its construction conforms to that of the full-sized ship, but also against the extent to which it fulfils its purpose, which differs from that of the ship.

A model may have been made to demonstrate a particular feature or fitting, in which case its overall appearance might not be as important. On the other hand, if a model was only made to show the overall arrangement or hull shape, some fittings or features may be simplified or even omitted.

The Navy Board models can be grouped together because they all share similar construction features such as their framing and planking patterns. However, not only do they reflect the handmade idiosyncrasies of particular model makers, but their construction sometimes also varies as a result of those who commissioned the work.[4] For example, the model of the *Mordaunt* (SLR0004) includes the coat of arms of the Mordaunt family.

Moreover, a model can only depict a single point in a ship's life, whether a proposal, fitted as launched, or at some particular point in its career. In some cases, a model was later modified or updated, such as the gunport arrangement in the models of the 50-gun Fourth Rate (SLR0218) and the 70-gun Third Rate *Royal Oak* (SLR0230). If the model's owner was a former captain, the model may show it as fitted when he commanded the ship. Naturally, this determined which features were included on the model.

Model with the coat of arms of the Mordaunt family. (SLR0004)

Materials

Materials are an important consideration when making any ship model and they needn't necessarily be the same as those used to build a full-sized ship. In fact, the issue of scale precludes the use of many of the types of wood that were used on full-sized ships. Oak, for example, was used extensively on ships in this period because of its strength, but was almost never used on ship models because of the difficulty of working it at such a small scale. The large grain of oak would look out of place at a much smaller scale, and timber strength was not so important on a ship model. Not only would the realism of the model be lost, but it was also liable to become distorted. Therefore, model makers chose different wood according to the desired properties. For example, the wood used for the frames of Navy Board models are generally thought to be English fruitwoods such pear and apple. These woods are fine-grained and are not generally prone to warping or splitting, provided that temperature and humidity do not fluctuate too dramatically.

For the planking, either fruitwood or boxwood could be used. The slow growth and lack of visible grain of these species makes their wood ideal for creating a fine veneer, and the crisp finish of its suitably small grain gives the impression of oak at a 1:48 scale.

The carved decoration on the models is often made of lime (*Tilia*), holly, or boxwood. In *Silva* (1679), John Evelyn's widely read book on trees, he wrote that because of lime's 'colour, and easie working, and that it is not subject to split, Architects make with it Modells for their designed Buildings, and small Statues, and little curious Figures have been Carved of the wood'.[5]

It is often difficult to identify specific species of wood on the Navy Board models, as varnish or paint often obscures the natural colour and grain. Occasionally it is possible to study the natural finish on the underside of the figurehead or gunport wreaths, where evidence suggests it is usually boxwood. The use of endoscopes

Ship of 40–44 guns (c.1660) with mica stern lights. (SLR0367)

with controlled lighting has improved our ability to study models further by giving access to the model internally and reaching areas where the wood has been left in its natural state, without the varnish and stained finishes applied externally. It is often difficult to detect later replacements, if the work has been done to a high standard. However, internal examination using an endoscope makes it possible to find the repairs and alterations that were not or could not be covered up. The question of wood species warrants further analysis under a microscope of cross-sections of samples taken from the models.

Mica is a type of naturally occurring silicate mineral. It was known as 'muscovite' or 'Muscovy-glass' in Elizabethan England due to its use in medieval Russia as an alternative to window glass. It was used in the seventeenth century because its physical characteristics made it easy to produce very thin sheets for use in the windows and lanterns of ships.[6] This practice is replicated on the ship models, and can be seen on a model of a yacht from around 1690 (SLR0379). It was relatively easy to work and could be scored and drilled to replicate the individual panes from which a full-sized window would be constructed. Mica was preferable for models because in this period it was difficult to manufacture glass thin enough to give a realistic impression of windows on a ship model. However, with its improved manufacture, glass was later adopted on ships.

Guns on the earlier seventeenth-century models, although rare, tend to be turned in wood. These were sometimes later replaced by more realistic brass versions. Other brass or iron fittings on the Navy Board models such as hinges, brackets, guns, and anchors were generally replicated using the same materials as on the original vessel.

Gold paint was common for decorative carving in the seventeenth and early eighteenth centuries. The rest of the model was finished in a way that did not completely obscure the natural look of the wood, such as varnish, shellac, and staining. By the mid-eighteenth century, carving too was often left in its natural wooden state and only the thick wales along the sides of the hull were painted black, following trends common on full-sized vessels.

The use of bone for decorative details on models started to appear in the early eighteenth century, as its structure allows it to be carved and turned at such a small scale. It was often used for the spokes on the ship's wheel, deck pillars, stair rails, and the more intricate decorative features on stern galleries. There are no surviving examples of seventeenth-century models that include the use of bone or ivory as part of the construction or decoration. This is possibly a result of the availability of sharp tools to cut and carve the bone.

Navy Board models are generally fastened with glue or brass pins. However, there is also evidence that wooden pegs called treenails were sometimes replicated in small scale and used to secure the planking to the frame in the same manner as a full-sized ship. While little is known about the specific glues used on the Navy Board models, woodworking glues in this period were generally made from animal bones or fish, which were heated in water to extract the collagen protein.[7] This type of glue would be applied hot, and the two surfaces held in place before being allowed to cool and completely dry.

Tools

Very little is known about the exact tools that model makers used, but during this period new techniques were developed that allowed ship modelling to reach a greater level of quality. The importation of higher grade steel from Germany in the seventeenth century allowed for finer and better quality tools to be made. When Charles II returned from exile, he inspired a taste for fine furniture, which utilised new techniques imported from continental Europe.[8] Marquetry (in which thin veneers are applied to create decorative patterns), as well as staining and polishing, were subsequently adopted by ship model makers to create far superior models than before.

One of the first tasks in model making would be to cut the materials into standard flat sheets from which the model's framing could then be cut. This would have been carried out using a frame saw, which comprises a blade held under tension in the centre of a rectangular wooden frame. Better steel used to make the saws enabled the blade to be held under greater tension, thereby allowing thinner veneers to be cut.

The tension of the blade was also particularly important for the fretsaw, which became widely used in furniture making in the seventeenth century. It was also known as the 'Buhl saw' after French cabinet-maker André-Charles Boulle (1642–1732), who mastered the process of inlaying bronze and brass into furniture. The fretsaw consisted of a very shallow blade strained tightly between the ends of a U-shaped frame. The shallow depth of the blade made it possible to turn the saw to cut the intricate curves of the frames accurately.

As well as saws, a number of small hand-carving tools would have been used. Model makers would have adopted these skills and tools from a variety of crafts but it is possible that specialist model makers each undertook different aspects of work on a model. A series of chisels and gouges would have been used, each with its own purpose, either with a flat edge for working the hull framing, or with a point or curved edge for intricate carved decoration. However, evidence of exactly which tools ship model makers used is scarce.

Model makers employed various tools to produce smooth finishes. Although not mass-produced in England until the nineteenth century, sandpaper was known in the eighteenth century, and may have been used on models.[9] It is also probable that files, scrapers, and sharp blades repeatedly run across the wood at an angle were used to achieve the desired smooth surface. For the application of fastenings and fittings such as gratings, it is known that small drills were used, as broken examples have been found in the lower hull where their recovery was not possible.

Construction

Advances in naval architecture meant that ship plans became increasingly common from the end of the seventeenth century. These draughts outlined the shape of the ship on paper at a 1:48 scale (¼in to 1ft) and included numerous details about the ship's construction. It is thought that model makers worked from ship plans to produce the Navy Board models, which may explain the fact that most models were also made to a standard 1:48 scale.[10] Hence ship models may differ structurally from the actual ships, particularly as most models were not crucial to the design or construction process. Many aspects of the models' construction were simplified or stylised for the practical reason that it was not necessary to include certain details.

Framing

The first thing to note is that models' exposed hull framing, in its various configurations, is a stylised interpretation of the various parts that make up the frames of a ship.[11] To make a model in which each individual timber is shaped and then assembled one by one, as was the case in shipbuilding, was not an efficient method to make a model when these elements could be simplified. The earliest surviving model that actually shows the true construction of the hull, a style known as 'in frame', dates to 1715 and was made to show the old and improved method of framing around the bow and stern of the hulls (SLR0405).

Navy Board models followed a construction sequence that had notable differences from that used for full-sized ships. Each complete frame was cut out from planks of wood, probably with a frame saw, rather than made up of separate floor timber, futtocks, and top timbers. The hull would then be constructed of a run of complete frames glued together.

Once the frames had been smoothed using sharp tools and scrapers, it was probably checked using wooden or card templates lifted from the ship's plan. Next, on

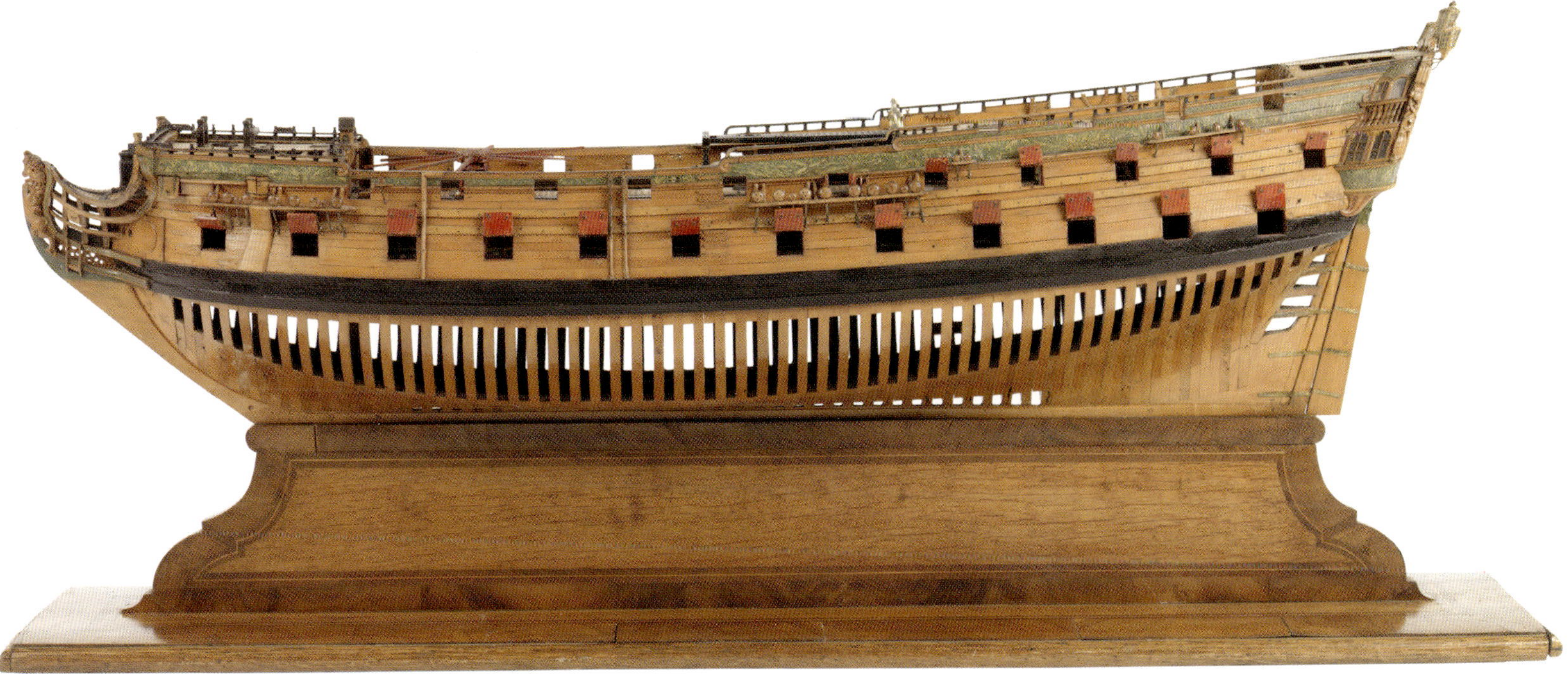

Model of a 50-gun ship, c.1715 (SLR0405), showing the hull framing as constructed, as opposed to the stylised hull framing as seen in the second example of a Navy Board model of 50-gun ship. (SLR0219)

every alternate frame, or pair of frames depending upon the style used, a section was removed using a chisel, cutting from the outside inwards, with the waste pieces falling into the hull. This process is evident by the scratch marks on the corresponding frames left from the edges of the chisel blade on either side and by the 'tears' of the grain left on the ends of the frames themselves.

There is visual evidence on the frames that the model maker would annotate the individual pieces using pencil marks to denote their position. These were a series

RIGHT
Schematic diagram of the first stage in the construction, complete frames are glued together to form the hull, before a section of each frame was removed. (Drawn by N. Ball)

FAR RIGHT
Schematic diagram of the standard Navy Board frame arrangement used for the majority of models, in which a section of every other frame is removed. (Drawn by N. Ball, after John Franklin)

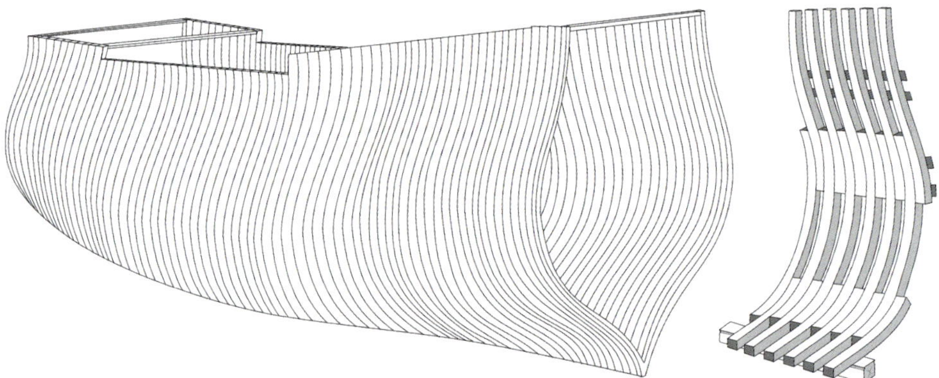

TOP
External view of the frames from below the main wale showing evidence of the scratch marks left by a chisel when removing a section of every alternate frame. The marks have darkened over time with the build-up of dust and grime. (SLR0374)

ABOVE
Endoscopic internal view of the frames at height of the main wale, showing the torn grain and the chisel marks between alternate frames. (SLR0390)

of numbers prefaced by the letters 'S' and 'L', an abbreviation for starboard and larboard (port). In most cases, similar to the ship's plans, the numbers run from the mid-ship section, denoted by a circle with a cross inside, towards the bow and stern. These annotations would have been added when cutting out the frames individually – they could not have been written on the faces of the timber after assembly due to the lack of space, although there are some cut and score marks where alternative frames have been removed with a chisel.

It is unclear why model makers chose this stylised form. One theory suggests that when the hull is viewed from bow or stern, the lighter colour of the wood contrasts with the dark shadow of the gaps and accentuates the complex curves of the hull, especially around the bow and stern.

At the bow, the framing system on a ship has to change where the hull shape curves round to a very bluff shape. The cant and hawse timbers form the area around the bow that takes the strain of the anchor cables when the anchor is deployed. On full-sized ships, the hawse pipes, where the cables enter and leave the hull, were often lined with lead to prevent the cables from chaffing. The timbers were 'canted' – leaning forward of the vertical – to take into account the shape of the bow as it rounds towards the stem. This complicated pattern of cant and hawse timbers was often simplified on the Navy Board models. For example, the *Royal William* of 1719 (SLR0409) does not include cant frames, and the hawse pieces are represented by a single wedge of wood curved to fit.

Keel, Stem, and Stern Post

One of the most significant differences between shipbuilding and model making is the construction sequence of the hull. On a full-sized ship, the keel is the first timber to be laid, hence the start of a ship's construction is referred to as the date the keel was 'laid down'. Once the keel is laid, creating the spine of the ship, the stem and stern posts are erected at either end, forming the bow and stern. Next,

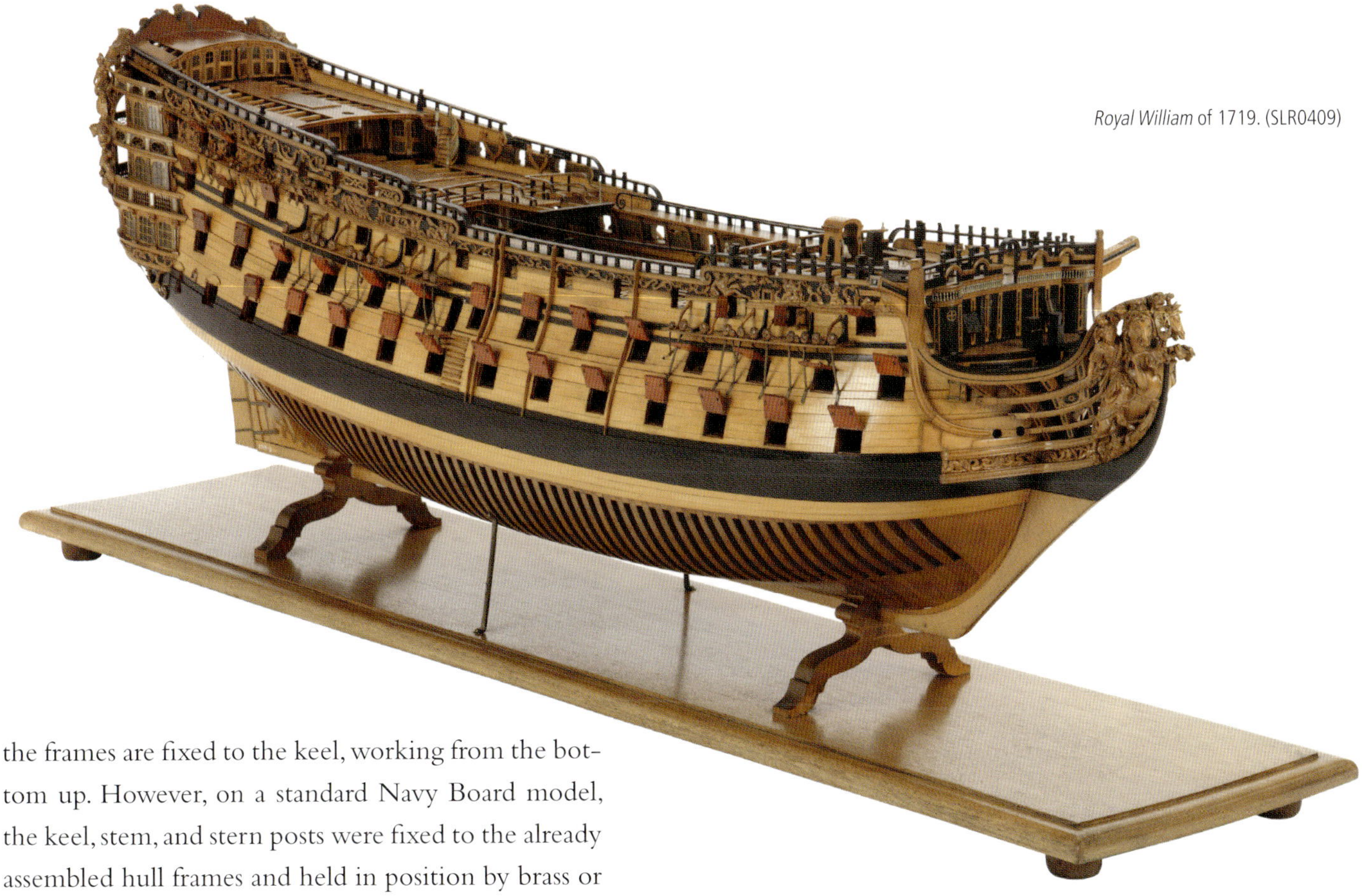

Royal William of 1719. (SLR0409)

the frames are fixed to the keel, working from the bottom up. However, on a standard Navy Board model, the keel, stem, and stern posts were fixed to the already assembled hull frames and held in position by brass or wooden fastenings together with animal glue. In most cases, the scarph joint of the keel and stem has been faithfully replicated and secured with brass pins.

Internal Structure

Before the model was decked and planked, internal fittings were fixed in place. The keelson was attached internally on top of the floor timbers, sandwiching them between this long timber and the keel below. Mast steps were often placed on top of the keelson: the mizzen mast at the stern, the mainmast near the middle, and the foremast towards the bow.

The model maker would next fit the limber strakes, footwaling, stringers, and deck clamps. These longitudinal timbers were fixed to the inside of the hull to add support to the framing, as well as provide support to deck beams and cross pillars.[12] The layer of inter-

The stem is scarphed to the keel and fixed in place with six brass pins on this model of a First Rate from around 1725. (SLR0422)

TOP
Internal view looking forward, showing the cross-pillars. (SLR0217)

ABOVE
Decorative internal cabin bulkhead, complete with a working hinged door and chequered floor decoration. (SLR0012)

nal ceiling planking is always omitted on the Navy Board models, allowing light between the frames into the hull. Often, just like on a full-sized ship, timber riders would be secured vertically to the inside surface of these longitudinal timbers on the lower part of the hull, for extra strength. Similarly, curved breast hooks were fitted horizontally to reinforce the inside of the bow framing.

Internal cross-pillars were diagonally crossed timbers used to add transverse strength to the hull of a ship, especially around the turn of the bilge. Although unnecessary on a ship model not exposed to the considerable forces impacting a real ship, they can be found in some Navy Board models (see SLR0217), possibly to demonstrate this feature, or simply pride in accuracy on the part of the model maker, illustrating a level of practical knowledge about the real process of shipbuilding.

The bulkheads, a series of vertical walls that partition the hull of a ship on all the main decks, generally take the same form on the models as on the ships. The most important are the quarter-deck bulkhead dividing the quarter deck from the waist; the forecastle bulkhead dividing the forecastle from the waist; and the beakhead bulkhead at the forward end of the forecastle. The heavy bulkheads dividing the hold are often omitted in models, however sometimes additional lighter bulkheads are installed inside the models to form individual cabins – these could often be highly decorative (see SLR0012).

Deck Planking and Beams

There are various styles of deck planking and framing, and most examples include partial planking, whereby some of the planking is omitted to expose the deck beams, carlings, knees, and ledges.

The deck beams span the width of the ship model to hold the frames in place and provide strength to the hull. They rest on the deck clamps and are supported by vertical deck pillars resting on the keelson, as well as knees. Knees were angled timbers, secured either horizontally as lodging knees, or vertically below the ends of the deck beams as hanging knees. The carlings, which run fore and aft between the deck beams, support the smaller ledges. On a ship this provided a strong structure that could support the deck planking and weight of the guns.

The most likely reason for the partial deck planking style was to let some light into the model to allow one to see the inside, whilst still providing a platform on which to mount the guns on their carriages. Moreover, on deck, there is also a section of planking along the centreline that supports the hatches, capstan, gallows, and riding bitts. However, the rest of the beams are left exposed.

Deck planking was often applied as a single sheet of wood veneer and scored to denote individual planks and butt joints. In other examples, individual planks were laid and held in place with metal and wooden fastenings or just glued.

Where a model represents a two- or three-decked ship, the deck planking below the upper deck is simpler and supports the guns on rather crude carriages without wheels, since they remain hidden from view. In addition to the deck planking, nearly all of the deck hatches are included, often with raised combings and sometimes with elaborate corner joints. Most are removable and allow access to the decks and the hold below.

Navy Board model of a 50-gun small two-decker, *c.*1703. The exposed deck beams can be seen where the planking has been omitted. In the centre is a drumhead capstan. On the right, the forecastle planking has been scored to denote individual planks. (SLR0218)

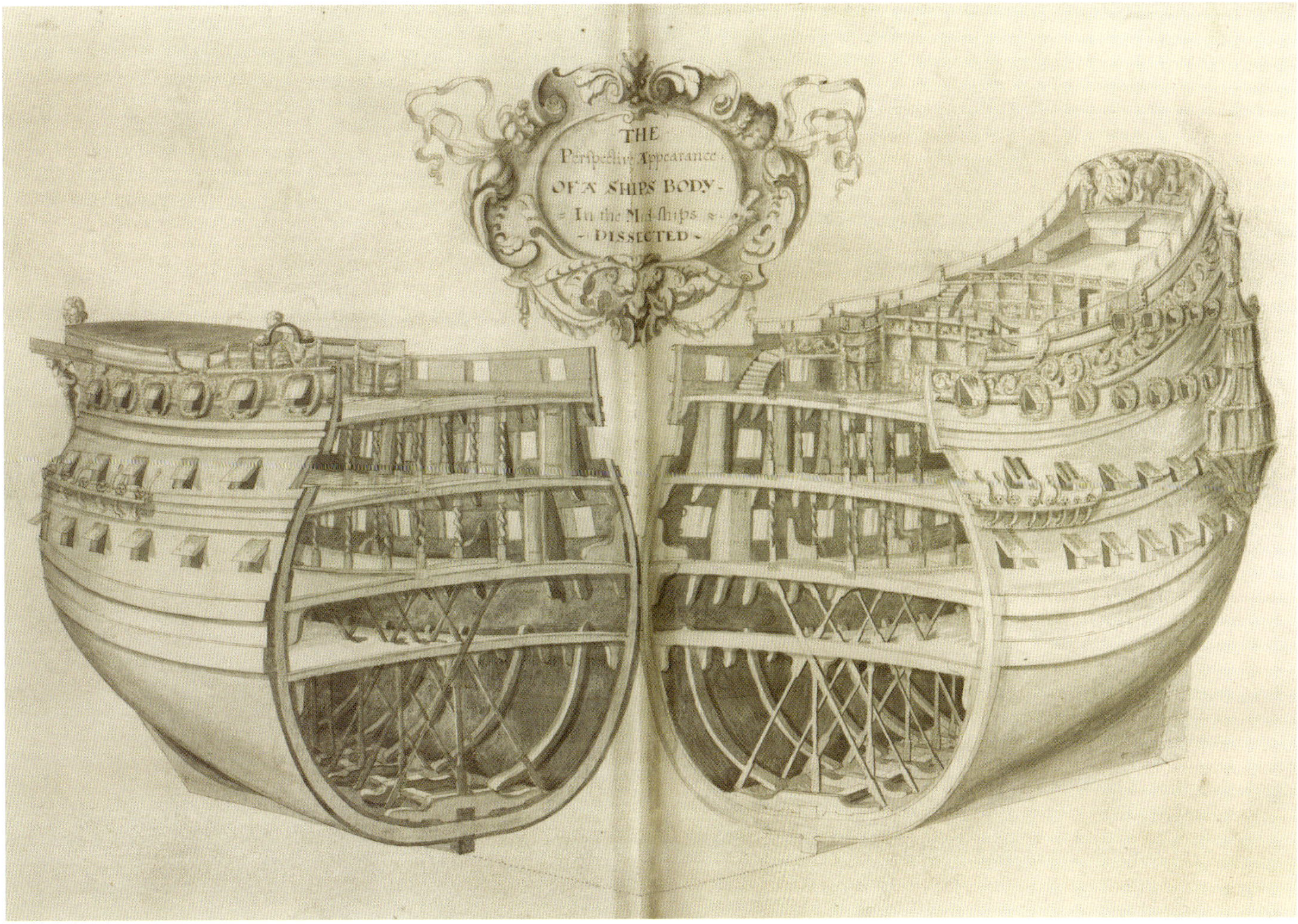

'The perspective Appearance of a Ships Body – in the Mid-ships Dissected'. (The Pepys Library, Magdalene College, Cambridge: Pepys Sea MS. 2934)

Hull Planking

The stern timbers, main wales (large horizontal timbers just above the waterline and normally painted black), and the upper wales were then fastened with either treenails or brass pins. This allowed for the correct positioning of the gunports and other external fittings such as planking, channels, and hawse holes. Purely from a practical perspective, once the wales were correctly fitted they would act as a guide for the rest of the external fittings to be positioned and applied. To position the

'Section Through a First-Rate, about 1690', after Thomas Phillips, about 1701. (BHC0872)

OPPOSITE PAGE

Three different styles of planking, from left to right: single piece of veneer secured with treenails; single flat veneer with scored planking and treenails; and individual planks. (SLR0374, SLR0389, SLR0409)

gunports and cut them out, it would be too complicated and time-consuming to make separate parts to fit between each gunport.

Partial hull planking is the main feature that distinguishes the Navy Board models from other styles. The earliest example of a Navy Board-style model (SLR0217) does not have any planking above the wales or along the upper deck. A slightly later model of a three-decker (SLR0372, *c.*1670), thought to have been made by Anthony Deane, shows planking between the main and upper wales, but is still largely left unplanked elsewhere. As the style evolved, by the end of the seventeenth century hull planking was included above the main wale and up to the bulwark screens.

Ships of the seventeenth and eighteenth centuries were usually constructed with the planks secured to wooden frames using treenails. These were wooden pegs that were hammered tightly into a pre-drilled hole through the plank and into the frame. There are some examples of models where the planks are secured with miniature treenails. In some cases planks were glued or secured to the frames using brass pins. It is rare to find Navy Board models with individual planks fitted: the more common method, particularly on seventeenth-century models, was to have a flat veneer that had the planks, joints and treenails scored or stamped on to mimic the construction of planking.

Fittings

One aspect of construction that differentiates the Navy Board from other styles of model is the high level of detail dedicated to the fittings. Rather than just showing the hull shape, the Navy Board models include numerous small details. After the major work of planking and decking, the head rails, poop deck rails, gunport lids, mouldings, bulwark screens, and cappings would be fitted. Stairs, which could be made up from individual pieces of wood or carved from a solid piece, would be fitted to lead up from the waist to the quarter deck.

One of the most noticeable fittings on the Navy Board models is often the capstan located in the waist or decks below. On a ship, this large cylindrical machine was mounted on a central spindle, fitted through a hole in the deck, and used manpower to lift heavy weights, such as the anchor, or to work the lower yards. On a Navy Board model, the large wooden barrel of the capstan was made from a single piece of wood turned on a lathe, then fitted with the whelps that gripped the cable. Bars, where the men would push, were either inserted directly through the barrel in early examples, or later into a drumhead, allowing up to ten bars to be fitted.

The rudder would be attached to the stern post with brass pintles and gudgeons. After 1703, when the ship's wheel was introduced, the wheel was mounted

Anchor secured to the port bow of the *Yarmouth* (1748, SLR0454). The anchor ring is secured to the cathead and the flukes are secured from the gravity davit.

Waist and foredeck of the *St Michael* (1669, SLR0002) showing a typical ornately carved seventeenth-century belfry, as well as wooden guns mounted on carriages.

Foredeck of the *Royal William* (1719, SLR0409) showing the plainer eighteenth-century style of belfry, as well as the galley chimney, and the foremast channel (fitted with deadeyes), on the port side.

on deck and rigged with ropes, which were led below and attached to the tiller through sheaves (see SLR0218).

Anchors are only included on some Navy Board models, often when a model was rigged. Rather than just having the anchors on the model swinging from the catheads, the inclusion of associated equipment such as the gravity davit, square span shackle, and buoys or floats give a good illustration of how the anchors were used (see SLR0454).

Furthermore, the presence of the shrouds enabled anchors to be stowed along the channels in their sea-going condition as they would have been when under sail. Linings of additional planking fitted to protect the hull where anchors are stowed can also be seen towards the bow and fitted under or near the channels.

The ship's bell was hung in the belfry located at the forecastle bulkhead. The Navy Board models often include a bell carved from wood and painted to replicate bronze – some are also fitted with working clappers and bell ropes. The belfries of the seventeenth-century models are often highly decorative, with gold-painted

The changing shape of the stern lantern. Top to bottom: *St Michael* (1669, SLR0002), First Rate, 96-gun (*c.*1702, SLR0386) and Fourth Rate, 50-gun (*c.*1714, SLR0396).

carvings, but by the early eighteenth century they became less ornate.

On the Navy Board models, the channels, which support the deadeyes for the rigging, were generally cut from the same wood as the planking, probably box-wood. The deadeyes are individually carved or turned, with a groove to take the metal strop that secures it to the brass chainplate fixed to the hull.

The position of the galley is shown on the models with a galley chimney penetrating the foredeck. Sometimes the galley stove itself is included, almost hidden in the forecastle below, illustrating the immense detail included by the model makers (see SLR0384 and SLR0012).

On three-deckers, entry ports were included to allow officers to board the ship without having to scale the high sides. These consisted of a doorway cut into the middle deck, only on the port side before the 1670s and later on both sides. Early examples were elaborately decorated, often with a small arched roof painted internally and gilt railing. Models of the larger vessels include an entry port, which was embellished either with carved wooden frames or fretted metal rails. These were painted gold on seventeenth-century models, but were left plain in the eighteenth century.

Lanterns are included at the stern on some models, and in rare cases the lanterns reserved for flagships and those leading a convoy can be found in the fighting tops, which were platforms surrounding the top part of the foremast, mainmast, and mizzen mast (see SLR0001). Larger ships would have had three mounted on the taffrail, and on the models these are made from a mixture of carved wood and gold-painted wire, glazed with mica. The Navy Board models are perhaps the best source for tracking these changes in lantern style, especially as they do not appear on plans: the lantern was spherical in the mid-seventeenth century, before the introduction of the hexagonal form at the beginning of the eighteenth century.

Armament

Few Navy Board models are fitted with guns, but the surviving examples show guns turned in a dark wood, or a lighter wood which has been stained or painted black. Some show different calibres, especially on two- and three-decker models, where the heavier, large-calibre guns are located on the lower decks. An early example, the *St Michael* (1669, SLR0002) shows guns mounted on wooden carriages with trucks. Turned brass guns started to appear on models in the early eighteenth century and are normally on more realistic carriages together with working tackles. Some models even include tompions, different shapes and mouldings on the barrels, and details of the trucks with their associated tackles.

Stern and Quarter Galleries

Before the carved and painted decoration could be added, the stern and quarter galleries needed to be fitted to the model. The stern gallery is a structure projecting aft from the stern, which in this period could either be open, taking the form of a balcony with ornate balusters, or enclosed with glazed windows (also known as lights).

The stern gallery's structure is contiguous with the quarter galleries, which are the two box-like appendages either side of the stern. Their primary function was to extend and improve the officers' accommodation. Not only did they allow more light into the cabin and better observation, but the overhanging structure of the quarter galleries was used to house the officers' toilets, where waste had an uninterrupted fall to the sea below.

Much like on the ships themselves, on the Navy Board models the galleries were built as additions to the main hull structure. Some of the more complex pieces such as the upper and lower finishing pieces and the drops are carved from a single block of wood, usually boxwood. As with most models of the Navy Board style, they are heavily decorated with carvings and paintings. Depending upon the size of warship depicted, the quarter galleries range from one tier on smaller ships to three tiers on big three-deckers. Small vessels such as sloops and yachts had a simple framed window surrounded with carved decoration, called a quarter-badge.

Small pieces of mica have been used on the stern and quarter gallery windows. They are held in place with brass or wooden fastenings together with animal glue, either as individual panes or as larger pieces covering three to four window spaces with the wooden frames overlaid. Glass was expensive and difficult to make in large sheets, so the smaller pieces had to be held in place with lead strips within a wooden frame. Often the model maker recreated the small individual panes by scoring and piercing the sheets within the wooden framework of the galleries (see SLR0005).

Decoration

The changes in decorative style from the mid-seventeenth to the late eighteenth century, and the Admiralty order of 1703, as noted in the Models and Art section, are reflected on the models themselves. This can be further appreciated through comparison of each Navy Board model in the Catalogue.

However, in the same way as each Navy Board model shares common construction features, all Navy Board models share certain decorative characteristics. It is possible to give an overview of typical decorative elements, while at the same time

Standard crowned lion rampant figureheads. On the left is a 40-gun ship from around 1685 (SLR0005); on the right is the 70-gun *Yarmouth* from 1748 (SLR0454).

pointing out significant changes between the seventeenth and eighteenth centuries. Throughout the period, the decoration on the Navy Board models, as on the ships themselves, took two forms, namely carving and painting. Despite changes to style, the position of this decoration on the vessel remained rather consistent.

The majority of the carved work can be found at the bow and on the stern, with additional decoration often adorning structural elements and fittings. Carvings, either sculptural or carved in relief, were ordinarily made of boxwood or lime, and unless the model was to be rigged these would usually be the last things to be added.

At the bow, the carved sculptural figurehead was mounted prominently on the stem knee, which was attached to the stem post. The standard Royal Navy figurehead for this period was a carved lion rampant, which appears on most models of lower-rated ships. Only First Rates or larger Second Rates would usually be fitted with a very ornate figure with further supporting embellishments, which would either have royal or mythological associations. Despite the Admiralty order of 1703 reducing the amount of decoration, during the eighteenth century this was still largely the case, and single figureheads could still even be found on a number of the lower rates such as frigates and sloops.[13]

Although the basic arrangement of the head rails at the bow remained similar over time, earlier models were painted gold, with caryatid figures adorning the head timbers. These were later replaced with more simplified moulded timbers. Below the figurehead, a carved trailboard was fitted to either side of the stem, often depicting dragons or scaled sea serpents.

Moving aft, behind the figurehead there was decoration on the bulkhead beak-

The change in style and reduction of decorations shown in the *Boyne* from 1692 on the left, and a Fourth Rate from around 1725 below. (SLR0006, SLR0431)

head, cathead and the knees. In seventeenth-century models, this took the form of sculptural figures that were later replaced by pilasters and arches made of plain mouldings. Typically, along the sides of the hull, earlier models included gold-painted wreathed gunports along the upper gun decks, and, where the rails stepped down, hancing pieces often took the form of a carved animal or scaled dolphins.

The reduction of carved decoration by the Admiralty Order of 1703 is reflected on the models themselves, most notably in the lack of carved wreaths around the gunports, the replacement of hancing pieces with simple curves, and decoration limited to painted scenes along the bulwark screens, painted with trophies of arms, floral motifs and scrolls, and animals.

Inboard, the forecastle bulkhead had carved embellishments together with the canopy of the belfry, ornate stairs leading onto the quarter deck, as well as carvings on the rails and bulkheads. The stern is the most heavily decorated part of the Navy Board models, where the structure provided a large area on which to display carved decorations. The taffrail at the top often took the form of a central bust or coat of arms, surrounded by high-relief allegorical figures, putti, and richly carved floral designs. The stern counters below were often painted with decorative trophies of arms, multicoloured drapes, and cordage.

At either side of the taffrail are the quarter figures, which were usually full-length carved sculptures. These were not only decorative, but a structural feature connecting the quarter galleries with the stern gallery. Decorative carved work enriched the lower finishing at the base of each quarter gallery. The stern and quarter gallery windows were divided by vertical carved decorations, taking the form of caryatid figures in earlier models, but by the eighteenth century, elegant pilasters, balusters, and mullions were used.

The change in style and layout of the stern shown on a model of an unidentified 90-gun ship (*c.*1675) on the left, and the *Barfleur* (*c.*1740) on the right. (SLR0003, SLR0424)

Rigging

There are very few surviving seventeenth-century Navy Board models with original rigging, and it is likely that most were not rigged at all. During the late seventeenth century the configuration of the rigging changed little, and to rig a model would have had an enormous impact on the cost and time needed to construct the model, as well as its finished size. Its size alone would have had implications for moving the model around, such as between the dockyard and the Navy Board. In the twentieth century, it became common practice to rig models for additional effect.

Even unrigged, the models give a good indication of the rigging of the ships they represent. The position of each mast is shown by a hole in the deck, and the channels and deadeyes, which appear on the majority of the models, can indicate the type of rig. For example, three holes indicated a three-masted ship-rigged (square-rigged) vessel, and a single hole would indicate a cutter-rigged yacht.

From a research point of view, rigged models are a valuable source for showing the detailed working of a sailing rig, in particular the location of the standing rigging in relation to the masts and spars, and where the running rigging was belayed or tied off. Apart from the very rare surviving early rigging warrants of 1719, most existing plans of a ship did not include this amount of detail, which was usually added once the ship had been launched.[14]

Although the rig on smaller vessels such as yachts could vary, all ships were square-rigged and consisted of three masts that supported the horizontal yards onto which the square sails were attached. Only the aft-most mizzen mast was rigged with a fore-and-aft lateen sail, and at the bow a large bowsprit, which extended forwards. The early years of the eighteenth century saw changes to the configuration of a ship's rigging, with the introduction of the jibboom and the change in shape of the fighting tops from round to square. These changes can be seen on the Navy Board models but rarely elsewhere.[15]

The jibboom was a spar used to extend the bowsprit. Before its introduction, the bowsprit normally included a small spritsail topmast standing upright at its end, such as in the *St Michael* (SLR0002). The fighting tops, which consist of trestle-trees, cross-trees, top and cap, are the structures at the masthead of the fore-, main- and mizzen masts. They are needed to support the topmast and its shrouds. From the few surviving models that are complete with largely original rigging, it is possible to determine the materials used for both the standing and running rigging.

In order to preserve a sense of scale, hemp or flax cordage could not be used on models, as the fibres were much too big. Much finer silk was used on models, laid

Rigging and sail plan of the Establishment of 1719 for a 70-gun ship.

The rigging of this Fourth Rate (*c.*1714) is almost entirely original, including the extension of the bowsprit and square fighting tops. (SLR0396)

The mainmast of the *St Michael* (1669, SLR0002), showing the circular fighting top, as well as the standing and running rigging.

into yarns and used as rope. Using the same method as for full-sized ropes, each rope on a model is hawser laid, meaning it is made from three yarns, which have been individually twisted, and then three of these are twisted together in the opposite direction to form a single rope. Rigging on models has often been stained or painted black. This represents the procedure of applying tar to a ship's cordage to protect it from the elements as well as warding off general wear and tear. Model rigging in its 'natural state' – unaffected by UV degradation or staining – can be found within blocks and deadeyes or by teasing open the larger anchor cable stowed within the hull of the model.

Summary

The Navy Board models provide a wealth of information about their construction and the skill of the maker in creating such detailed and complex models. There is evidence of an intimate knowledge of shipbuilding in the yard, even though a model maker may have made conscious decisions to ignore the overall process of construction. The models also hint at skills brought over from the Continent in the 1660s, such as the marquetry and exotic wood veneers used by cabinet-makers. The divergence between the construction of the model from the actual ship is a reflection of the practicalities of using woods that suited their purpose, like the fine grain of boxwood to create the intricate carved figureheads and stern boards. As these models are analysed further, they will continue to increase our understanding about how they were created, constructed and finished to produce delicate works of art.

Catalogue of the National Maritime Museum's Navy Board Ship Model Collection

Introduction

The Navy Board ship model collection at the National Maritime Museum consists of fifty-four models dating from about 1650 to 1775, as well as two high-quality twentieth-century models which replicate the Navy Board style.

The models have been chosen on the basis of their construction method and style. There are some variations: all of the fifty-six models have exposed stylised frames below the wale, but three are block models that have been painted to replicate this style. These have been included because they are important for understanding the influence of this 'Navy Board framing', not only to ship model construction, but also to how the style of the Navy Board models was perceived by contemporary model makers.

As style rather than function has been the basis for inclusion in this catalogue, the two modern models have been included because their standard of work is of such high quality that it rivals the originals. Furthermore, having been in the collection for over seventy years (since 1944), these two models are an integral part of the National Maritime Museum collection and it is felt that they should not be separated from the other Navy Board ship models.

The origins of this collection are diverse and include transfers from four major collections – namely the Royal Naval Museum Greenwich, Greenwich Hospital, the Mercury collection, and R.C. Anderson – as well as various acquisitions from other organisations and private individuals.

The first major national collection of ship models in Britain was started by the Surveyor of the Navy, Sir Robert Seppings, in the Model Room at Somerset House in around 1813. This collection was transferred to the new School of Naval Architecture at South Kensington, and became part of the South Kensington Museum.

The South Kensington models were then relocated to Greenwich in 1873 when the School of Naval Architecture moved to join the Royal Naval College, which had already transferred from Portsmouth 1869. The models were displayed in the Royal Naval Museum, along with some models from the Greenwich Hospital collection, which had also been at the Royal Naval College since the hospital had ceased activity in 1869.

The Model Room at Somerset House set up by Seppings, in an engraving from George Virtue's *London Interiors*, 1842. (PAI8083)

The Mercury Collection before it was acquired by the Society for Nautical Research. In the foreground is a Fourth Rate (SLR00374), as well as the Royal Yacht (SLR0375).

When the National Maritime Museum was founded in 1934, these two collections were then transferred to the Museum, those models belonging to the Admiralty on a permanent basis, and those that belonged to Greenwich Hospital on indefinite loan. These models, which included twelve from the Royal Naval Museum, formed the core of the National Maritime Museum ship model collection.

The Mercury collection – a large historic collection of ship models belonging to the Mercury Nautical Training School based on the Hamble river, Hampshire – was put up for sale in 1921. There were fears that the collection would possibly follow the ship model collection previously owned by Charles Sergison, which was sold to the American collector Colonel Henry Huddleston Rogers in December 1922 (and can now be seen in at the US Naval Academy in Annapolis, Maryland).

In the 1920s several important Navy Board models were sold by J.M. Botibol of London. This advertisement for the sale of the then-unidentified model of *St Michael* (SLR0002) was published in *The Connoisseur*, May 1929. The flags shown in this image have not survived, but were known to be modern additions.

Bronze bust of Sir James Caird (1864–1954), by William Reid Dick, 1935. (ZBA4374)

Dr Roger Charles Anderson, by Bernard Hailstone, 1962. (BHC2513)

The National Maritime Museum's founding benefactor, the wealthy Scottish shipowner Sir James Caird (1864–1954), stepped in and provided the money for the Society for Nautical Research to purchase the collection for the Museum. The Mercury collection of over a hundred ship models included six made in the Navy Board style, which appear in this catalogue.

As well as the Mercury collection, Caird purchased numerous other paintings, artefacts and models which he donated to the NMM, including ten Navy Board models at auction and from private individuals. In the 1920s, the *St Michael* model was advertised for sale by the dealer J.M. Botibol. In 1939, it was entered into an auction by Robert Spence and purchased by Sir James Caird, who presented it to the Museum later that year.

Dr Roger Charles Anderson (1883–1976) was a noted naval scholar specialising in the rigging of seventeenth- and eighteenth-century warships and was one of the founding trustees of the National Maritime Museum. Anderson was an avid collector of ship models and in 1949, he donated twenty-five models to the National Maritime Museum, ten of which were Navy Board models – including the oldest made in this style, thought to date from around 1650 (SLR0217).

The Royal United Services Institution Museum was founded in 1831, and was housed at Inigo Jones's Banqueting House from 1895. When it closed in 1963, fifty ship models, including two Navy Board models, were transferred to the National Maritime Museum.

In addition to models from these major collections, since the end of the Second World War, the NMM has acquired a further twelve Navy Board ship models from private individuals, the details of which are included in this Catalogue.

The Catalogue is organised in chronological order by the date or approximate date of the launch of the vessel depicted, along with the NMM's four-digit catalogue numbers with the prefix 'SLR' or 'ZBA'.

Along with the scale and the date the model is thought to have been made, a table of dimensions lists the scaled-up dimensions of each model, next to the dimensions of a comparative vessel. In some cases, the ship model can be identified as a specific ship, in which case the dimensions of that ship are used for direct comparison, when available. In other examples, the vessel for comparison has been chosen for similarity in hull dimensions, class, date, or number of guns.

The Royal United Services Museum in the Banqueting House, Whitehall.

Third Rate, 50–58 guns (*c.*1650)

NMM NUMBER: SLR0217

SCALE: 1:48

DATE MADE: *c.*1650

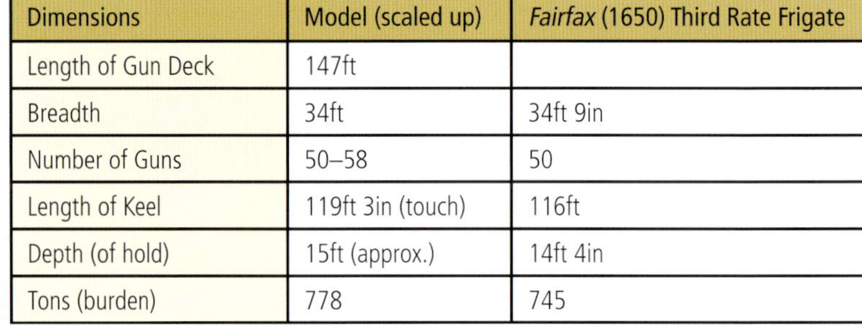

Dimensions	Model (scaled up)	*Fairfax* (1650) Third Rate Frigate
Length of Gun Deck	147ft	
Breadth	34ft	34ft 9in
Number of Guns	50–58	50
Length of Keel	119ft 3in (touch)	116ft
Depth (of hold)	15ft (approx.)	14ft 4in
Tons (burden)	778	745

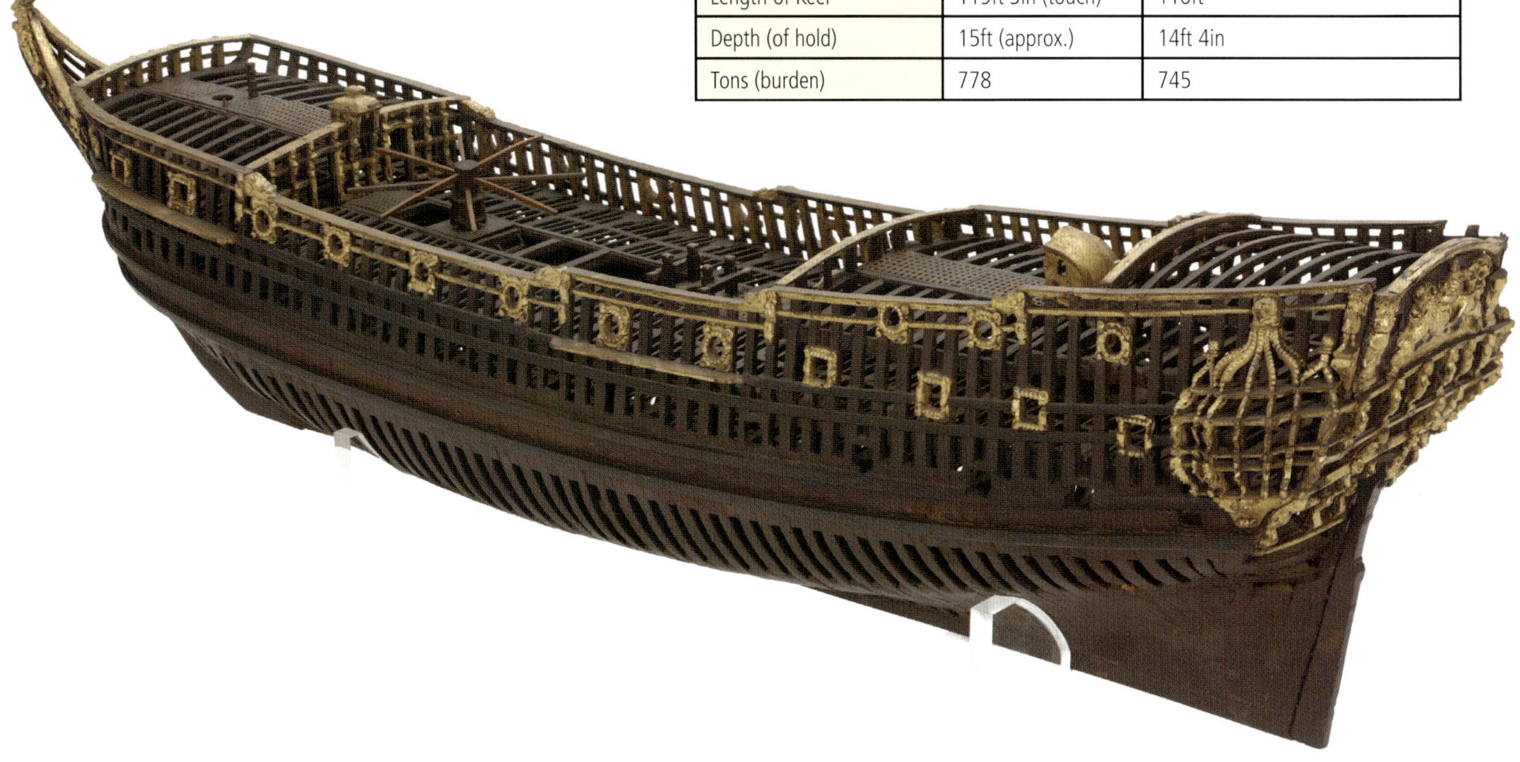

Introduction

This is the oldest 'true-scale' model in the NMM collection and is one of the oldest in Europe. It is also the earliest known example of a model in the Navy Board style.

Identification

The model depicts a sleek, fast ship of the Commonwealth period, characterised by the fine lines, and long, raking stem and stern posts. The proportions of the model agree closely with the Third Rate frigates built during the Commonwealth period, such as the *Fairfax*. However, the Stuart coat of arms displayed on the stern suggests that the model was probably made after the Restoration of Charles II in 1660. In fact, as internal evidence suggests, the arms were a later addition, as was the practice with the full-sized ships with the return of the monarchy.

Provenance

The model was formerly held at Dartmouth Castle in Devon, but was acquired by Dr R.C. Anderson, who presented it to the NMM in 1935.

Construction and Materials

Unlike other Navy Board models, this model is unusual in the fact that it has been left completely unplanked, although it does follow the standard Navy Board framing pattern. The type of wood is obscured by a layer of dark brown paint, which has been applied thickly in some parts. Inboard, there are deck beams as well as knees, and on the upper deck there are hatch gratings. Internally, there are diagonal cross-braces, which were a seventeenth-century invention to improve the lateral strength of the ship's hull.

LEFT
Detail of the capstan below decks, complete with wooden bars.

MIDDLE
Detail of the double companionway leading down from the upper gun deck.

RIGHT
Detail of the single companionway leading down from the upper gun deck. Notice it is flared at the base with the lower step notched, as it was located up against the mast.

Fixtures and Fittings

Along the sides of the hull are the main and upper wales, and channels for the main- and foremasts (but not mizzen), as well as gunports. Between the mainmast and foremast in the waist sits a jeer capstan with bars fitted to the barrel on the upper deck, and a main capstan on the gun deck just before the quarter-deck bulkhead. Both of these are the old-type capstans where the bars pass through the octagonal-shaped head. The model includes an early example of a belfry positioned at the forecastle bulkhead. On the quarter deck there is a covered companion with a forward-facing entrance.

Decoration

The model is limited in its overall finish, but has some elegant, gold-painted, carved decoration, including an early uncrowned lion figurehead. The gunport wreaths are of an unusual square design. The single quarter galleries are painted gold, as is the royal coat of arms of the Stuarts on the stern.

Naseby (1655), 80–86 guns

NMM NUMBER: SLR0001

SCALE: 1:48

DATE MADE: *c.*1943

Dimensions	Model (scaled up)	*Naseby* (1655)
Length of Gun Deck	162ft	161ft
Breadth	40ft	42ft
Number of Guns	80–86	80
Length of Keel	134ft 3in (touch)	131ft
Depth (of hold)	17ft (approx.)	18ft
Tons (burden)	1174	1274

Introduction

Made in 1943 by Robert Spence, this modern version of a Navy Board model faithfully represents the style and construction features. The *Naseby* was renamed the *Royal Charles* upon the Restoration of King Charles II in 1660, and as flagship took part in many actions against the Dutch from 1659–66. The ship is arguably most well known as a result of the Dutch raid on the Medway in 1667, where it was captured and taken back to the Netherlands, and eventually broken up in 1673. The royal coat of arms from the stern was saved and can now be seen in the Rijksmuseum, Amsterdam.

Identification

Although the model represents the *Naseby*, no plans of the ship survive. It was made using contemporary drawings of the ship by Willem van de Velde (PAF6460 and PAH1723), the known recorded dimensions of the ship, and the lines taken from a contemporary model of an English two-decker of similar date in the collection of the Statens Sjöhistoriskaat Museum in Stockholm, Sweden.

Provenance

Presented by Robert Spence, 1946.

Construction and Materials

Spence has followed the style and materials, using fruitwood for the hull and boxwood for the carving and planking. The profuse carved decoration is painted gold, and mica was used for the windows throughout. As a known sculptor, artist, and model restorer, Spence had access to a number of contemporary seventeenth-century ship models and was able to produce an accurate and convincing patination to the wood surfaces, especially the planking.

Fixtures and Fittings

As with the original early Navy Board models, the guns are turned in wood, and have been painted to resemble bronze, and are fitted on carriages with wheels. At the bow, two anchors are rigged to the cat block on the cathead. The belfry is ornately carved, complete with bell and the canopy has a pair of stylised dolphins. The double capstan in the waist is of the early (pre-drumhead) form, and is fitted with bars. Behind the shrouds of the mainmast channel on the starboard is an early form of roundhouse, where officers could relieve themselves at sea. It is a wooden, semicircular structure with two circular windows, and a hole below through the channels to allow drainage. The quarter deck has been raised to increase headroom below, and is fitted with a grating to allow light and ventilation. Just aft of the mizzen mast is a curved canopy protecting the entry to a bell-shaped stairway to the upper gun

deck. The stern lanterns are made in the early circular form, and are complete with small panes of mica, and another is fitted to the main fighting top for communication.

Rigging

The model is rigged with typical mid-seventeenth-century three-masted ship-rig, complete with circular fighting tops and a sprit topmast over the bow.

Decoration

At the bow is an equestrian figurehead painted gold, depicting Cromwell trampling the nations of England, Ireland, Scotland, the Netherlands, Spain, and France. A winged female figure, representing peace, holds a wreath above his head. The upper rail is made up of a carved screen between head timbers formed from caryatid figures. In the waist, as well as the belfry, there is additional carved work on the bulkheads and where the rails step up. The foredeck bulkhead has gold-painted female caryatid figures. Along the sides, the hancing pieces are formed from carved sea serpents being ridden by male figures. On the bulwarks there are gold-painted, carved mermaids, and gunports with circular wreaths or decorative square frames on the upper and quarter deck. On the quarter-deck bulkhead above the main entrance to the cabin is a carved Commonwealth coat of arms.

The quarter galleries are of an early form, with a large canopied gallery at the top, with a glazed window and tiled roof. Below is an ornately carved figure of Justice, holding scales and a sword, with a lion at her foot. The lower finishing is ornately carved, with a pair of seahorses pulling a putto in a carriage. The quarter figures are male and female figures in Greco-Roman dress. At the stern is a central carved George Cross on a central shield, flanked by seated male and female figures. On the taffrail, two carved dragons sit above a seated female figure blowing two horns, flanked by two sphinx-like creatures. The model sits upon carved stylised dolphin crutches, replicating the typical seventeenth-century examples.

Fourth Rate, 40–44 guns (*c.*1660)

NMM NUMBER: SLR0367

SCALE: 1:48

DATE MADE: *c.*1660

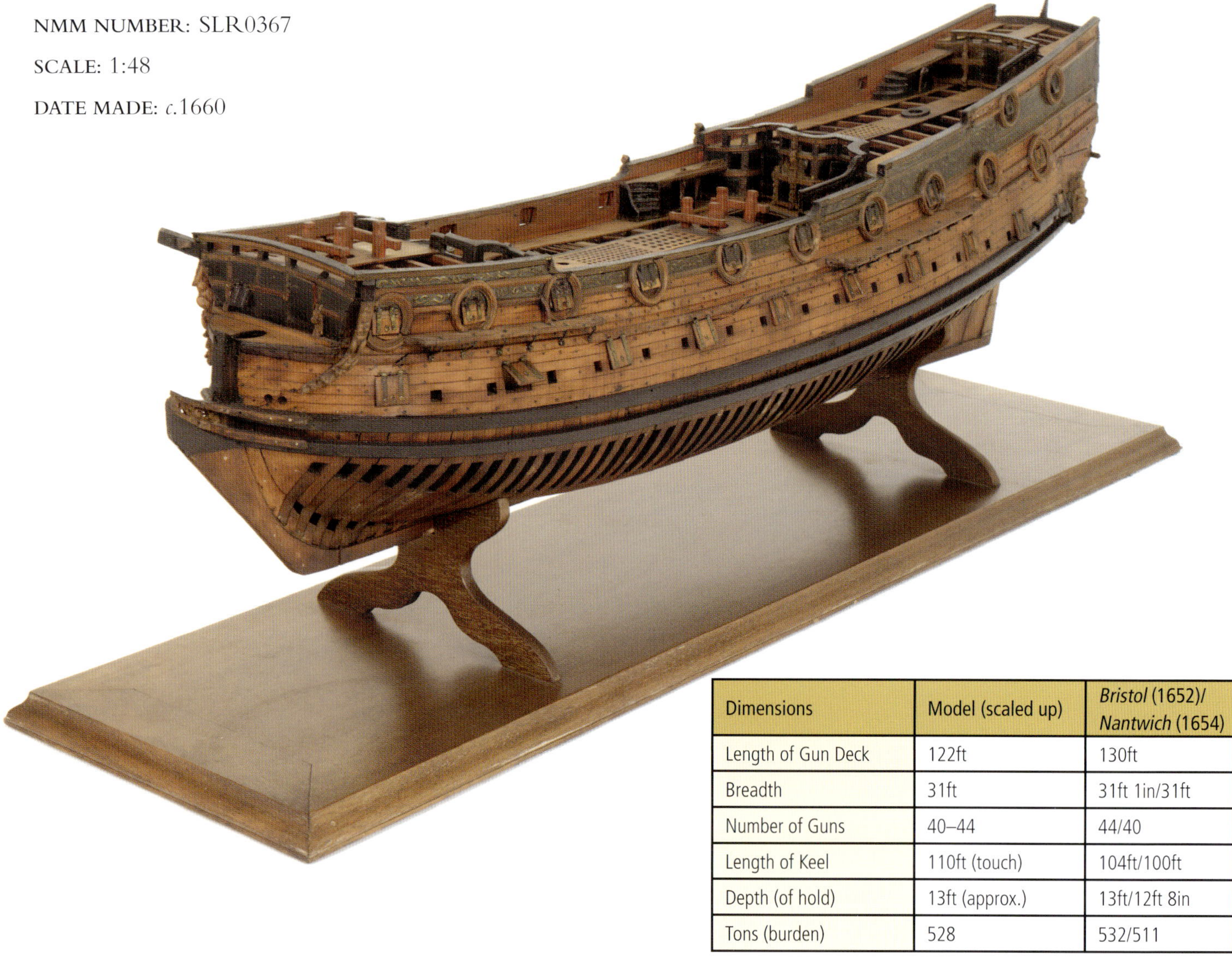

Dimensions	Model (scaled up)	*Bristol* (1652)/ *Nantwich* (1654)
Length of Gun Deck	122ft	130ft
Breadth	31ft	31ft 1in/31ft
Number of Guns	40–44	44/40
Length of Keel	110ft (touch)	104ft/100ft
Depth (of hold)	13ft (approx.)	13ft/12ft 8in
Tons (burden)	528	532/511

Introduction

This model illustrates the development of the two-deckers during the early years of the Restoration with the fine lines of the earlier frigates and the use of sweep ports employed in light airs. The combination of these design features and increased armament led to the description 'galley-frigate'.

Identification

It is very difficult to identify this model with any certainty as there is so much conflicting evidence. The inscription on the stern clearly shows 'Bristol 1666', but the dimensions do not accurately match the *Bristol* launched in 1652. The dimensions are very similar to the *Nantwich* built at Bristol in 1654. The date may refer to the year in which that ship was wrecked: 1666.

Provenance

Previously in the Royal Naval Museum, Greenwich, and transferred to the NMM in 1934.

Construction and Materials

This model has been heavily restored in the past and nearly all of the upper-deck planking, quarter and forecastle deck beams are twentieth-century replacements. The hull frames are of the standard pattern of floors and futtocks. The planking above the main wales consists of a single piece with individual planks scored and fastened mostly with wooden treenails and some brass pins. Some of the original mica is present in the stern and quarter galleries, as well as the quarter-deck bulkhead.

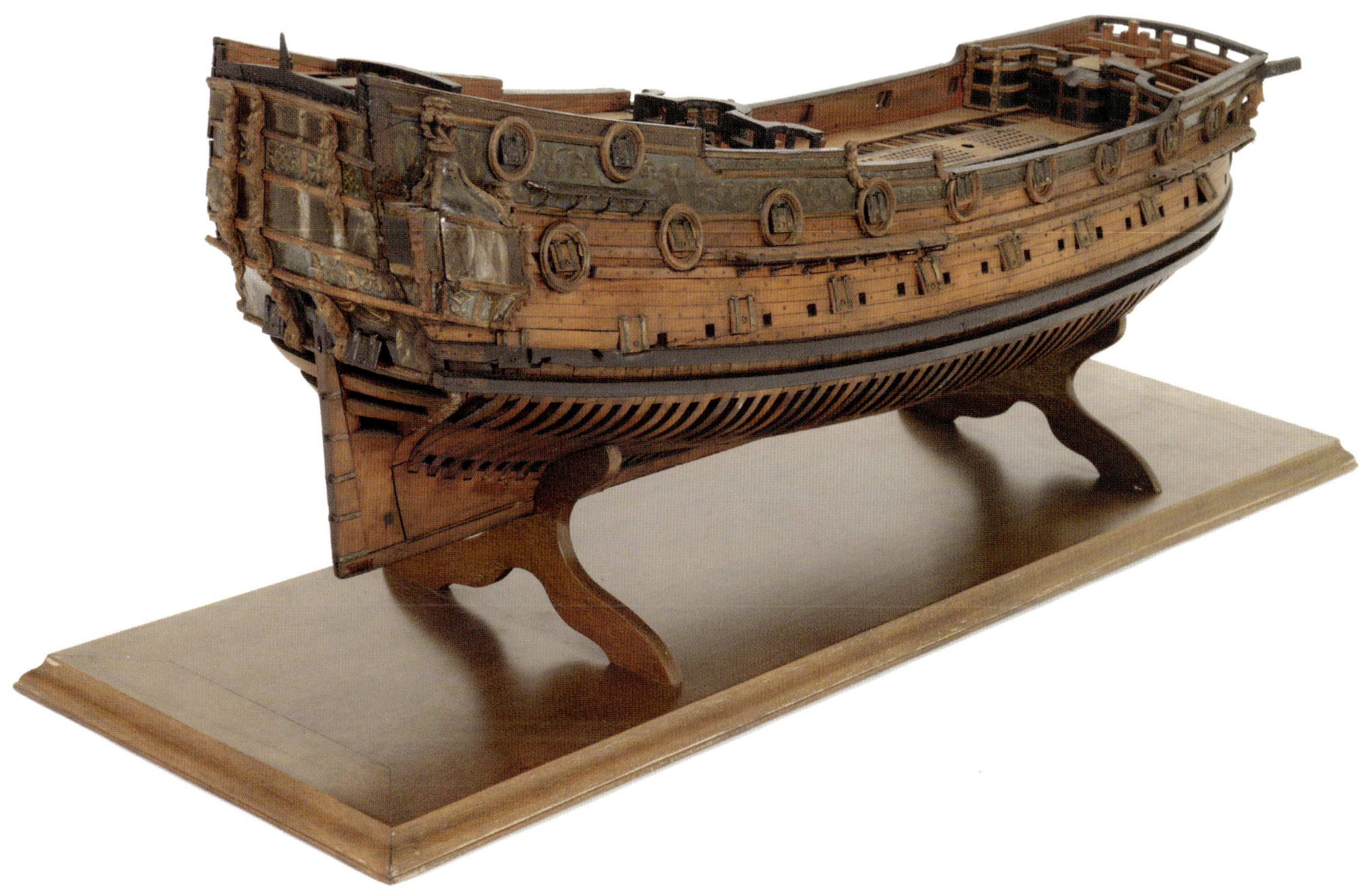

Fixtures and Fittings

The hull is fitted with twenty-two gunports with modern brass hinged lids and eighteen sweep ports each side. The forecastle bulkhead is largely complete with the galley preparation space present inboard, just below the remaining lower portion of the belfry. Most of the stairs, gangways, and bulkheads appear to be original, some with their glazing in place. The only surviving quarter gallery is on the starboard side and has painted and carved decoration. Some of this is now missing, which reveals the construction of these 'half-bottle'-shaped structures, the purpose of which was to provide light for the stern cabins and a dry, protected location for the captain's toilet.

Rigging

The wooden channels are secured above the upper wales supported by brass chainplates. All of the deadeyes are missing, although there is evidence that they were once rigged.

Decoration

Only the carved rail, running from the hawse pipes to supporting the catheads, survives from all of the bow area. Only two original hancing pieces remain and are located at the break of the main deck and quarter deck. One depicts a putto, whilst the other is a female with a lower body of a horse. The bulwark friezes are original and consist of mixed foliage, with acanthus leaves slightly obscured by the dark varnish layer. This also continues on the quarter and stern galleries in the same fashion, with the lower complete with drapes and cordage. The gunports are surrounded by simple circular mouldings rather than the familiar carved decoration.

Fourth Rate, 36–40 guns (*c.*1660)

NMM NUMBER: SLR0368

SCALE: 1:48

DATE MADE: *c.*1660

Dimensions	Model (scaled up)	*Adventure* (1646)
Length of Gun Deck	116ft	116ft 2in
Breadth	26ft 9in	27ft 9in
Number of Guns	36–40	32
Length of Keel	92ft (touch)	94ft
Depth (of hold)	14ft (approx.)	13ft 10in
Tons (burden)	380	385

Introduction

This model represents a 36–40 gun vessel of the Restoration period, but it includes a number of interesting features. Unusually, it has a name painted across the stern, as well as a non-standard type of framing.

Identification

There are many anomalies that appear on this model, and although the name 'Shearness' is inscribed on the stern that appears to be contemporary with the surrounding painted decoration, it is certain that this model cannot represent a ship of that name as the first, built in 1691, had fewer than 32 guns. This model is clearly of an earlier date with different proportions from that ship, and at this scale, the dimensions and gunport configuration are very close to the *Adventure* launched in 1646. These frigates of 32–34 guns, built 1646–50, or the Fifth Rates of 1666–71, were longer and narrower. The noticeable rake of the stem, the absence of the belfry on the forecastle, and the lack of outboard channels for the mizzen rigging, all suggest an earlier date. However, the shape of the bulkheads and the general character of the decoration point to a date after the Restoration in 1660.

Provenance

Caird Collection, 1944 via the London dealer Spink's.

Construction and Materials

The style of the hull framing is a very early example of double frames and quite different from the traditional Navy Board style, and similar to the *Boyne* (SLR0006). All the timbers are butted together and comprise of floors, first and second futtocks, and a single top timber. They are fastened together with wooden treenails at the ends of the timbers, as well as a rather curious set of wires which have been tensioned up with windings internally. It is not clear as to whether these wires are later additions, as it would require the dismantling of the decking and beams to gain access. There are also a number of vertical timbers between the transoms on the stern which are not common, but may reflect the actual practice of ship construction. Some of the original mica still survives in the stern and quarter galleries, whilst a number of the deadeyes are turned in bone, which may be later replacements. The whole model is mounted on its original hull crutches and walnut-veneered baseboard.

Fixtures and Fittings

Sadly, this model has suffered from damage and loss of parts over the years and a number are either missing or are modern replacements. In particular, a large proportion of the upper deck beams and planking are later, as they appear to be a different type of wood and lack the older patination of the original parts of the hull. However, the capstan below decks looks to be contemporary and is of the old type with a head where the wooden bars pass through the octagonal head. It would also appear that the rudder, with its gudgeons and pintles, and most of the gunports are later replacements, as well.

Rigging

These early ships were three-masted ship-rigged and even though the model has three mast positions, the mizzen shrouds are not fitted as they were probably fastened inside the bulwarks.

Decoration

Again, due to the incomplete condition of the hull, a lot of the carved and painted decoration is either later or modern replacements. However, the quarter galleries are a fine example of carved decoration for this period and are thought to be original. The painted decorative scheme tends to date to post-1660s for the Restoration period and, as is typical, would have been added or modified later.

St Michael (1669), 84–86 guns

NMM NUMBER: SLR0002

SCALE: 1:48

DATE MADE: *c.*1669

Dimensions	Model (scaled up)	*St Michael* (1669)
Length of Gun Deck	155ft	155ft 2in
Breadth	40ft 9in	41ft 89in
Number of Guns	84–86	80/90 (reclass. as 98-gun First Rate in 1672)
Length of Keel	126ft (touch)	122ft 2in
Depth (of hold)	18ft (approx.)	17ft 7in
Tons (burden)	1153	1200

Introduction

The *St Michael* model is one of the most impressive ship models in the collection. Launched in 1669 at Portsmouth as a Second Rate, the model depicts the ship before she was reclassified as a First Rate 98-gun ship in 1672.

Identification

The *St Michael* represents the earliest English ship model that can be identified with any certainty. Its identity was confirmed by R.C. Anderson, who compared the model to several van de Velde drawings held at the Museum (see 'Ship Models and Art' section).

Provenance

Sir James Caird purchased the model from Robert Spence in 1939, and presented it to the Museum later that year. It is thought it was owned by Sir Robert Holmes, former captain of the *St Michael*. His will, dated 1692, states that he owned 'two moddles of shipps'.

Construction and Materials

Unusually, the frames are made of walnut, but they match the standard pattern and are fastened with a mixture of brass pins and wooden treenails. Most of the internal surfaces remain in their natural state without any varnish or stains, allowing better identification of the woods used. The planking consists of large pieces of boxwood with individual planks scored horizontally and secured with wooden treenails. The double main wales are painted black, the middle wales are left in their natural state and there are no upper wales, just a gilt moulded rail, above which the top of the sides is painted black. Internally, there is a keelson; two footwales either side; a longitudinal beam shelf runs lengthways around the height of the wales; pillars are fitted under every other gun-deck beam, and fore and aft knees at the wing transom. Like most of the larger English ships of this period, *St Michael* had a round tucked stern. The beakhead bulkhead is two decks deep, and contains chase ports on both the middle and upper decks. The quarter deck bulkhead has a large central pair of doors opening to an enclosed 'bell'-shaped stairway leading down to the middle deck. There are no side gangways or stairs leading up to the quarter deck and forecastle from the waist.

Fixtures and Fittings

The model is equipped with guns, most of which are thought to be original, turned in wood, stained, and mounted on simple carriages on the deck, although some deck planking is omitted, revealing deck beams. The hatches have been fashioned from a single piece of end-grain wood, with the holes punched through. Amidships there is an entry port with gilt railing on the port side. There is a fore jeer capstan, with five whelps, fitted just forward of amidships. The single main capstan is abaft the mainmast on the lower deck and fitted with an original, although slightly damaged, swifter. Of particular interest is the decorated belfry at the forecastle bulkhead, which has a highly elaborate structure with ornate carvings. It is complete with a bell turned in wood and carved dolphins with tails entwined on the canopy.

Rigging

The model is complete with masts and spars; the three masts rest straight onto the keelson with no mast steps. The rigging is largely original, apart from the running cordage which is modern and dates from when the model was re-rigged in 1930 before it was acquired by the NMM.

Decoration

In the seventeenth century, the powerful warship was as much a statement of royal power as it was a piece of military hardware. As such, the highly decorative nature of the models is thought to be true to the original ship. The figurehead is of a seated figure in a chariot drawn by a pair of eagles. Behind the eagles, holding the reins, is a winged putto. The figure is probably Ganymede, who was, in Greek mythology, taken at the order of Zeus to Mount Olympus to live with the gods.

This model shows one of the earliest examples of two-tier quarter galleries, one on the middle gun deck and one on the upper gun deck, which are ornately decorated with carved gilt work. Each tier is supported by carved and gilt window mullions and horizontal gilt quarter rails with the planking between painted black. Mica window panes have been scored lightly to show each square pane. At the top of each quarter gallery, the upper finishing is crowned with a gilt carved badge, and below the lower finishing is a gilt winged putto head. The gunports on the upper gun deck and the quarter deck are all wreathed. The starboard quarter gallery shows the highly decorative nature of the two-tiered quarter galleries, as well as the Greco-Roman quarter figure.

At the stern, the taffrail is decorated with a putto holding a pair of cornucopias, and more putti sitting astride seahorses. In the centre panel is the crowned monogram of Charles II. Above this is the royal coat of arms of the Stuarts, a replacement carved by Robert Spence in 1931–32, together with the carved initials 'CR' for Carolus Rex. The lower counter features painted trophies of arms and the rudder head is decorated with a lion's head. The quarter pieces appear to represent St Michael himself, below which the cloven-hooved figure of the Devil crouches. The stern lanterns are a circular design with a gilt frame and glazed with mica.

First Rate, 90–94 guns (*c.*1670)

NMM NUMBER: SLR0372

SCALE: 1:54

DATE MADE: *c.*1670

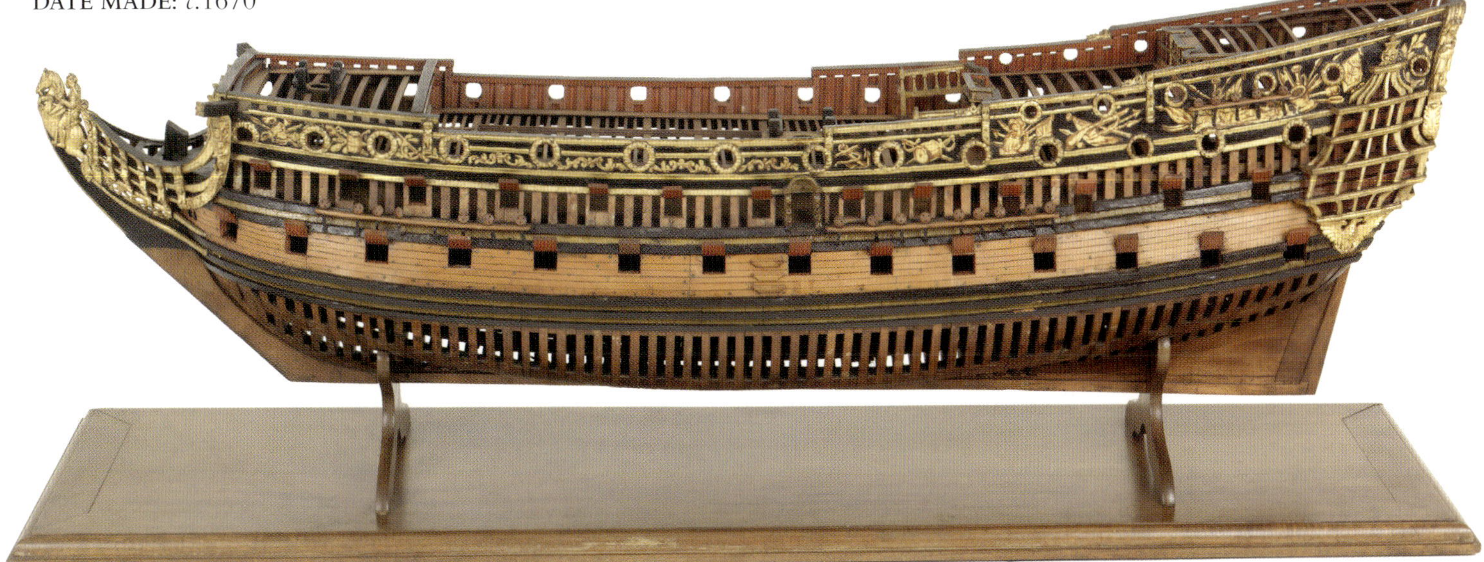

Dimensions	Model (scaled up)	*St Andrew* (1670)
Length of Gun Deck	163ft	159ft
Breadth	44ft	44ft
Number of Guns	90–94	96
Length of Keel	110 (touch)	128ft
Depth (of hold)	19ft (approx.)	18ft 8in
Tons (burden)	1407	1318

Introduction

The model is in a partially finished state and when compared to other models of this period, such as the *St Michael* (SLR0003), this model is of a much simpler finish.

Identification

Although possibly a design for a three-decker of 1670, the model agrees in many respects with a ship whose plans appear in Sir Anthony Deane's *Doctrine of Naval Architecture* of 1670. The very unusual feature of the three lower wales, instead of the normal two, appears in Deane's drawing. His first three-decker was the *Royal James* of 1671, although this model probably represents a slightly smaller ship and it has been associated with the *St Andrew* of 1670.

Draught from *Deane's Doctrine of Naval Architecture*, 1670, Pepys Library, Magdalene College, Cambridge.

Provenance
Mercury Collection.

Construction and Materials
It is rather unusual in that very little of the hull is planked, the deck beams are left unplanked, and the stern and quarter galleries are in frame only. In this respect it is similar to the early frigate model (SLR0217). However, the lower and middle decks are planked with a single sheet of vellum which has been secured with treenails and brass pins.

Fixtures and Fittings
Along the sides it does include an arched entry port on each side and channels, chainplates, and deadeyes for three masts. It also has hinged gunport lids on the middle and lower gun decks and wreathed gunports on the main gun deck. It has bitts in the waist and on the foredeck, as well as a single pair of riding bitts fitted on the lower deck. The middle deck is equipped with an old-style capstan with spaces for four through bars.

Decoration
At the bow, the figurehead is a crowned figure on horseback, possibly representing King Charles II. The head rails are supported by gold-painted, carved caryatid busts, and the beakhead bulkhead is decorated with five full-length figures. The catheads are supported by carved lions. The bulwark screens, above the upper wales, have been decorated with painted trophies of arms and are complete with wreathed gunports. The lower finishing on the quarter gallery is a carved, gold-painted eagle and the quarter figures are carved male figures.

Yacht, 8 guns (*c.*1674)

NMM NUMBER: SLR0378

SCALE: 1:32

DATE MADE: *c.*1674

Introduction

This model possibly represents the second Stuart Royal Yacht *Katherine II* (1674). Royal yachts were used primarily by the king for leisure and personal transport, but were also used by the Royal Navy during wartime. Their speed and manoeuvrability made them very useful for communication between ships. Originally built to replace the earlier *Katherine* (1661) captured by the Dutch at the Battle of Texel in 1673, the second *Katherine* saw service throughout the reign of William and Mary, and Queen Anne. She was rebuilt in 1720, during the reign of George I, before finally being sold in 1801.

Dimensions	Model (scaled up)	*Katherine II* (1674)
Length of Gun Deck	74ft	
Breadth	21ft	21ft 1in
Number of Guns	8–10	8 x 3pdrs
Length of Keel	59ft (touch)	56ft
Depth (of hold)	7ft 4in (approx.)	8ft 4in
Tons (burden)	144	132

Offset drawing of the starboard-bow view of what may be the *Katherine II* by Willem van de Velde, *c.*1677. (PAH1864)

Identification

The dimensions match very closely to the *Katherine II*, which was launched at Chatham Royal Dockyard in 1674 by Phineas Pett. The model bears a striking resemblance to a van de Velde drawing of an 8-gun yacht, thought to be the *Katherine II*.

Provenance

The model was previously in the possession of Rear-Admiral F. Proby Doughty (1833–1892). It was loaned to the Science Museum by Mrs Marion E. Drogo Montagu before being transferred to NMM as part of the permanent collection on the death of Mrs Montagu in 1951.

Construction and Materials

The model is an excellent example of late seventeenth-century craftsmanship. It is made using the typical fruitwoods such as apple and pear, as well as boxwood for the decking, planking, and the carved decoration. Left unplanked below a double strake black main wale, above which the planking is a single panel fixed with treenails. The decking is formed from single panels of boxwood fixed with brass pins. At some point it has had some woodworm, but it is no longer active.

Fixtures and Fittings

Much of the fittings and fixtures are thought to be modern additions – including anchor, six guns, and carriages. The stern lanterns were found inside the hull of the model when the model was being restored at the Science Museum in the 1930s. On the short poop there is a brass tiller for steering, attached to a rudder hung on the stern post on brass pintles and gudgeons. On the portside of the stern post there are water draught marks in Roman numerals.

Rigging

The model was re-rigged in the 1930s at the Science Museum using modern sails. The model is gaff-rigged on a single mast just forward of amidships with a square topsail, as well as two headsails on a long bowsprit. This rig was common for Stuart Royal Yachts, but by the 1690s Royal Yachts were larger and switched to a ketch rig. The mast gaff and spars are all original, but most of the rigging, including the sails, are modern additions.

Decoration

The model is highly decorative with fantastic high-relief, gold-painted carvings. The figurehead is a woman holding a child, flanked by putti and caryatids along the head rails. The stern depicts a draped female figure in front of a large laurel with her left hand resting on an anchor. She is flanked by two standing putti, holding anchors, and two cornucopias. Below, stern

timbers with five gold-painted, carved putti, standing on four carved lion's heads, and a central fish head sit between the four stern windows, which let light into the cabin. On the counter, four carved emblems illustrate the monarch's realms, from left to right: a thistle for Scotland; a rose for England; a fleur-de-lis for France; and a harp for Ireland. The Stuart monarchy still had not relinquished an historic claim to the French throne, despite their co-operation with the French in the Third Anglo-Dutch War. Below are two stern-chaser gunports. The quarter pieces are male figures standing above an animal. Each quarter badge consists of two small windows surrounded by ornate, gold-painted carvings. Along the sides, the bulwark screens are decorated with low-relief, gold-painted carvings on a red background and wreathed gunports.

Second Rate, 90 guns (*c.*1675)

NMM NUMBER: SLR0003

SCALE: 1:48

DATE MADE: *c.*1675

Dimensions	Model (scaled up)	*Neptune* (1683)
Length of Gun Deck	158ft	157ft
Breadth	42ft	44ft
Number of Guns	90	90
Length of Keel	136ft (touch)	136ft
Depth (of hold)	18ft	
Tons (burden)	1246	1344

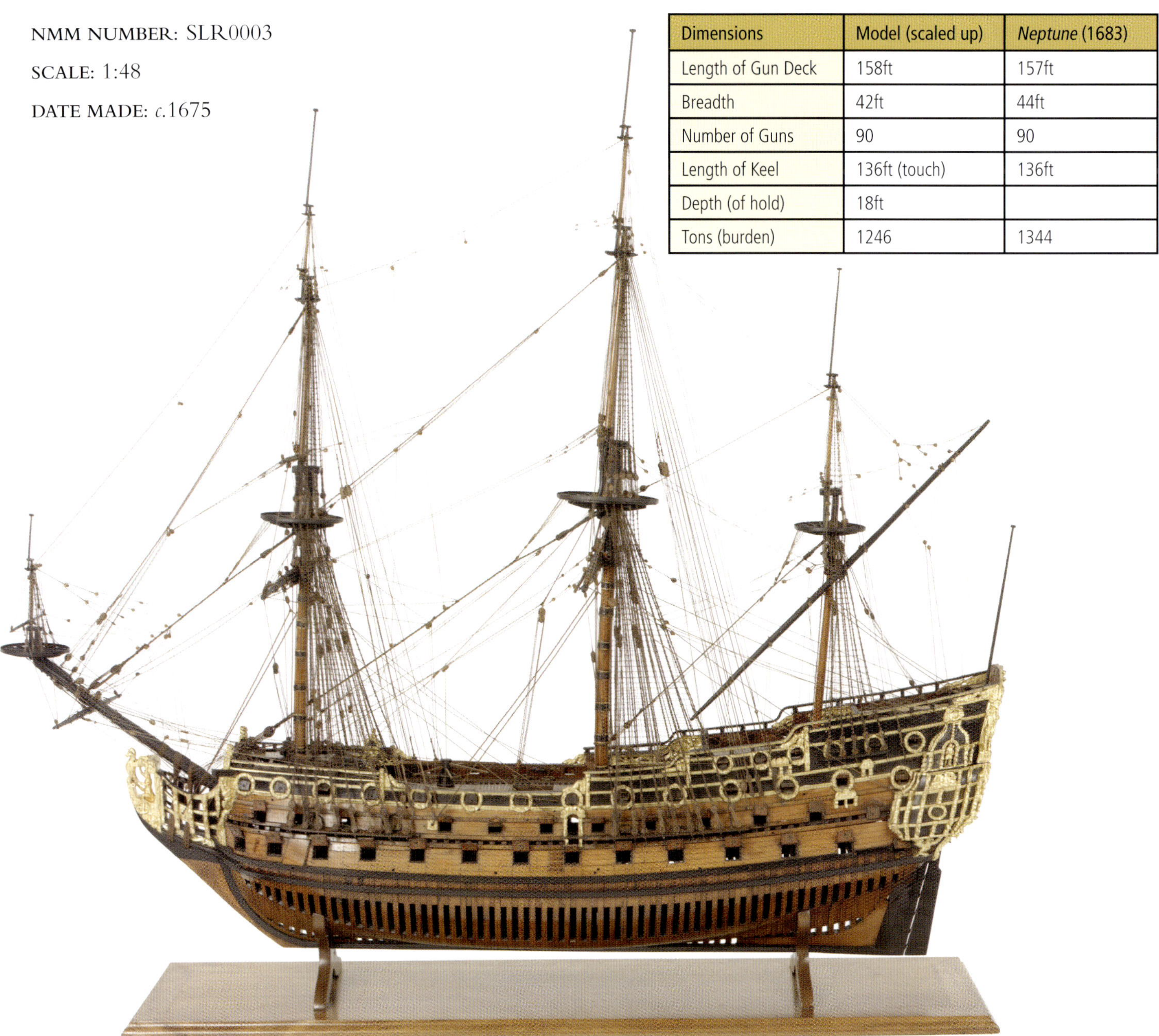

Introduction

The 'Thirty Ships' programme was given the seal of approval by Parliament on 5 March 1677 and included nine Second Rates to carry ninety guns. Charles II took a very active role in the design of these ships and he insisted on an increase to the dimensions of the original design based upon the *St Andrew* (1670). This model may depict one of these designs, even though the dimensions are too small for any of the ships that were actually built.

Identification

Even though the dimensions of the model do not correspond to any known ship of the period, historically it was thought to represent one of these nine Second Rates. Recent research has suggested that the gunport arrangements are very similar to the *Neptune* launched in 1683.

Provenance

Previously in the possession of Dr R.C. Anderson and acquired by Sir James Caird in 1933.

Construction and Materials

The hull planking is a series of large pieces of, possibly, boxwood, which have been scored and stamped to show the individual planks and butt joints with their respective treenail fastenings. The main wales have been left unplanked and are attached with metal fastenings. Above the wales are a number of holes drilled through the planking indicating the position of the scuppers – used for freeing the main gun deck of water.

Fixtures and Fittings

On the forecastle deck is fitted the galley stove chimney, painted black. On the aft side of the bulkhead is small set of steps leading up to the belfry for operating the bell. Behind these appears to be a small half-round serving table with glazed windows underneath, presumably to provide for light for the galley.

In the waist area are a number of gratings along the centreline, which are cut from the end-grain of the wood so as to allow the holes to be punched through. There is also a single old-type capstan (modern replacement) which is rigged with the wooden bars held in place with a rope swifter. At the break of the quarter deck and directly below the royal coat of arms is a rounded canopy to protect the stairway leading down to the middle gun deck. At the stern, the taffrail includes an oval-shaped grating to provide light for the accommodation on the quarter deck and four small 'trumpeter's' cabins on the poop, either side of the ensign staff.

As to whether guns were fitted originally, an internal inspection of the gun decks has not produced any evidence of old glue marks or holes for pin fastenings to hold the carriages in place.

Rigging

Only the lower fore- and mainmasts are thought to be original. They illustrate how the masts were made in several sections and held together with rope wooldings. Both the standing and running rigging was replaced by Anderson in 1929.

Decoration

When Anderson repaired the model in the 1920s, he wrote that:

> A few years ago we stripped off all the carving and replaced the plaster-of-Paris repairs of a previous restoration with fresh carvings. We also removed an unauthorised heightening of the stern. As it is, no-one can possibly tell the new carvings from the old, while there is no possible doubt that the new ones are correct.[1]

All of the carved decoration has been repainted gold, probably when the rigging was repaired or replaced. The bulwark screens have been painted black at a later date, and now possibly obscure original painted decoration.

At the bow is an ornately carved figurehead comprising of a crowned figure being carried over water in a wheeled chariot drawn by a pair of eagles. The figure, which holds a rolled scroll in her right hand whilst holding the reins for the eagles on the right, bears remarkable similarity to the figurehead of the *St Michael* (SLR0002). Along the sides of the hull the gunports of the upper deck and above are decorated with gold wreaths. There are also four pairs of hancing pieces in the shape of crouching greyhounds. On the port broadside on the middle gun deck is the entry port with an ornately carved canopy, on which is a pair of lions crouching with their tails entwined. The quarter-deck bulkhead includes a gold-painted, carved royal coat of arms above the companionway. Notice also the etched mica windows that provide light for the accommodation below.

The 'half-bottle'-shape quarter galleries are in two sections, with the upper canopy complete with glazed windows surrounding a small male figure holding a staff in his left hand. Only the middle section of the lower gallery is glazed to illuminate the cabins of the middle gun deck. The gunport directly cutting through the upper part of the main wale bears a similar resemblance to the *Neptune*.

The stern galleries are quite magnificent in detail and execution, with the monogram 'JR' on a roundel surmounted by a pair of putti and eagles on either side. The quarter and upper decks have open stern galleries, but the middle and main decks are enclosed. Amongst the wealth of carved decoration are the Scottish thistle, the Welsh leek, and the English rose situated on the windows of the middle gun deck.

Yacht, 8 guns (*c.*1675)

NMM NUMBER: SLR0379

SCALE: 1:32

DATE MADE: *c.*1675

Dimensions	Model (scaled up)	*Charles* (1675)
Length of Gun Deck	75ft	
Breadth	21ft	20ft 6in
Number of Guns	8	8 x 3pdr
Length of Keel	60ft (touch)	54ft
Depth (of hold)	7ft 4in	7ft 9in
Tons (burden)	146	120

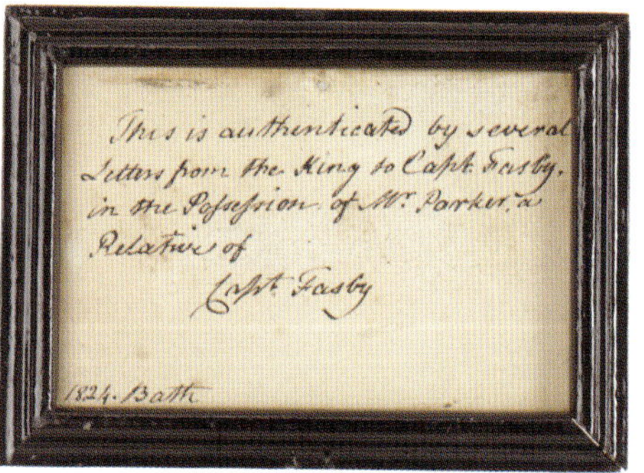

This is authenticated by several Letters from the King to Capt. Fasby, in the Possession of Mr. Parker, a Relative of

Capt. Fasby

1824. Bath

Introduction

This model of a yacht has been associated with the Royal Yacht *Charles* launched at Rotherhithe in 1675. These small, fast vessels, which originated in the Netherlands, were popularised by King Charles II and his brother James. The original Dutch yachts had a shallow draught ideal for Dutch waters, and leeboards were used to prevent leeward drift. However, with the deeper English waters, a more pronounced keel and greater draught gave the English yachts better directional stability.

Identification

A framed paper label dated to 1677, which may be original but cannot be verified, is mounted on the baseboard and identifies the model as the *Charles*. Another, dated 1824, supports this claim by citing several letters, which are now unknown.

Although the model is similar to the Royal Yachts of the period, neither the appearance nor measurements seem to fit the smaller *Charles*, which measured 54ft on the keel by a 20ft 6in beam.

Furthermore, a van de Velde the Elder drawing of the *Charles* shows a yacht of similar layout: the hull shape is similar, and the wales, mast, and channels are fitted in similar positions. However, the gunports, decoration, and stairways are notably different. This means that at present the model cannot be identified with any certainty.

Provenance

The model is thought to have belonged to Captain William Fasby. An additional label dated 1824, states that the model 'is authenticated by several letters from the King to Capt. Fasby, in the possession of Mr. Parker, a relative of Capt. Fasby'.

Fasby, a contemporary of Pepys, commanded several of the Royal Yachts between 1666 and 1688. The model was previously in the possession of the Earl of Normanton and was purchased by the NMM from Godden's of Worthing on 13 May 1959.

Construction and Materials

The model is built of fine-grained wood, and finished with varnish and mounted on original crutches. The exposed frames are the standard type, and it is decked with large single panels with hatches, and a small grated foredeck.

Fixtures and Fittings

The model includes a windlass, as well as a chimney for the galley at the bow. The channels, chainplates, and deadeyes are fitted for a single mast, just forward of midships. The model is shown with a set of painted paper launching flags. The Union Jack flown from the jackstaff at the bow was adopted by the Royal Navy from 1606, despite not being adopted on land until the 1707 Act of Union. Amidships is the Stuart Royal Standard used at sea between 1603 and 1689 and again between 1702–07. However, the red ensign at the stern, which includes the Union flag in the canton, was not adopted by the Royal Navy until 1707. This may suggest the flags (or at least the red ensign) are later additions.

Decoration

The decoration on this model is of a high quality, but the carved work is not as elaborate as some of the Royal Yachts of the period. At the bow there is a standard Navy lion figurehead, with caryatid figures on the head rails as well as quarter-deck bulkheads. The sides are decorated with wreathed gunports (the aft four being 'dummies'), and carved Order of the Garter stars. The quarter pieces are naked male figures holding swords.

The stern also includes a large Order of the Garter star, which is a heraldic shield of St George's Cross encircled by a garter with the motto *Honi soit qui mal y pense* with a buckle at the bottom left, encircled by an eight-point star. This is flanked by two eagles and four putti heads, two of which have puffed cheeks and pursed lips to symbolise blowing wind. The insignia of the Order of the Garter is of particular significance in the reign of Charles II, as he reinstated the first order of chivalry when he was restored to the throne in 1660.

The model has a separate additional carved royal coat of arms of the period of William III, which has been framed. It is of a similar size to the Garter star on the taffrail, which it may have been intended to replace.

Drawing of the yacht *Charles*, by Willem van de Velde, c.1676. (PAI 7277)

Shallop (*c.*1691)

NMM NUMBER: SLR0380

SCALE: 1:16

DATE MADE: *c.*1691

Dimensions	Model (scaled up)	Queen Mary's shallop (1689)
Length overall (on deck)	33ft 3¾in	41ft 7in
Breadth	6ft 6in	6ft 7in
Length of Keel (touch)	26ft	
Draught	1ft 10in	2ft 11in

Queen Mary's shallop of 1689 (BAE0039), previously on display at the NMM, complete with a carved royal coat of arms above the rudder.

Introduction

This model depicts a shallop of the 1690s, built plank-on-frame in the Navy Board style. Thames shallops were light barges used for transporting the monarchs between the royal palaces along the Thames, as well as visiting warships at anchor in the river and estuaries.

Identification

It is thought that this model may represent a design for a barge built for William III, which was built in clinker fashion and would have been rowed by up to ten oarsmen. It is very similar to the full-size Queen Mary's shallop in the NMM collection (BAE0039) and the Royal Barge of Charles II on display at the National Museum of the Royal Navy, Portsmouth.

Provenance

The model was originally part of the Admiralty Model Room at Somerset House. It was transferred to the South Kensington Museum and then the Royal Naval Museum, Greenwich. Finally, it was transferred to the NMM in 1934.

Construction and Materials

Whereas most of the Navy Board models are built in stylised framing patterns, strictly speaking, this model of a shallop depicts the construction accurately. The construction consists of twenty-two frames, with each frame made up of a thin floor timber and a single futtock either side. Inboard, there is a light deck fitted just above the floor timbers. The model shows two strakes of the overlapping or clinker planking below a thicker gunwale. The lower strakes have been omitted in order to show the hull section. It has been built from an unidentified fruitwood fixed with small brass pins, and sealed with a layer of varnish.

Fixtures and Fittings

Internally, thwarts are fitted across the hull, providing strength, as well as a place for the rowers to sit. Interestingly, each thwart has a small groove on either side where a central gangplank could be mounted. This would allow passengers to board from the bow and walk to the benches at the stern. At the stern, the boat curves upwards to allow a raised position for the helmsman. The rudder would have been operated with a short tiller rather than a yoke with lines, allowing more space for passengers in front. The stern post has pintles indicating where a missing rudder once hung. Staggered along the gunwales are ten carved and gold-painted rowlocks, indicating the position of the oarsmen.

Decoration

For an otherwise functional boat, the model shows a high level of decoration. This is an indication of the types of prestigious passengers this type of vessel would have carried. At the bow it has a small, gold-painted horse figurehead, carved either side of the stem post. Along the sides, the gunwale is painted red and with ornate, gold-painted frieze decoration highlighted with gold leaf along the stern bulwark and inside the gunwale. At the stern, the transom is decorated with a simple gold crown on a red background.

In Focus: 3D Scanning – Shallop (1691)

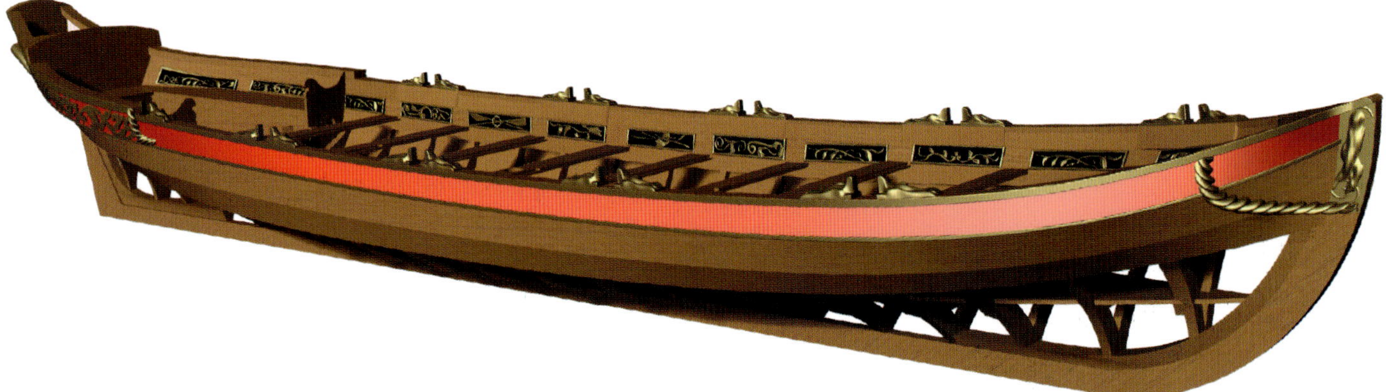

One aspect of ship model research that has expanded greatly is the use of 3D laser scanning technology, which has enormous potential for use with ship models. 3D scanning is a non-contact technique, which limits object handling, making it ideal for use within a museum context where traditional measuring may be impractical with old or delicate ship models. 3D laser scanning can accurately measure a ship model to produce a digital model which opens up the potential for detailed analysis, illustration, or interactive display.

This shallop model (SLR0380), dated to 1691, was chosen as a case study to demonstrate the use of 3D laser scanning. The model is small, with a relatively basic style of construction, with a keel, stem and stern post, twenty-two frames left open below the waterline, with three clinker planks above, and internal thwarts.

A FARO Arm laser scanner was used to record the surface of the model to produce a digital 'point cloud' made up of a lot of data points. This point cloud can then be used to create a digital 3D model, for analysis on a computer, or for 3D printing.

The point cloud that resulted from scanning the shallop model was used to 'reverse engineer' the model and to create a CAD (computer-aided design) model. This digital 3D model was then manipulated to correct the slight warpage that had occurred in the wood of the original model. The keel was digitally straightened, so the 3D model showed how it was originally constructed.

From this model, it was possible to produce 2D diagrams, showing the internal as well as external construction. The longitudinal section shows the boat cut lengthways along the centreline, illustrating the internal arrangement. A plan-view diagram of the construction was also drawn, which shows the boat from above, with thwarts, the small central deck below, and the frames underneath.

The digital 3D model was also used to create a lines plan, which shows the boat in three perspectives. This not only documents the shape of the vessel, but allows for further analysis and comparison with other boats. The sheer plan shows the longitudinal vertical section of the ship, with vertical station-lines spaced evenly along the hull, and curved buttock-lines in green.

The body plan shows the vertical cross-sections, split into two, showing the boat from the stern on the left and from the bow on the right. This time the buttock-lines are shown straight and vertical, and the curved station-lines in red show the shape of the hull at different points along its length.

The half-breadth shows the longitudinal transverse section at the deck line, with the station-lines appearing straight, and the blue waterlines showing the shape of the hull at different heights above the keel.

Finally, the model was rendered to give a realistic surface finish. The potential for utilising a render model in interactive museum displays is great.

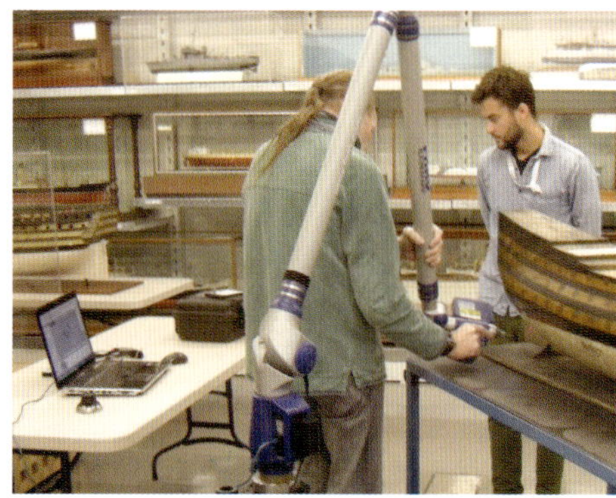

TOP
3D rendered model by Pat Tanner.

ABOVE
Pat Tanner of 3D Scanning Ireland, scanning using the FARO arm.

OPPOSITE PAGE TOP
Longitudinal section construction drawing, longitudinal external construction drawing, and plan-view construction drawing. (SLR0380; drawn by Pat Tanner, 3D Scanning Ireland)

OPPOSITE PAGE BOTTOM
Lines plan produced by 3D laser-scanning the original 1:16 scale model. Lines are drawn to the outside of the planking. (Drawn by Pat Tanner)

10.154m (33 feet 3 3/4 inches)

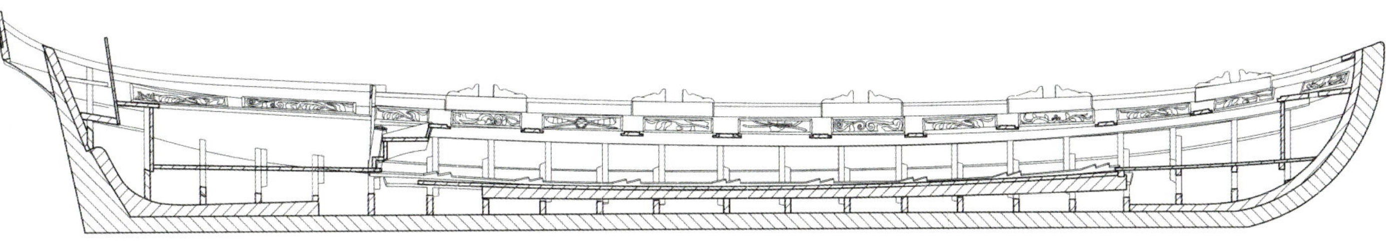

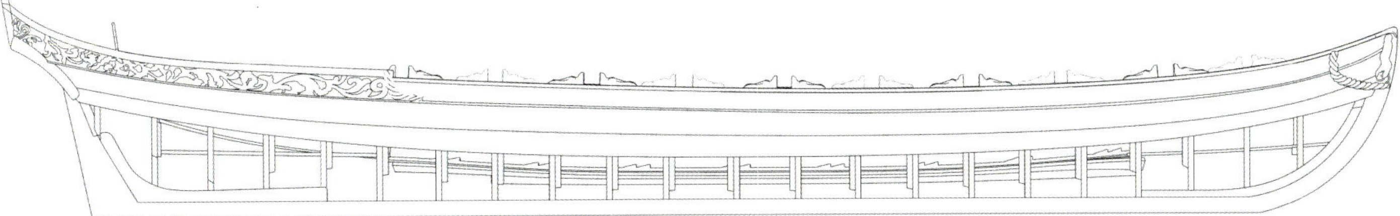

10.154m (33 feet 3 3/4 inches)

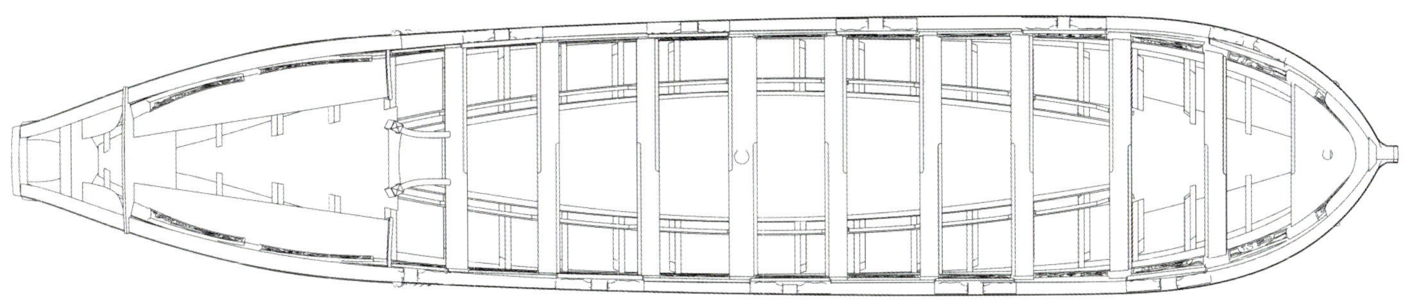

10.154m (33 feet 3 3/4 inches)

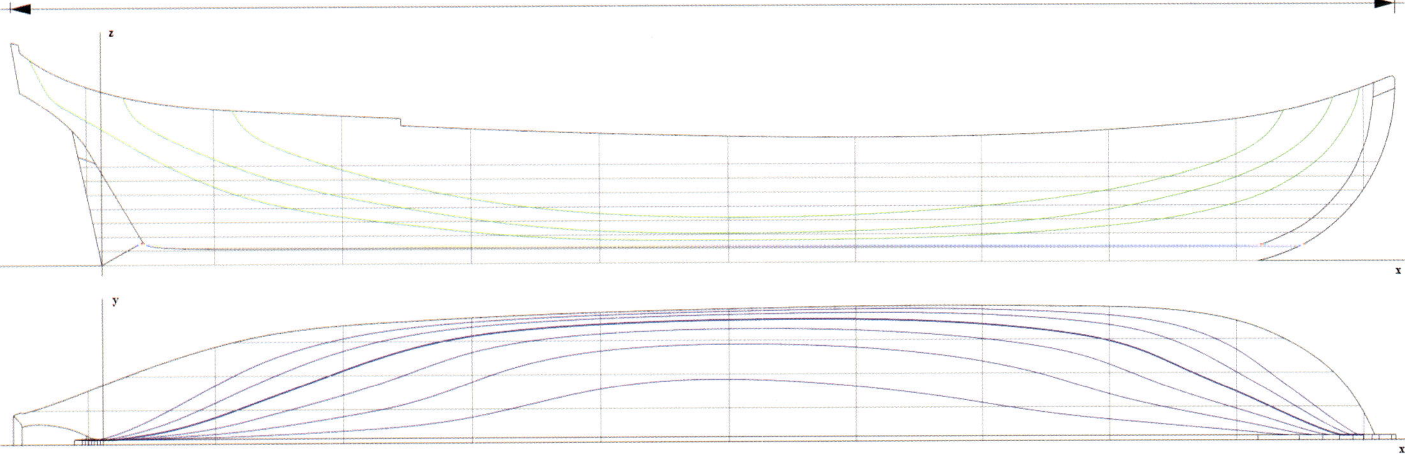

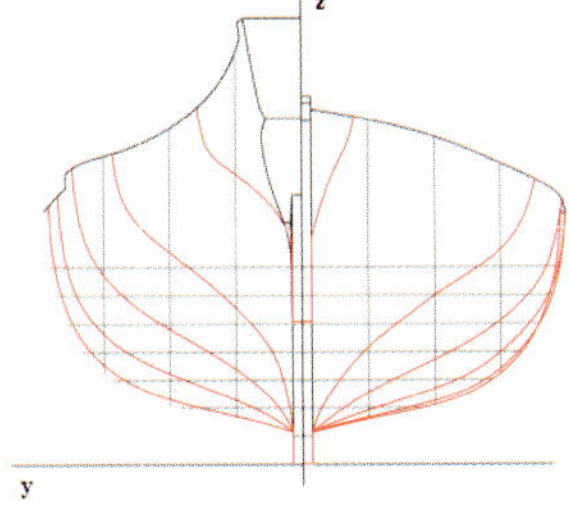

PRINCIPAL PARTICULARS

Length Overall (On Deck)........10.15 m (33' - 3¾")
Length W.L..............................9.27 m (30' - 5")
Beam......................................1.98 m (6' - 6")
Draught ....0.56 m (1' - 10")
Displacement............................2.26 tonnes (2.23 tons)

Mordaunt (1681), 48 guns

NMM NUMBER: SLR0004

SCALE: 1:48

DATE MADE: *c.*1681

Dimensions	Model (scaled up)	*Mordaunt* (1681)
Length of Gun Deck	122ft	122ft
Breadth	32ft 2in	32ft 4in
Number of Guns	40–48	48
Length of Keel	105ft 9in (touch)	101ft 9in
Depth (of hold)	14ft	13ft
Tons (burden)	565	567

Introduction

The ship was originally built for a syndicate headed by Lord Mordaunt, later Earl of Peterborough, as a heavily armed privateer until bought by the Royal Navy in 1682. Privateers were ships built for wealthy individuals or syndicates and were operated at a time of war under a commission of war, sometimes known as a letter of marque.

Identification

The model's measurements agree very closely with the ship's known dimensions, and the coat of arms for the Mordaunt family is located between the two scrolls on the break of the poop deck. There are also four contemporary drawings by the Dutch artist Willem van de Velde the Elder showing detailed views of the stern and broadside, both of which bear a close resemblance to the model (PAH3925, PAH4120, PAH9367, PAI7281).

Not surprisingly, there are several conflicting features that throw doubt about the date of the model. The lion figurehead without the familiar crown suggests a date before acquisition by the Navy, but the Admiralty badge mounted on the break of the quarter deck would suggest the opposite.

Provenance

Mercury Collection.

Construction and Materials

The planking on both the frames and deck beams is a mixture of individual planks fastened with wooden treenails and scored planks with treenails stamped on. The scarph joint of the keel to the stem post is accurate and reinforced with brass fastenings. Most of the deck gratings are cut end-grain wood to enable the openings to be punched through. The stem, keel and stern post are complete with rabbit lines – where the planks land to form a watertight joint. There is also a faint waterline scored along frames just below the main wales.

Portrait of the *Mourdaunt* by Willem van de Velde, *c.*1681. The figures on board give a nice idea of scale. (PAH3925)

Fixtures and Fittings

The belfry is mounted at the break of the forecastle bulkhead and is complete with an ornately carved roof of two crouching lions with entwined tails. Sadly, the bell itself is now missing. Unusually, the main riding bitts and the main capstan, complete with wooden bars, are fitted on the upper deck. To overcome the problem of leading the anchor cables from the hawse pipes below, a pair of shallow troughs have been cut through the forecastle bulkhead to enable the cable to be taken around the capstan and then down to the orlop deck for stowage.

Rigging

The hull has the channels mounted just above the upper wales and are complete with chainplates and wooden deadeyes, indicating the standard three-masted ship-rig.

Decoration

Of all the Navy Board models in the collection, this example is the most complete, especially the carved decoration in terms of the quality of the craftsmanship. Along the bulwarks, the mouldings, hancing pieces, wreathed gunports, and channels with deadeyes have been painted gold. The friezes along the quarter and poop decks have very fine, deeply carved acanthus leaves on a blue ground which continues round the stern galleries.

The quarter galleries are of the traditional 'half-bottle' shape, with a single light (window) surrounded by a mixture of foliage and small figures. Below is a pair of ornately carved finishing pieces in the form of winged dragons. The taffrail has a shield in the centre with a putto riding a scaled dolphin either side. Both the open and closed galleries' lights are of mica, with the frames either painted in blue or etched on for the smaller panes. A royal coat of arms is centrally mounted between the galleries.

Fourth Rate, 50 guns (*c.*1682)

NMM NUMBER: SLR0374

SCALE: 1:48

DATE MADE: *c.*1682

Dimensions	Model (scaled up)	*Bonaventure* (1683 rebuild)
Length of Gun Deck	130ft 4in	124ft 10in
Breadth	33ft 6in	32ft 2in
Number of Guns	50	40
Length of Keel	107ft 2in (touch)	102ft 6in
Depth (of hold)	14ft	12ft 4in
Tons (burden)	658	564

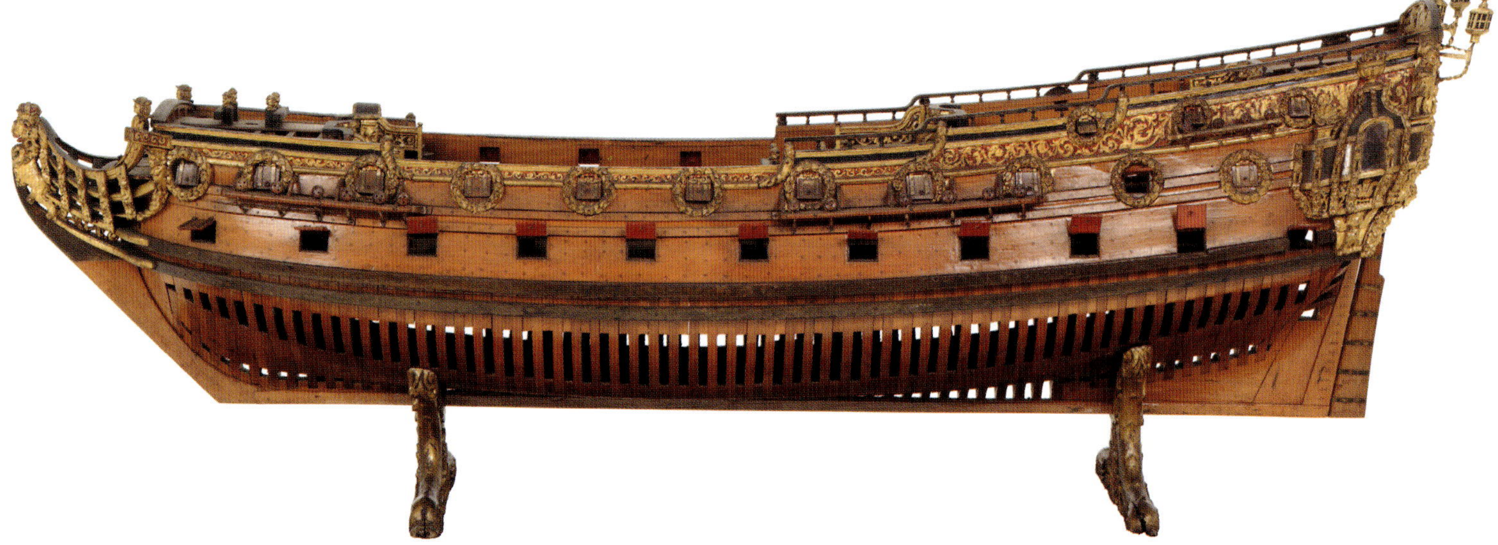

Introduction

This detailed model from the period of Charles II possibly has a link to James, Duke of York, because it prominently displays the plume of feathers of the heir apparent.

Identification

The model is unidentified, but has 1682 painted across the stern. The only similar Fourth Rate built around this date was the 40-gun *Bonaventure*, which was rebuilt in 1683. The model is of a ship a fair bit bigger than the *Bonaventure* so the identity of the model cannot be confirmed.

Provenance

The model was purchased in 1920 by Dr R.C. Anderson from Mr F. Morrice of Brompton Hall, Sussex, as a present for his wife and co-researcher Romola Anderson. In 1983, the model was purchased by the Museum.

Construction and Materials

It is built in fine-grained wood, most of which is probably apple or pear wood. The model has standard framing. The planking above the black main wale is made up of a single piece and fastened with treenails. It is partially decked and includes hatch gratings, and bitts in the waist and foredeck and riding bits on the gun deck.

Fixtures and Fittings

It includes a number of particularly fine details for a model of a smaller ship. There are stairways between the waist, forecastle, quarter, and poop decks. Roman numerals on the port side of the stern post and the starboard side of the stem show the draught of water, which can be used to confirm the scale. At the break of the forecastle, the gold-painted belfry has a turned wooden bell in place. At the stern there are three gold-painted stern lanterns made in the hexagonal parallel-sided design which was an early eighteenth-century design.

Decoration

The decoration is the most striking aspect of this model, and a particularly good example for a model depicting a Fourth Rate. Gold-painted carved work adorns the bow, stern, quarter galleries, gunports, and belfry and beautiful frieze work in red

and gold covers the bulwarks. The figurehead is the typical Royal Navy carved lion, this one with the mouth and coronet picked out in red. At the bow, ornate carved caryatid figures support the head rails, beakhead bulkhead and catheads. Decorative heads adorn the bitts in the waist and on the foredeck. The stern carving, particularly, is sumptuous, even for the Restoration period, which was known for decorative carved work. At the top, the taffrail has an ornate lion and a unicorn as part of a crowned royal coat of arms.

Below, four panels are elaborately painted with the date '1 6 8 2' and in the centre a plume of feathers, the symbol of the heir apparent, at this point Charles II's brother James, Duke of York. Notably, the model maker chose to honour the Duke, despite his having lost the office of Lord High Admiral in 1673 after the Test Act excluded Catholics from public office. The lower counter is decorated with painted trophies of arms, and the rudder head is a carved, gold-painted, bearded head. The stern timbers are adorned with female caryatids and male quarter figures in classical dress stand above wreathed portraits. The quarter galleries are equally ornate, and include the plume of feathers above a winged lower finishing. Along the upper deck and quarter deck the gunports are surrounded by large gold-painted wreaths.

Fourth Rate, 44–50 guns (*c.*1685)

NMM NUMBER: SLR0005

SCALE: 1:48

DATE MADE: *c.*1685

Dimensions	Model (scaled up)	*Deptford/Sedgemoor*
Length of Gun Deck	123ft	125/123
Breadth	34ft	33ft 6in/34ft 6in
Number of Guns	44	44–50
Length of Keel	113ft	103/109
Depth (of hold)	13ft 5in	14ft 4in
Tons (burden)	631	614/692

Introduction

Small two-decked ships were extremely versatile, as they were able to hold their own in line of battle, but were also capable of being part of minor squadrons, providing presence on a station as well as attacking and defending trade.

Identification

The dimensions and style of this model tend to agree with a group of three ships launched in 1687, in particular, the *Sedgemoor* and the *Deptford*. In fact, recent research suggests that the shape of the bow and angle of the forefoot is a feature of the shipwright Thomas Shish, who built the *Deptford*.[2] Shish died before the ship was completed and it was eventually finished by Joseph Lawrence, whose son was known to have made models of yachts.

Provenance

Previously in the Rufford Abbey collection at the seat of Lord Savile, the model was purchased by Sir James Caird in November 1938 at a Christie's sale, with Spink's & Sons acting as Caird's agent. It is possible that the model once belonged to George Savile, 1st Marquess of Halifax. In 1938, *The Times* reported 'A seventeenth century carved wood model of a frigate, probably a Stuart 44-gun two-decker similar to the one in the Metropolitan Museum, New York, was sold to Messrs. Spink for £283 10s.'[3]

Construction and Materials

The hull is of the standard type of framing

with the planking consisting of large veneers of wood with both a plain finish as well as scored individual planks, held in place with treenails. The angled planking on the square tuck stern is also scored on. Most of the original mica has survived, with some later replacements in glass.

Fixtures and Fittings

The forecastle bulkhead has a pair of doors, between which is the ornately decorated belfry, complete with a turned wooden bell which has been painted a green-bronze colour. The quarter-deck bulkhead is also fitted with doors and glazing of mica. There is a pair of short gangways with stairs landing on the upper deck. At the stern there are a pair of quarter badges, as opposed to galleries, fitted with two windows scored with individual panes.

Rigging

The masts and spars are original, but the standing and running rigging was replaced in 1939 by Arthur Waite, under supervision of Dr R.C. Anderson. It shows the unusual rigging detail of lower catharpins for drawing or 'tightening' in the shrouds.

Decoration

The carved decoration is particularly striking in terms of its details and depth. A typical lion figurehead is mounted on the bow and is supported by the upper cheek and hair bracket which finished just forward of the cathead. Along the upper works are the circular wreathed gunports for the upper gun deck and two pairs of hancing pieces at either end of the bulwarks in the waist.

The taffrail has been carved with depth and has the 'CR' monogram of Charles II on a cartouche with a crown above. It is supported by a pair of standing putti holding the tails of scaled dolphins, who in turn are being ridden by putti. Below is an open gallery with a screen that has a series of busts painted directly onto a black ground. Either side is a pair of classically dressed figures resting on small platforms supported by female figures.

Royal Yacht, 6 guns (*c.*1685)

NMM NUMBER: SLR0375

SCALE: 1:32

DATE MADE: *c.*1685

Dimensions	Model (scaled up)	*William and Mary* (1694)
Length of Gun Deck	73ft 4in	76ft 6in
Breadth	22ft	21ft 7in
Number of Guns	6	8
Length of Keel	58ft 8in (touch)	61ft 5in
Depth (of hold)	8ft	9ft 6in
Tons (burden)	154	156

Introduction

Yachts became popular during the reign of King Charles II and were characterised by sleek lines and luxurious and highly decorative features. Royal Yachts were reserved for the use of royalty on state business as well as pleasure.

Identification

This model has not been identified with any particular vessel, but with the royal coat of arms on the stern it is highly likely that it depicts a Royal Yacht.

Provenance

Mercury Collection.

Construction and Materials

Above the standard framing, the model has two open wales painted black and planked above with a single panel fixed with treenails. The deck planking is omitted to show the deck beams and interior, which in the cabins has a laid marquetry floor and panelled bulkheads.

ABOVE
Detail of the inlaid floor decoration in the main cabin.

ABOVE RIGHT
Detail of the bell-shaped stairs leading into the main cabin, with the decorated floor and panelled bulkhead in the background.

Fixtures and Fittings

Fittings include a short forecastle with a grating deck and windlass abaft it. Just aft of the mainmast is a single pair of bitts, with decorative carved heads.

Along each side there are six gunports with gold-painted, carved decorative wreaths, the forward three each having guns that are run out, the aft three all having gold-painted circular lids. The guns themselves are turned in wood and mounted on carriages, both of which are painted black. Above the quarter deck there is a rare example of an awning frame, painted black and mounted forward of the long poop deck accommodating a tiller.

Rigging

The model is unrigged, but there is a stump bowsprit and single mast (probably modern additions), with a single channel, chainplates, and deadeyes fitted either side.

Decoration

At the bow there is a gold-painted figurehead in the form of a putto figure on horseback, with gold-painted caryatid figures along the head rails and supporting the anchor catheads. Large, square quarter badges are surrounded by carved putti painted gold on the port and starboard stern quarters, and an ornately carved and gold-painted stern gallery with four large stern lights. The model is mounted on a pair of decoratively shaped wooden crutches and displayed on a rectangular wooden baseboard. The decoratively carved acanthus-leaf frieze on the beakhead bulkhead and along the bulwarks is painted gold on a red background. The quarter-deck bulkhead is glazed with glass and supported with vertical gold-painted carvings.

The stern is decorated with gold-painted carvings, a royal coat of arms of the Stuarts is mounted on the taffrail, and five carved figures adorn the stern timbers, between which there are glazed panes of glass. The counter is decorated with low-relief rose and thistle carvings with winged putti above. The quarter figures depict a female figure entwined with a snake or serpent, and the quarter gallery is comprised of a square window surrounded with putti.

St Albans (1687), 50 guns

NMM NUMBER: SLR0376

SCALE: 1:48

DATE MADE: *c.*1944

Dimensions	Model (scaled up)	*St Albans* (1687)
Length of Gun Deck	127ft	128ft 4in
Breadth	33ft	32ft 10½in
Number of Guns	50–54	50
Length of Keel	118ft (touch)	107ft 3in
Depth (of hold)	15ft	13ft 3in
Tons (burden)	621	615

Introduction

This model depicting the *St Albans*, a 50-gun two-decker launched at Deptford in 1687, was made in the 1940s by Robert Spence. However, some carved decoration and frames are thought to have been reused from an original seventeenth-century model.

Identification

The model has been identified based on comparison with an original model of *St Albans*, now at Trinity House, London.

Provenance

The model was purchased from Robert Spence on 24 April 1944, for £275 12s 6d.

Construction and Materials

The model differs from the usual framing pattern in that every other frame is omitted, which produces a hull with a much wider room-and-space between frames. The futtocks are pinned to the floor timbers laterally with brass pins. Internally, stringers give longitudinal strength to the hull. This style suggests that the model was made by constructing the frames on the keel, rather than making a full hull of frames and chiselling out each frame – as was common practice for the majority of Navy Board models. The vessel has a square tucked stern, similar to the construction of many of the other surviving Fourth Rates from this period, a technique which was later replaced by the round tuck stern for all but the smallest English ships. Above a black two-strake main wale, the model is planked with individual strakes secured by brass pins.

Fixtures and Fittings

There is a capstan in the waist, and a gold-painted arched belfry at the break of the foredeck, as well as elegant companionways and stairs from waist to quarter deck. There are deck hatches, bitts with carved gold-painted heads on the foredeck and in the waist, and channels, chainplates, and deadeyes fitted for three masts.

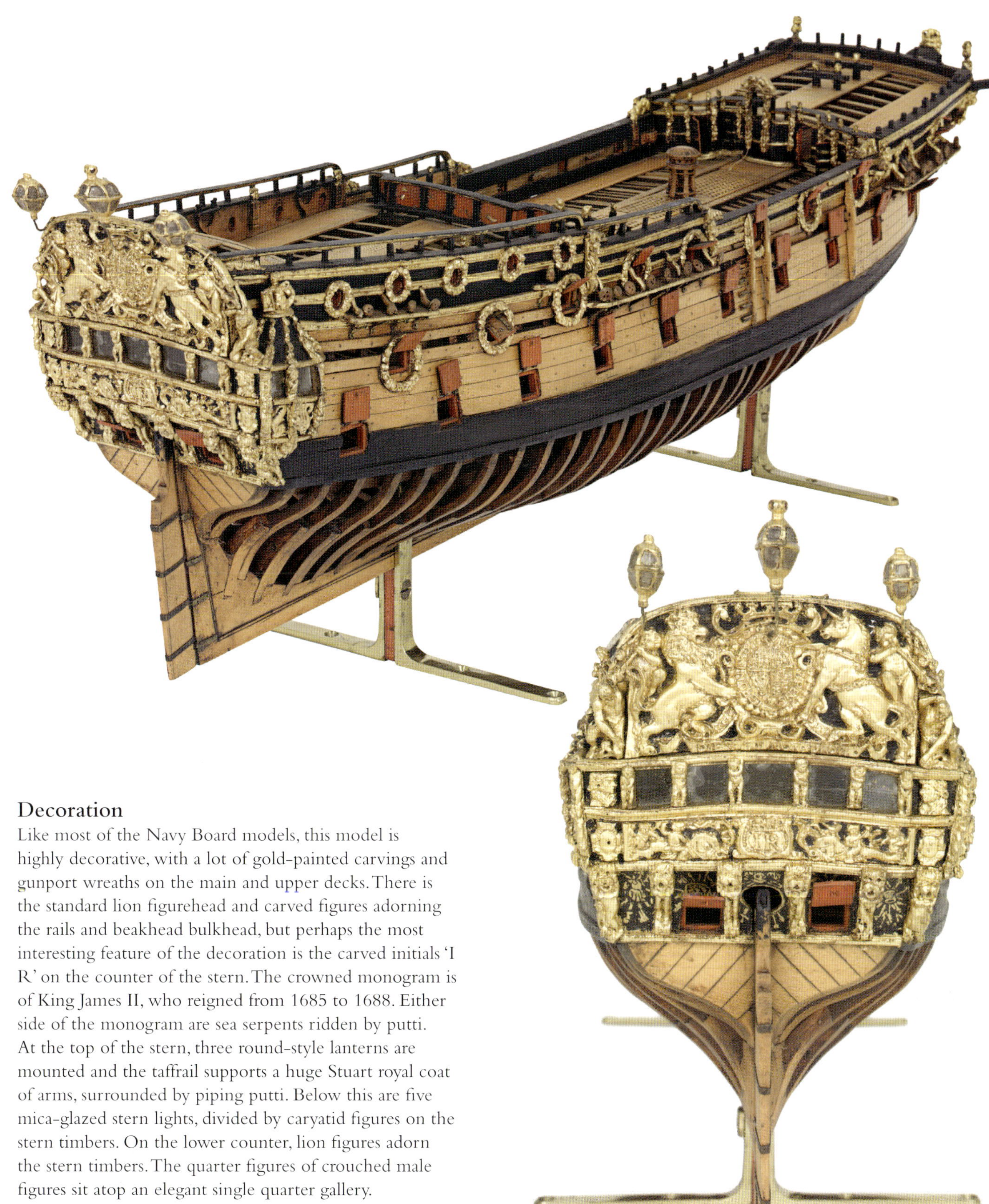

Decoration

Like most of the Navy Board models, this model is highly decorative, with a lot of gold-painted carvings and gunport wreaths on the main and upper decks. There is the standard lion figurehead and carved figures adorning the rails and beakhead bulkhead, but perhaps the most interesting feature of the decoration is the carved initials 'I R' on the counter of the stern. The crowned monogram is of King James II, who reigned from 1685 to 1688. Either side of the monogram are sea serpents ridden by putti. At the top of the stern, three round-style lanterns are mounted and the taffrail supports a huge Stuart royal coat of arms, surrounded by piping putti. Below this are five mica-glazed stern lights, divided by caryatid figures on the stern timbers. On the lower counter, lion figures adorn the stern timbers. The quarter figures of crouched male figures sit atop an elegant single quarter gallery.

English Yacht, 6 guns (*c.*1690)

NMM NUMBER: SLR0377

SCALE: 1:32

DATE MADE: *c.*1690

Dimensions	Model (scaled up)	*William and Mary* (1694)
Length of Gun Deck	65ft 4in	76ft 6in
Breadth	20ft	21ft 7in
Number of Guns	6	8
Length of Keel	60ft 8in (touch)	61ft 5in
Depth (of hold)	8ft	9ft 6in
Tons (burden)	113	152

Introduction

An English yacht from the period of William and Mary. Yachts were recorded in England from the middle of the seventeenth century with the return of Charles II from exile in the Netherlands, and together with enthusiasm from the Duke of York, the sport of yachting became popular amongst the nobility.

Identification

The identity of this model is unknown, but the level of decoration suggests a yacht built for someone of importance.

Provenance

Donated to the NMM by Dr R.C. Anderson in 1949.

Construction and Materials

Each frame is unusual in that it is made up of a single floor timber which spans the lower hull up to the height of the main wale, and a futtock which scarphs the floor timber and extends upwards to the deck beams. The model is planked above the wale with broad panels. The deck planking is entirely omitted, allowing one to view inside the hull.

Fixtures and Fittings

At the bow there is a windlass, which was typically used instead of a capstan on these smaller vessels. It is a typical horizontal barrel windlass with three pawl rims, where the pawls would click into place to prevent the windlass from turning in the opposite direction. There are two elaborate pawls carved in the form of lions. The hull is complete with sixteen wreathed gunports, of which ten are 'false ports' which do not pierce the sides of the hull.

No guns are shown on the model, but this type of yacht could have typically carried six 3pdr guns. There are gilt channels, chainplates, and deadeyes for a single mast. This type of vessel would have been cutter-rigged and steered by a tiller, shown on the poop deck.

Decoration

The model can be dated by the double-headed figurehead reflecting the dual monarchy of William and Mary (1689–94). The deeply carved taffrail above the stern depicts a laureate-crowned female figure with cuirassed bust, holding a staff, with left hand resting on a shield, surrounded by putti. It is possible that this represents the figure of Britannia, which had seen a return to usage on coins during the reign of Charles II. A 'quarter badge' on either side provides light into the state cabin.

Fourth Rate, 50 guns (*c.*1691)

NMM NUMBER: SLR0349

SCALE: 1:48

DATE MADE: *c.*1691

Dimensions	Model (scaled up)	*Centurion* (1691)
Length of Gun Deck	126ft 3in	125ft 8in
Breadth	33ft 6in	33ft 2in
Number of Guns	48–50	50
Length of Keel	108ft 6in (touch)	105ft
Depth (of hold)	13ft	13ft 5in
Tons (burden)	633	614

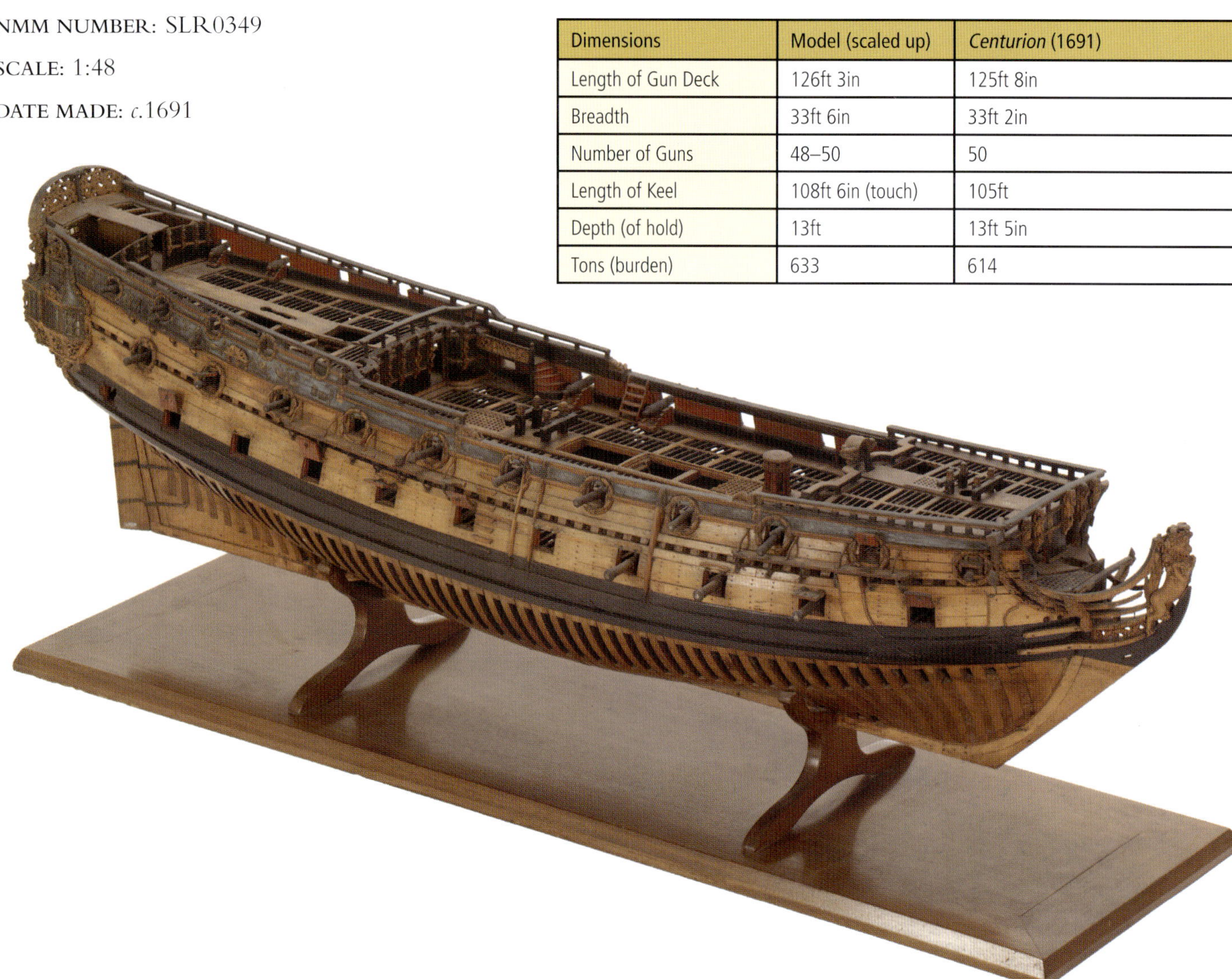

Introduction

This 50-gun Fourth Rate is a good example of very well-made model from the period of William and Mary.

Identification

The monograms of co-monarchs William and Mary, 'WR' and 'MR', feature on the ornately decorated stern and date the model to between 1689 and Queen Mary's death in 1694. The model has been associated with the *Centurion* on the basis of the date and dimensions. The *Centurion* was a 50-gun Fourth Rate built by Fisher Harding and launched at Deptford Dockyard in 1691.

Provenance

The model was donated by Sir James Caird after he purchased it for £350 on 30 December 1935 through his agent Spink's.

Construction and Materials

The model is constructed with the standard Navy Board frame arrangement. It has a square tuck stern, which gives the hull very fine lines at the stern. By this period, the Royal Navy had abandoned this building technique for larger ships in favour of the stronger round tuck stern.

The wood is thought to be pear, and the model is partially decked and equipped in a high level of detail. It is planked above the main wale with individual strakes, but noticeably between the upper wale the top timbers of the framing are left exposed. On the upper deck, the ledges (which run athwartships between the fore and aft carlings) have been made from ebony.

Fixtures and Fittings

The curved stairways from the waist to the quarter deck have gracefully carved fretwork rails with the monograms 'WR' and 'MR'. Towards the forward end of the waist is a jeer capstan without bars. The guns are simple turned wooden barrels mounted on truckless carriages painted red. They are positioned on narrow strips of deck planking either side of the deck. The gunport lids are fixed with brass hinges and painted red inside.

Rigging

The model includes channels, with chainplates for three masts, but some deadeyes are missing. An interesting detail is the hooked block of the cathead purchase which is hanging off the cathead at the forward end of the forecastle. This was the method by which the anchor was secured after weighing anchor.

Decoration

The lack of gold paint makes for a much more subtle decorative style, but allows the intricate carving to be seen in much greater detail. At the bow, there is a small amount of damage around the head rails. However, the crowned lion figurehead and the figures at the beakhead bulkhead are particularly elegant left in their natural finish. The bitts on the forecastle and in the waist are decorated with carved heads. The belfry is an elegant arch supported by carved caryatid figures, and is left in a natural finish. The bell mounted inside is metal with a fixed clapper.

The carved work adorning the stern is superb – the twin charioteers on the taffrail are cut clear through to create a beautiful fenestrated affect. Each of the eight stern lights consists of nine brass-framed panes of glass. On the counter panes are intricate high-relief carvings, including the monograms 'WR' and 'MR'. On the vertical stern timbers are high-relief figures, and five human heads at the bottom of the lower counter. Roman figures stand at the quarter pieces above finely constructed quarter galleries. Along the bulwark is a delicate frieze work of gold trophies of arms painted on a blue background. The hancing pieces at the end of the drift rails of the quarter deck are carved putti. The gunports along the main, forecastle, and quarter decks are wreathed and those on the lower deck left plain.

Boyne (1692), 80 guns

NMM NUMBER: SLR0006

SCALE: 1:48

DATE MADE: *c.*1692

Dimensions	Model (scaled up)	*Boyne* (1692)
Length of Gun Deck	157ft	157ft
Breadth	40ft 9in	41ft
Number of Guns	80	80
Length of Keel	130ft 6in (touch)	128ft 2in
Depth (of hold)	19ft (approx.)	17ft 3in
Tons (burden)	1160	1160

Introduction

The *Boyne* was one of seventeen two-decker 80-gun ships ordered under the 1691 programme. They were generally not that successful, owing to the over-gunning on the crowded quarter deck and forecastle. As a result of this, the hulls tended to sag at the extremities under the weight of the additional guns, causing structural problems and, in some cases, compromising stability.[4]

Identification

This is one of the rare seventeenth-century models that can be identified with certainty. Not only do the measured dimensions of the model agree very closely with the known dimensions of the ship, but there is a carved scroll on the break of the poop inscribed with 'Ye BOYNE Bt By Mr Harding DEP SA'. Fisher Harding was the Master Shipwright at Deptford during the period of the *Boyne*'s construction (see page 29).

Provenance

Presented to Greenwich Hospital by King William IV in 1830 and subsequently transferred to the Royal Naval Museum in 1874. The Royal Naval Museum Collection was later transferred in 1934 at the founding of the NMM, where it is part of the Greenwich Hospital Collection.

Construction and Materials

The most striking feature of the construction of this model is the alternate double spacing of the hull frames which throws more light into the interior of the hold. It is complete with the floors and then a single solid frame up to the open main wales. This would have been constructed frame by frame, using the keel, internal stringers, and keelson to hold them in place during assembly. The hull planking, deck, and punched gratings are all fastened with brass pins. The hull planking above the main wale is a single

piece scored with individual planks, but without the butt joints. Brass has been used throughout on gunport hinges, hatch doors open flat on deck for companionway, 'barley twist' stern lantern brackets, and the rails on the beakhead next to gratings. The stem and stern posts are realistically scarphed to the keel and secured with a number of brass pins.

The model was probably rigged with launching flags, as the turned wooden plugs inserted into the mast apertures together with a brass clamp on the aft side of the figurehead still survive. The baseboard and mounts follows a style of the second half of the eighteenth century.

Fixtures and Fittings

The quality and originality of this model is quite extraordinary and is complete with a whole range of fittings as well as a profuse amount of carved and painted decoration. Of particular interest are the heads, or 'seats of ease', located just forward of the beakhead bulkhead by the gratings, whilst the forecastle is complete with a square galley-stove chimney, and a large square span shackle, used to locate the large wooden fish davit for working the anchors. There is also an ornately carved belfry above the bulkhead housing a turned wooden bell complete with clapper. In the waist is a single jeer capstan of the drumhead type, a pair of piss-dales located on the inwales, and a set of curved stairs leading up to the quarter deck.

The poop deck has a pair of trumpeters' cabins, fitted with wooden cots inside, which are mounted up against the taffrail. Just aft of the mizzen mast is the helmsman's companion, a small raised box structure with windows and a grating roof. There is also the oval-shaped rowle through which the whipstaff was worked and connected to the tiller, which in turn manoeuvred the rudder. This was the method of steering the larger warships before the introduction of the wheel in around 1703 (see SLR0218). Projecting out from the taffrail are three stern lanterns of the rounded oval shape, fitted with mica glazing.

Rigging

The hull has the channels mounted just above the upper wales, which are complete with chainplates and wooden deadeyes, indicating the standard three-masted ship-rig.

Decoration

The bow has a typical crowned lion figurehead supported by a pair of putti, together with ornately carved rails, cheeks, cathead, and hawse pieces. The hawse pipes are surrounded with a large carved sea serpent. Along the hull side are painted friezes of trophies in a chinoiserie style, wreathed gunports for both the upper gun-deck and quarter-deck guns, and four hancing pieces in the form of crouching dogs in the waist.

The monogram of the co-monarchy of William and Mary is carved on the quarter and enclosed stern galleries together with a pair of busts. The quarter galleries are topped with a pair of putti holding shields, with the lion rampant indicating the House of Nassau. There are also four swans, the two large quarter figures are bearded men holding a staff and wearing a helmet, standing on scaled dolphins and serpents. The taffrail is very ornate and inward: there are a pair of crouching male lions, putti holding foliage, two females blowing horns either side of a central helmet and breastplate trophy with the entwined monogram 'WM'. The middle gallery has the royal coat of arms, while the lower has three putti supporting a royal crown, flanked by a pair of swans, which are repeated on the lower quarter galleries.

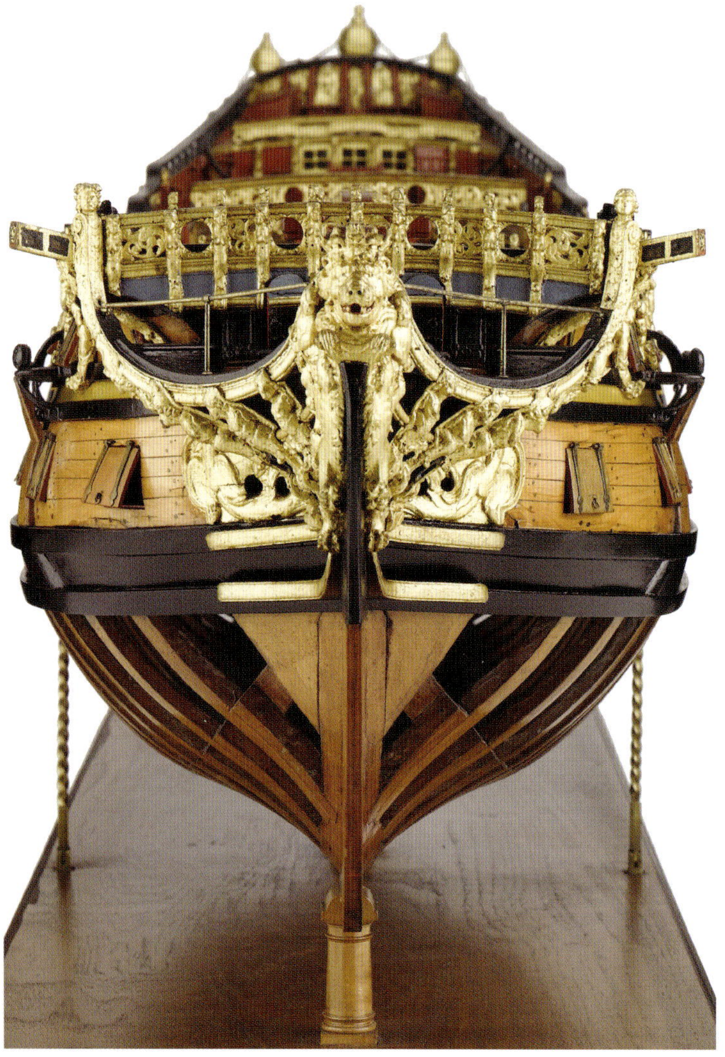

Fourth Rate, 50 guns (1695–1702)

NMM NUMBER: SLR0381

SCALE: 1:48

DATE MADE: 1695–1702

Introduction

The model depicts a 50-gun two-decker Fourth Rate of the late seventeenth century, which would have carried 32pdr guns on the gun deck, 12pdrs on the upper deck, and 6pdrs on the quarter deck. Ships like this were ideally suited as heavy cruisers to protect English commerce from French privateers during the Nine Years War (1688–97).

Dimensions	Model (scaled up)	*Greenwich* (1699)
Length of Gun Deck	132ft	135ft 10in
Breadth	36ft	36ft
Number of Guns	50–52	50
Length of Keel	112ft (touch)	110ft
Depth (of hold)	13ft	13ft 6½in
Tons (burden)	761	785

Identification

On the stern, the royal arms and single monogram 'WR', representing William III, provides a date of between 1695 and 1702 (the single monogram being an indication of the death of Mary, his queen, in December 1694). The model is quite broad and doesn't quite fit the dimensions of the Royal Navy ships known to be launched between 1694 and 1703. The beam is the same as the larger Fourth Rates built at that time, such as the *Greenwich*.

Provenance

The model was given to Greenwich Hospital by King William IV in 1830, and it was lent to the National Maritime Museum in 1936. William IV had served in the Royal Navy as a young man and was later dubbed the 'Sailor King'.

Construction and Materials

The framing is of the standard floor-futtock-top timber arrangement. A unique feature of this model is the large amount of walnut veneer between the wales. Although unrealistically made from vertical sections, as opposed to horizontal planks, it highlights the links between model making and furniture making. It uses a technique popular in furniture making at the time called 'oyster shell marquetry', whereby wood was cut diagonally across the grain, producing a shell-like pattern. Above the upper wale the planking is of a lighter, fine-grained wood. The presence of a square tuck stern like many of the other surviving models of Fourth Rates indicates that this construction technique was still used for ships of this size, despite its gradual abandonment in favour of the stronger round tuck stern for larger English ships.

Fixtures and Fittings

The model has twenty-four gunports on the lower deck, another twenty-two on the main deck and six on the quarter deck, totalling fifty-two. The brass guns, larger on the lower deck, represent the 12pdrs and those on the upper and quarter decks, the smaller calibre. It is not certain if they are original, but they are turned in brass and have a green patina. The gunport lids are painted inside with a gold lion's head on a red background.

Rigging

The model was re-rigged in the Museum in 1937 by A.H. Waite using contemporary evidence. The rigging illustrates the typical features of the late seventeenth century, notably the short mizzen mast with its lateen yard, the round fighting tops, a bowsprit unsupported by a bobstay, and the spritsail topmast and yard situated at the end of the bowsprit. Rigging from this period has been fairly well documented, but a certain amount of interpretation is always needed to restore rigging. Therefore, unlike the rest of the model, the rigging should not be treated as a primary source.

Decoration

The model clearly illustrates the profuse amount of carved decoration, typical for the late seventeenth century. At the bow is a particularly fine crowned lion figurehead, flanked by two putti. The head rails are supported by carved male figures and on the beakhead bulkhead and below the catheads there are carved female figures. The bulwark screen is painted blue, and mounted with gold stars. On the break of the quarter deck there is a crowned 'WR' monogram of William III. At the stern, the taffrail is adorned with two winged female figures, the upper counter is mounted with a carved royal coat of arms of William III, flanked either side by a low-relief gilt rose of England and Scottish thistle. On the lower counter in the centre is another crowned 'WR' monogram. To either side are carved lions rampant of the House of Nassau; on the right, a palm frond across a sceptre, and on the left, a sword across an olive branch. Below the quarter galleries are Irish harps in low relief, as well as male laureate busts in profile below carved Roman-warrior quarter figures.

The decoration was in part a political statement: both royal symbols and symbols of the nations of the British Isles are displayed prominently with the monogram of William III. Since taking the throne with his wife Mary in 1688, William had been under enormous pressure from external forces, including Jacobites loyal to James II, supported by William's long-standing rival, Louis XIV of France. The combined symbolisms used on Royal Navy ships, such as is shown on this model, were designed to reinforce William's position as king.

In Focus: Ship Model Conservation

Historically, ship models have often been restored or 'improved' by experienced model makers or restorers. Sometimes this led to over-zealous restoration, where new structures, decoration, or rigging models have been added to models. Although early model makers and restorers were often highly skilled, with a high degree of concern for objects in their care, this practice has the potential to undermine the value of ship models as historical sources.

This approach was never adopted at the NMM, which has always treated models as historical sources as much as display objects. Shortly after the Museum opened in 1937, the ship model collection was put under the care of the Assistant in Charge of Models, supported by a modeller and a rigger, each of whom had an assistant. It is debatable whether additional work should be made obvious or hidden. In the 1920s, R.C. Anderson replaced earlier restoration from a model of a three-decker of 1675 (SLR0003) and ensured that 'no-one can possibly tell the new carvings from the old'.[5] In the 1970s, a model of the *Bedford* was restored using new parts made in a lighter wood, so that the restoration work is immediately obvious.

Since 1980, restoration at the NMM has been 'only considered on the basis of indisputable evidence and when absolutely necessary for the preservation of the model'.[6] Today, rather than restore objects, conservators work to preserve objects for future generations. Museum conservation involves objects of great historical value and is bound by a strict code of ethics. To maintain its accredited status, the National Maritime Museum must follow strict guidelines when any work is carried out. Conservators must record all stages of their work and any work must be reversible.

Furthermore, the scientific training of the modern ship-model conservator has

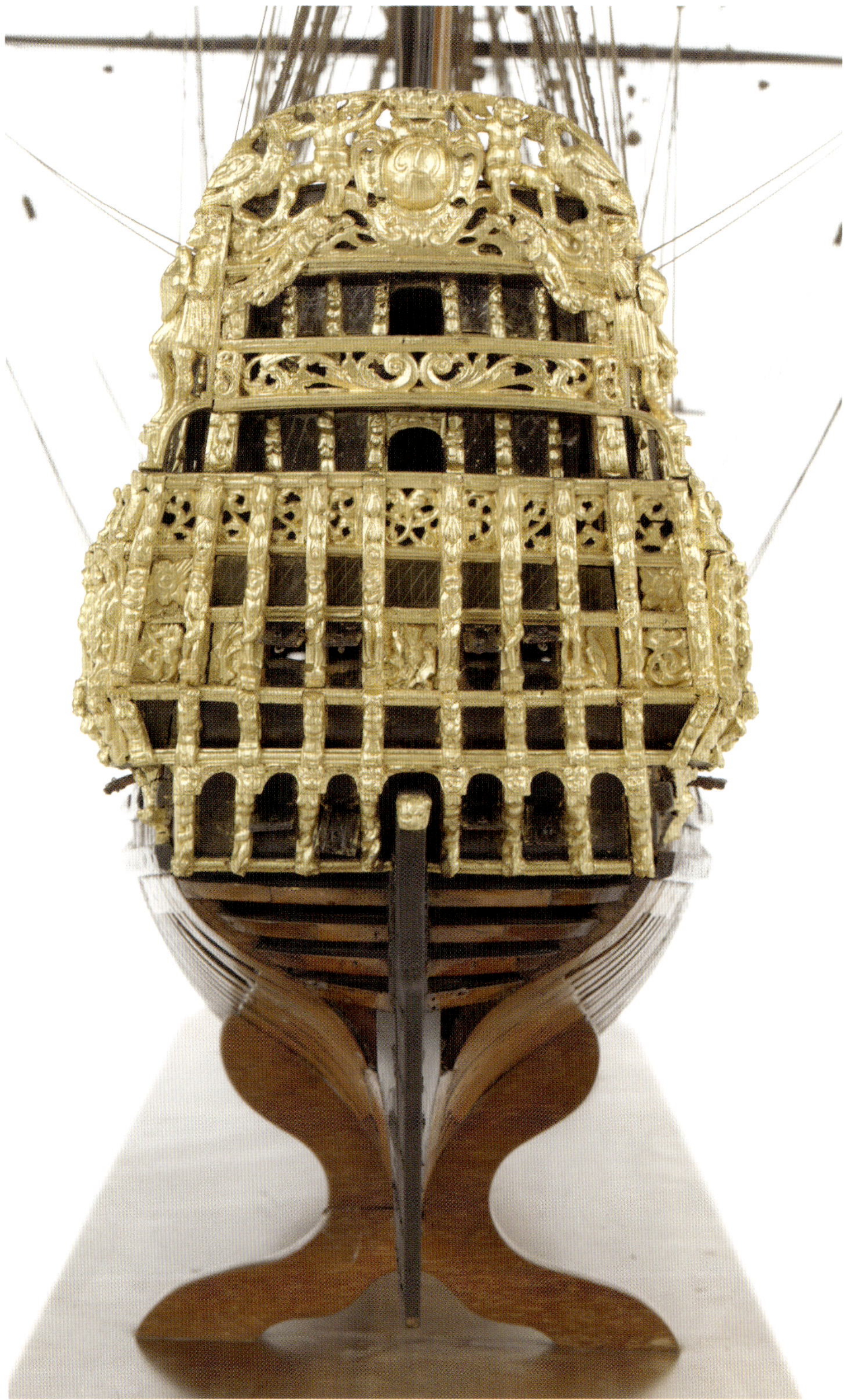

Model of a three-decker of 1675 which was extensively repaired in the 1920s. (SLR0003)

LEFT

Navy Board model of the *Bedford*. (SLR0384)

ABOVE

A conservator cleaning the baseboard of a model on display.

TOP

A curator measuring a model. Conservators regularly collaborate with curators to ensure the best possible care for ship models.

led to a much greater understanding of damage by humidity, contaminated air, insects, and other natural agencies. This can pose a particular challenge in ship model conservation owing to the mixed materials used in their construction, which often include wood, metal, textiles, and bone. Ship models have to be kept in a stable environment, because the different materials can react in different ways to sudden changes in climatic conditions. Low temperature helps to keep a stable humidity level, which is constantly monitored so that staff can take suitable action.

Preparation for new displays and routine cleaning of models carried out by conservators allows an unrivalled opportunity to investigate ship models and understand how they were made. Dust can be removed with a small vacuum cleaner or soft brush. A weak solution of detergent or a scalpel may be used where the dirt is ingrained. Degraded varnish or lacquer can be removed with solvents.[7] Wood, the primary material of most models, needs to be protected from insect life, rot, damp, and from conditions that may cause warping in small parts. Metal, such as iron or brass, is treated as little as possible, unless corroded.

Broken ends of rigging cord are common, and are impossible to repair adequately; they are replaced where necessary, but the old ones are stored for possible research. In terms of textiles, flags are easy to remove for treatment, but sails are treated *in situ* if possible. A model's rigging is also vulnerable to light damage, which means the model can only be displayed for shorter periods and in lower lighting. Painted areas of models are normally retained, even when they are cracked or flaking, and the layers are consolidated and re-adhered. Missing areas might be retouched if enough evidence is available: analytical work on the paint can provide useful evidence on the dating of the construction or restoration of the model.[8]

Bedford (1698), 70 guns

NMM NUMBER: SLR0384

SCALE: 1:48

DATE MADE: *c.*1698

Dimensions	Model (scaled up)	*Bedford* (1698)
Length of Gun Deck	147ft	151ft
Breadth	34ft	40ft 4in
Number of Guns	50–58	70
Length of Keel	119ft 3in (touch)	124ft 1in
Depth (of hold)	15ft	16ft 9in
Tons (burden)	1072	1073

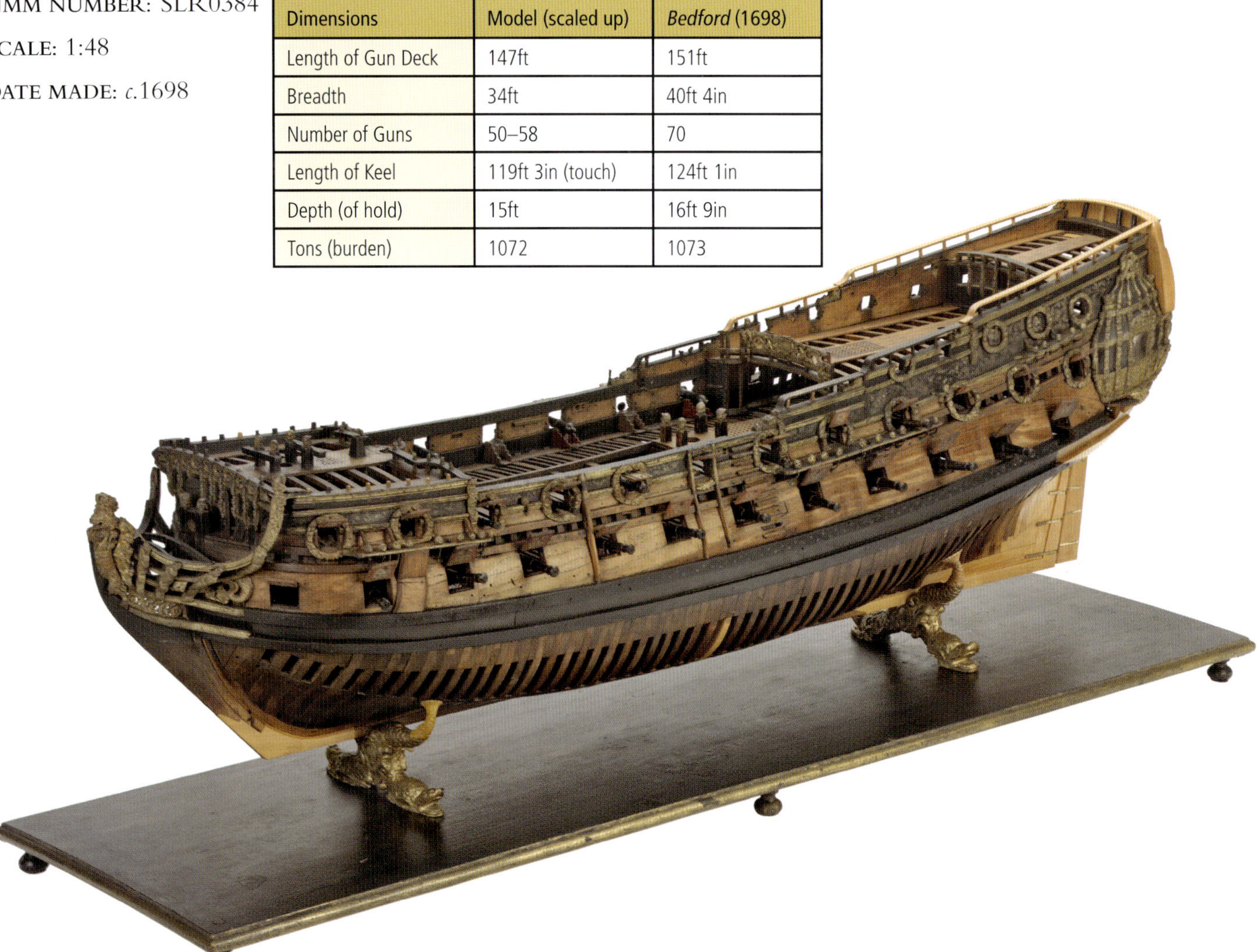

Introduction

Apart from the newly introduced 80-gun ships of the 1690s, the 70-gun Third Rates remained the most prolific during the first half of the eighteenth century, up until 1756 with the introduction of the new 74-gun ship. Under the 1695 building programme, Parliament granted funds for three new 70-gun Third Rates to be built. All three of these ships were named after senior officers of the Admiralty. The *Bedford* was named after Admiral Edward Russell, who was First Lord of the Admiralty and later created Duke of Bedford in 1694.

Identification

This model has now been positively identified[9] as the *Bedford*, launched in 1698, by comparing known dimensions, together with contemporary drawings by van de Velde. This is backed up further with the carved dolphin cradle supports bearing the initials 'FH' and the date 1698. This refers to Fisher Harding, Master Shipwright at Woolwich and designer of the *Bedford*. The dimensions of the model depict a ship of seventy guns, although it only shows sixty broadside ports. The reason behind this apparent anomaly is that the ship was built and launched during peacetime with its reduced armament.

Provenance

On loan to the National Maritime Museum from the Marquess of Salisbury.

Construction and Materials

The hull and frames are built in the standard form, but with the floor and top timbers extending further than usual. The planking above the main wales is a single piece of oak with the individual timbers scored on. The model had suffered from

FAR LEFT

An internal view of the lower portion of the whipstaff angled towards the top left of the picture. It is connected to the wooden tiller by the metal 'gooseneck' and securing pin.

LEFT

Detail showing the brick galley stove located in the forecastle.

a major worm infestation at the bow and stern in the past. The NMM stabilised the damaged areas and subsequently replaced them with new boxwood, which has been left in its natural state.

Fixtures and Fittings

As part of the model's restoration in the 1970s, it was decided to reinstate a fully working whipstaff. This method of steering the ship predated the more familiar ship's wheel, which was introduced in 1701–03 (see SLR0218).

There is also the original stove in the forecastle, painted with red bricks, and a copper chimney ventilating through the deck.

Most of the lights (windows) on the remaining bulkheads inboard and stern galleries are still fitted with the original mica. The guns have been turned in wood and stained a dark brown and mounted on simple wooden carriages. The model is supported by a contemporary pair of scaled dolphin supports on a painted oak baseboard trimmed in gold with four small bun feet.

Rigging

There is no evidence to suggest that this model was once rigged, which would be a rarity for a seventeenth-century model. The channels, chainplates, and deadeyes are mostly original and support the traditional three-masted rig of a ship.

Decoration

Most of the surviving carved decoration is complete with original finish, and in some places there is evidence of gesso, a type of undercoat paint, where the gold paint has worn away. At the bow, most of the carved decoration has remained largely intact. The lion figurehead is complete with putti supporters adjoining it to the head rails. There is also a very ornate carving of sea dragons around the hawse holes, just above the cheeks. Along the side of the hull, the painted bulwark friezes are in original condition and consist of an assortment of trophies of war and foliage which have been painted directly onto the model, but are slightly obscured by the dark varnish layer. The carved decoration on the quarter-deck rails has an indistinct coat of arms at its centre.

However, the stern frames, stern post, and upper portions of the galleries have suffered from worm infestation. The later restoration, seen here in the lighter and unstained boxwood, was a convention followed during the 1970s. Of particular importance is that this model is one of only a handful that is complete with its late seventeenth-century baseboard and 'dolphin' support cradles.

Peregrine Galley (1700), 20–24 guns

NMM NUMBER: SLR0394

SCALE: 1:44

DATE MADE: *c.*1700

Dimensions	Model (scaled up)	*Peregrine Galley* (1700)
Length of Gun Deck	84ft 4in	86ft 10in
Breadth	22ft	22ft 10in
Number of Guns	20	20
Length of Keel	71ft 6in (touch)	71ft
Depth (of hold)	8ft	10ft 7in
Tons (burden)	183	197

Introduction

The *Peregrine Galley*, launched at Deptford in 1700, was designed by Admiral Sir Peregrine Osborne, Marquess of Carmarthen, often known by his lesser title of Lord Danby. The hull has a fine entry and run and had reputation as a fast sailer. It was officially classed as a 20-gun Sixth Rate, but designed as a yacht-like fast transport for members of the royal family and other important dignitaries. It was used to carry the Duke of Marlborough to his Continental campaigns, and was the ship that brought King George I from Germany to take the British throne in 1714.

In 1716, it was refitted, renamed *Carolina*, and formally redesignated as a Royal Yacht. It was rebuilt again in 1733 and subsequently known as *Royal Caroline*. In 1749, it returned to the Navy as the *Peregrine*, and continued in service until 1762. Although the *Peregrine Galley* was built as a one-off, its design continued to be admired for generations – it was borrowed for a replacement *Royal Caroline*, which served as a Royal Yacht from 1750 to 1820, and adapted for a series of frigates launched between 1757 and 1806.

Identification

The model was identified as the *Peregrine Galley* due to three factors. First, the hull dimensions match closely to the *Peregrine Galley*. The model is made to the unusual of scale of 1:44, compared to most (although not all) Navy Board-style models, which were built to 1:48 – the same as the draughts. Secondly, the *Peregrine Galley* was just two-masted, and likely rigged as a brigantine with a square rig on the foremast, and fore and aft on the mainmast. The absence of channels for a mizzen mast suggests that the model depicts a vessel intended to be rigged as such.

Finally, the galley on the *Peregrine Galley* was unconventionally built, with the fire facing the magazine, something which the Duke of Marlborough criticised on a voyage to his Continental campaigns. The model itself shows this unusual and somewhat dangerous feature. However, the stern decorations, which depict Queen Anne and include the monogram 'AR' and the date '1708', suggest that the model was made, or altered after the accession of Queen Anne.

Provenance

Mercury Collection. NMM Caird Collection, 1934.

Construction and Materials

The model is made with the standard

framing. Above the black main wale, the planking is made up of several large panels secured with brass pins. On the port side these panels are scored to represent individual planks, but left unscored on the starboard side.

Fixtures and Fittings

Twenty guns was the nominal number of guns for this rate; however, the aft five gunports on either side are glazed with mica. This is not surprising considering the intended use of the *Peregrine Galley*. It was not intended to engage the enemy, which it could easily outrun. In fact, the extra guns made way for the stern of the ship to be fitted out luxuriously and comfortably for transporting for royalty and other dignitaries.

Rigging

The *Peregrine Galley* was initially built with two masts, and the model has no evidence of ever having had a mizzen mast. The position of the mainmast, forward of the midpoint between stem and stern, suggests that unlike the foremast, the mainmast was rigged fore and aft. If both masts were square-rigged it would make sailing to windward very difficult indeed.[10] In fact, due to the unbalanced nature of this rig, the full-sized vessel was later re-rigged as a three-masted fully rigged ship in January 1703.

Decoration

There is a standard gold-painted lion figurehead at the bow, but the stern is decorated with gold-painted high-relief carvings. At the centre of the large taffrail is a crowned female figure, probably Queen Anne, shown holding a sceptre and orb – the symbols of monarchy. She is flanked by two winged putti holding wreaths and to her left is a male bust, and to her right is a seated figure. The quarter figures are male sculptures shown in classical military dress holding shields.

Between the four mica-glazed stern windows is the monogram 'AR' and the date '1708' painted in gold on a blue background, in the style matching the other painted decoration of gold on a blue background. The quarter galleries have a square window with ornate, low-relief, gold-painted carvings in a floral design, and topped with a star, similar to the Order of Garter. There is a large amount of decoration around the bulwark screens in a gold-painted floral motif on a blue background.

Detail of the galley and chimney situated in the waist.

First Rate, 96 guns (*c.*1702)

NMM NUMBER: SLR0386

SCALE: 1:60

DATE MADE: *c.*1702

Dimensions	Model (scaled up)	*Royal Anne* (1704)
Length of Gun Deck	170ft	170ft
Breadth	49ft	48ft
Number of Guns	96	100
Length of Keel	140ft 4in (touch)	140ft 6in
Depth (of hold)	17ft 5in	19ft 4in
Tons (burden)	1796	1730

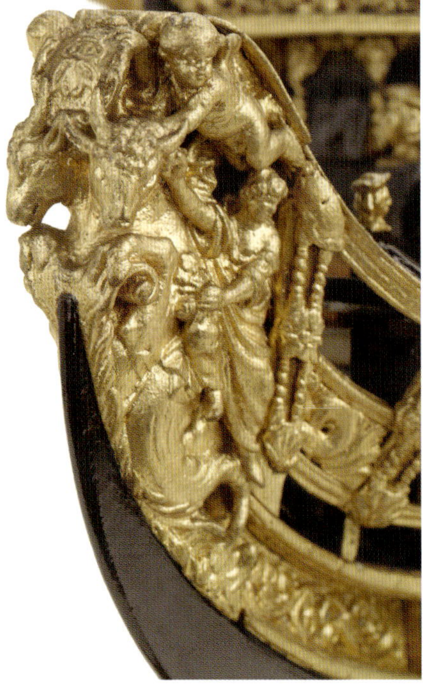

Introduction

During the late seventeenth century, the Royal Navy began building more of the smaller ships, such as the Fourth, Fifth, and Sixth Rates, to protect against increasing French attacks on British commerce. As a result, few large three-decker First and Second Rate ships were built between 1689 and 1705.

Identification

This model is something of an enigma, but there are several factors which have led to its being dated to around 1702. At a scale of 1:60, the model is of similar size to the 100-gun First Rate *Royal Anne* launched at Woolwich Dockyard in 1704. However, the number of guns and the gunport arrangement differs. The royal monogram 'AR' of Queen Anne on the figurehead seemingly makes 1702 the earliest possible date, but it is possible that the model was started some years before. The figurehead was often one of the last pieces to be added when making a model. The profusion of gold-painted carving suggests that the model was made before the order of 1703, restricting such decoration. However, as we have seen, these models could fulfil a decorative as much as technical function. Therefore, it seems plausible that the decoration could be present on a model, despite the restriction on ships. Finally, positioning the fore and main channels above the middle deck ports was common practice after 1702.

Provenance

The model was one of a number presented to Greenwich Hospital by King William IV in 1830. Many of these models were displayed in the Painted Hall, which from

1824 to 1934 was a gallery of marine art. In 1934, the models, including this one, were transferred to the NMM on long-term loan.

Construction and Materials

The model is decked, equipped, and mounted on three turned boxwood pillars along the keel with two 'barley twist' brass rods supporting the wales amidships. A noticeable feature of this model is that the exposed frames of the hull have been made from several different coloured woods, so as to highlight the main station frames that correspond with the ship plan.

Fixtures and Fittings

The model is finished with a high level of detail and in a somewhat more realistic fashion. For example, fittings like deadeyes are realistically painted black, rather than painted gold as on some other Navy Board models. As a result of changes in hull design, the reduction in tumblehome meant that the channels were raised to just below the upper gun deck to prevent the shrouds, the rigging that supports the mast, from interfering with the top of the bulwarks. The very unusual second entry ports on the upper deck would have allowed the officers to enter the vessel near the break of the poop deck. At the beakhead bulkhead the roundhouses, which accommodated toilets at the bow, are glazed with mica panes. This model is unique in that it is fitted with a windlass on the quarter deck which has ropes running down to the tiller. This is the earliest known evidence of a rope-operated steering mechanism, and was probably an experimental fitting prior to the introduction of the steering wheel in about 1703 (see page 19).

Decoration

At the bow, the figurehead shows a female figure being pulled by a double-headed bull, illustrating the story of the abduction of Europa by Zeus. Above, winged putti carry an escutcheon bearing the 'AR' monogram of Queen Anne. A profusion of relief carving on a red background adorns the stern. The taffrail shows a warrior and female figure with shields, possibly representing Perseus (on the port side), who slew the gorgon Medusa, and Athena (starboard), to whom Perseus gave Medusa's severed head to place on her shield. The counter panes and quarter galleries include an array of low-relief carvings of putti, trophies, and birds all painted gold, on a red background.

Two of a set of six small paintings of mythological figures in a maritime theme decorate the long quarter-deck area. They measure approximately 1 inch square.

Second Rate, 90 guns (*c.*1702)

NMM NUMBER: SLR0387

SCALE: 1:60

DATE MADE: *c.*1702

Dimensions	Model (scaled up)	*Marlborough* (1706)
Length of Gun Deck	162ft	162ft 8in
Breadth	47ft	47ft 4in
Number of Guns	90	90
Length of Keel	107ft (touch)	132ft 6in
Depth (of hold)	19ft (approx.)	18ft 6in
Tons (burden)	1572	1579

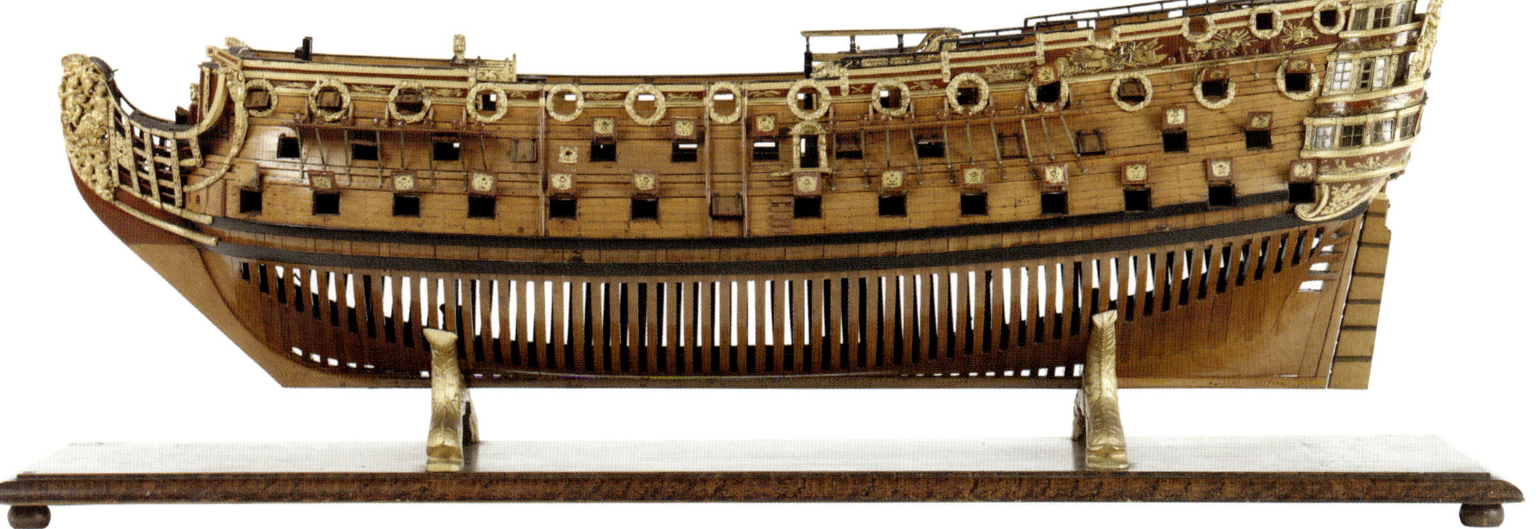

Introduction

This model exhibits many features which demonstrate the transition from the large tumblehome, pronounced sheer, and high baroque decoration of seventeenth-century ships, to the fuller-hulled and more restrained decoration of the eighteenth century, which began with the ships of Queen Anne's navy.

Identification

The limited decoration and position of the channels, above the middle-deck ports, would indicate a date after 1702. This is also confirmed by the royal arms of Queen Anne, displayed on the figurehead and stern, which were in use 1702–07. However, the model cannot be identified as a specific ship, although its dimensions fit those listed in the 1706 Establishment for a 90-gun Second Rate ship. The Royal Navy built seven 90-gun Second Rates under the 1706 Establishment. Of these, the only one launched between 1702 and 1707 was the *Marlborough*, which was a rebuild of the *St Michael* (1669). It is unlikely to represent the *Marlborough*, of which there is a particularly fine model now in the private collection of Arnold and Henry Kriegstein. That model, despite representing a ship of similar dimensions, has a different gunport arrangement and a figurehead representing the Duke of Marlborough. This model possibly represents a generic model showing the dimensions of the Establishment itself, rather than an individual ship.

Provenance

Previously at the South Kensington Museum, the model was transferred from the Royal Naval Museum to the NMM in 1934.

Construction and Materials

The overall construction is highly detailed, and shows some similarities to the First Rate 96-gun SLR0386 in terms of materials and finish. It is made in a fine-grained wood, of uniform colour with the standard-pattern framing. A notable feature on this model is the long gangway projecting forwards from the quarter deck to the position of the mainmast.

Fixtures and Fittings

The reduction of tumblehome in the design of a ship's hull meant that after 1702 it was necessary to raise the channels on the three-decker ships from the middle wale to the upper wale, and after 1745 even higher above the upper-deck gunports. The chainplates themselves were still bolted to the middle wales, and therefore had to become longer to reach up to the channels and deadeyes in the new higher position.

This model illustrates one of the earliest examples of a feature perhaps considered important to many who sailed on these ships: the toilets. In addition to the 'piss-dales' in the waist, to give some shelter from the weather as well as privacy, these 'roundhouses' as they were known, were built just forward of the beakhead bulkhead and behind the figurehead. They were quite light in construction, and the actual 'seat of ease' within was fitted on the outboard side, overhanging the ship's side.

Decoration

In decorative terms, this model represents a transition from the highly decorative seventeenth-century ships to the more restrained decoration on eighteenth-century ships, changes made primarily to save money. Notable features include the presence of round gunport wreaths, which means that it was likely that the model was made before Admiralty restrictions limited their use after 1703. The model includes a large and ornate figurehead, which is an elaborately carved scene depicting a female figure, possibly representing Queen Anne, holding a crown. She is shown seated in a shell-like vessel supported by a putto, with a stylised scaled dolphin below. Above, winged putti support the crowned royal arms prominently displayed at the front of the figurehead.

At the stern, the taffrail includes a high-relief carving of the crowned monogram of Queen Anne, supported either side by two winged putti, two wheeled field guns, and two more putti each holding an escutcheon with the cross of St George. The quarter figures are high-relief female figures shown in classical dress. Further decoration painted in raised gold and red chinoiserie on the counterpanes depicts a fantastical scene with sea creatures, including Neptune, dolphins, flying fish, mermen, and mermaids. Chinoiserie was a European interpretation of the Chinese artistic tradition that became particularly popular after increasing trade with the Asia in the late seventeenth century. This demonstrates knowledge of the latest styles and tastes by the model maker, or his patron. The model is mounted on an original grained baseboard on carved dolphin crutches.

Fourth Rate, 54 guns (*c.*1703)

NMM NUMBER: SLR0218

SCALE: 1:48

DATE MADE: *c.*1703

Dimensions	Model (scaled up)	*Bristol* (1711)
Length of Gun Deck	129ft	130ft
Breadth	34ft	35ft
Number of Guns	54	54
Length of Keel	107ft (touch)	108ft
Depth (of hold)	15ft	14ft
Tons (burden)	668	703

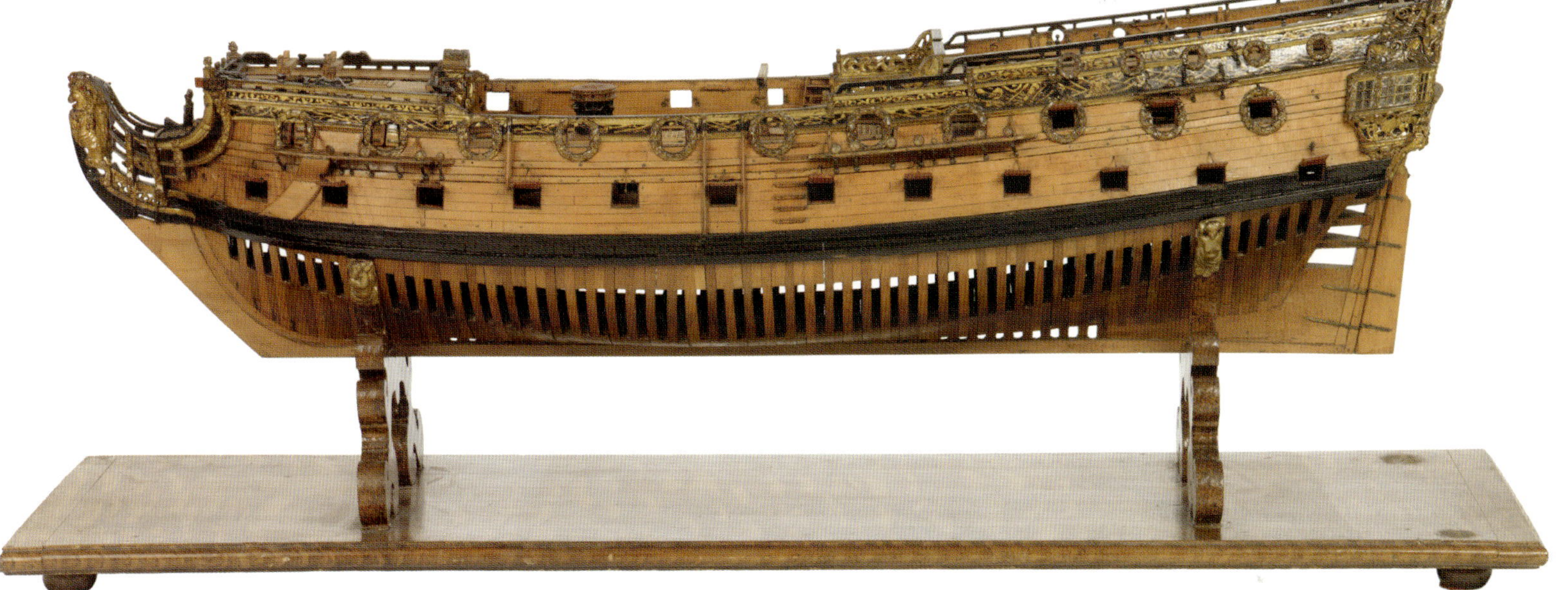

Introduction

A large number of these Fourth Rates were built during the late seventeenth and early eighteenth centuries. However, there was a small group of eight built from 1702–03 during the early years of Queen Anne's reign, the dimensions of which agree very closely with this model.

Identification

Past research has linked this model with several ships based upon the model's dimensions and the existence of the initials 'IL' or 'JL' and date '1701[?]' painted on a small cartouche on the stern. These ships were launched from 1699 onwards and the two sets of initials may represent John Lock, Master Shipwright at Plymouth from 1705; or Joseph Lawrence Senior, Master Shipwright at Woolwich from 1686. Lock launched the 54-gun *Bristol* at Plymouth in 1711, and the dimensions are quite similar. To confuse the matter further, the style of decoration would fit within the reign of William III and the presence of Queen Anne's monogram on the stern makes a positive identification difficult.

Provenance

Somerset House Museum, Royal Naval Museum 1874, transferred to NMM in 1934.

Construction and Materials

A relatively unique feature of the hull frames is that the line of the top timbers towards the bow and stern disappear into the main wales. Also, upon closer inspection of the framing, the quality of workmanship is not of the usual standard, as the uniformity of the dimensions varies and their assembly is poor, with a number of packing pieces inserted. Only by careful examination from inside the model using an endoscope was it discovered that the hull was originally pierced for twenty-four ports on the upper deck. Located just aft the cathead supporters, the original sills for the port are still in place but have been externally covered from view by planking. The model is complete with its original wooden crutches and baseboard, both of which have been finished with a graining effect, imitating a more expensive wood veneer.

Fixtures and Fittings

By far the most important fitting on this

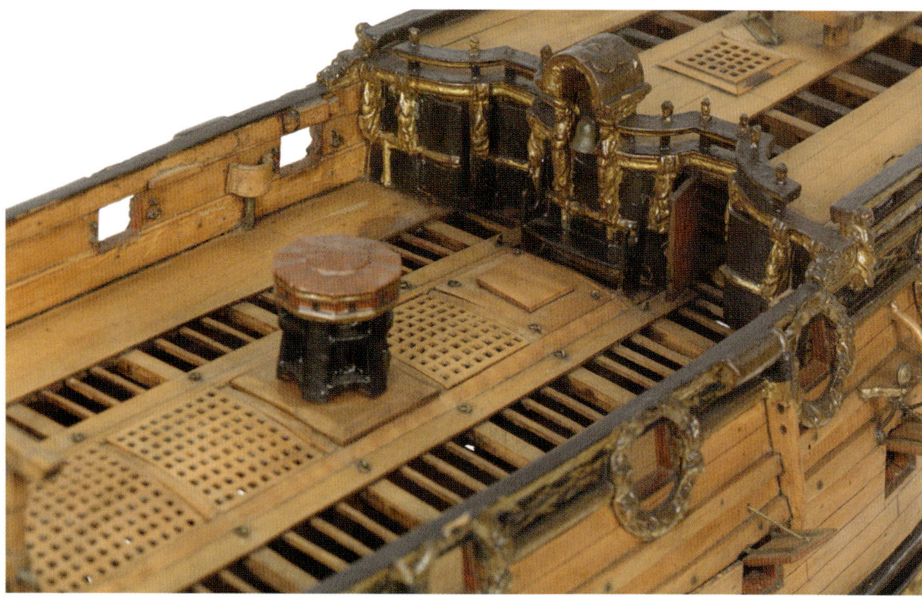

model is the presence of the steering wheel on the quarter deck. It is thought to be the earliest contemporary evidence of its introduction and combines the former steering method using a whipstaff located below on the gun deck. The 'rowle', or pivot through which the staff was operated and connected to the tiller, can clearly be seen below. The small box structure under the wheel on deck, known as the helmsman's companion, is fitted with windows to provide light for the helmsman below.

Also in the waist area are a pair of piss-dales complete with brass drainage tubes leading through the ship's side. Another interesting piece of furniture is the wooden bench located just under the belfry on the break of the forecastle. It is not known what it was used for officially, but it has been suggested in the past that it was used by members of the crew waiting to take the officers' food from the galley to the cabins aft. On the forecastle deck is the span shackle, a large square metal ring amidships, in which the end of the long and heavy wooden fish davit was housed for use when lowering and raising the anchors (see *Royal Oak*, SLR0230). The belfry is complete with a bell fitted with a clapper. In the waist is a double capstan with a drumhead fitted for ten bars, whilst below it is the older style of capstan, rigged with five whelps.

Decoration

The model illustrates the old style of wreathed gunports and carved bulwark screens before the introduction of the order in 1703 for the reduction of carved decoration, issued on the grounds of cost and maintenance. Both the decoration and style of the stern and quarter galleries still show the influences of the late seventeenth century. A unique feature of the overall scheme is that includes a large number of birds, ranging from eagles supporting the lion figurehead to various wildfowl, possibly cranes or herons, around the stern galleries and bulwark friezes. The initials 'AR' of Queen Anne's monogram can clearly be seen in the middle of the counter, just above the rudder head. The ornately carved taffrail comprises three crowns surrounding a trophy assembly, which again is a common feature used during the reign of William III over England, Ireland and Scotland.

Yacht, 10 guns (*c.*1705)

NMM NUMBER: SLR0390

SCALE: 1:24

DATE MADE: *c.*1705

Dimensions	Model (scaled up)	*Portsmouth II* (1702)
Length of Gun Deck	56ft	52ft 10in
Breadth	16ft	17ft
Number of Guns	10	6 x 2pdrs
Length of Keel	45ft (touch)	50ft
Depth (of hold)	8ft	8ft 6in
Tons (burden)	63	66

Introduction

As well as being used as fast manoeuvrable boats for transport of naval officers and communication, yachts were also used as private transport for wealthy individuals. Although fitted with guns, yachts were not large enough to engage the enemy.

Identification

Because of the amount of both painted and carved decoration, this model is thought to represent a yacht, as opposed to a small warship. During this period there were several yachts built at the Royal Dockyards, many of which were elegantly decorated for the use of important Royal Navy officers and commissioners, although one, the *Portsmouth II* launched in 1702, was later fitted in 1752 for the 'use of the young gentlemen of the [Naval] Academy' at Portsmouth.[11]

Provenance

Donated to the NMM in 1949 by Dr R.C. Anderson.

Construction and Materials

It has been constructed from the traditional English fruit woods such as apple, pear, and also box. The framing follows the standard pattern and the individual strakes of the planking above the wale are fastened with regularly positioned pairs of brass pins.

Fixtures and Fittings

The model shows a lightly armed vessel, probably fitted with ten 8pdr guns on both the upper and quarter decks. On deck, the fittings are very detailed, including capstan, belfry, riding bitts, deck hatches, and tiller. Of particular interest are the pumps, fitted just behind the mainmast. Although not

shown on all models, pumps were fitted in all vessels, primarily for removing water from the bilges and discharging it overboard. Water that pooled in the bilges, either through leakage of the hull or deck above during heavy weather, made for unsanitary conditions and could reduce the stability of the vessel. The type of pump fitted on this model is the 'elm tree pump', normally fitted on smaller vessels owing to its simple design. The pump itself was made up of a long hollowed tube of elm wood, chosen because of its durability in salt water, into which a piston and a valve were fitted. When the pump handle was pulled, the upper piston was lifted to bring up water through the tube and discharged. At the same time, water would be sucked up from the bilge through the fixed lower valve, ready to be taken up by the upper piston in the next pull of the pump handle.

Rigging

Although the model is unrigged, the presence of only two sets of channels would suggest that the vessel was two-masted, possibly rigged as a brig, snow, or ketch. There is some question as to how this vessel may have been rigged. The presence of a 'stool', which was a small deadeye just abaft the main channels, indicates that the mainmast included a topmast.

Decoration

Of special interest is the wealth of carved decoration, especially the belfry, quarter-deck rail, and the figurehead. The figurehead depicts a merman with scaled tail, his left hand resting on a scroll and his right hand above his head. Caryatid figures adorning the head rails, and wreathed gunports along the sides, indicate a somewhat anachronistic style for the eighteenth century. At the stern, the taffrail includes carved putti supporting an escutcheon bearing the 'AR' monogram, which indicates that the model was probably made during the reign of Queen Anne. In the centre, between glazed mica windows, a male figure is shown holding a sword, standing above a dolphin-like creature. Large, classically dressed male quarter figures are included either side of the stern. All the carved decoration is painted gold.

Third Rate, 60 guns (*c.*1706)

NMM NUMBER: SLR0389

SCALE: 1:48

DATE MADE: *c.*1706

Dimensions	Model (scaled up)	1706 Establishment 60-gun Third Rate
Length of Gun Deck	144ft	144ft
Breadth	37ft	38ft
Number of Guns	60	60
Length of Keel	120ft (touch)	119ft
Depth (of hold)	16ft	15ft 8in
Tons (burden)	887	914

Introduction

In the early eighteenth century, the Third, Fourth and Fifth Rate two-deckers were arguably more important to the Royal Navy's strategic goal of protecting trade than the big First, Second, and Third Rate three-deckers.

Identification

The model cannot be identified with a specific ship. Its dimensions are very similar to the Third Rates built to the Establishment of 1706, although the beam is slightly narrower.

Provenance

The model was donated to the NMM in 1945 by Frederick William Burton Conyngham, 6th Marquess Conyngham.

Construction and Materials

It is constructed of fruitwood, with standard framing. The deck is left unplanked, revealing carlings and ledges. The hull planking above the main wale is secured with individual treenails. The stern is constructed with a mica-glazed screen bulkhead inboard on the upper deck, providing a single open gallery, in what is in fact a flush stern. This contrasts with the seventeenth century, when the majority of ships had closed sterns, and to the later eighteenth century, which saw the addition of overhanging balconies.

Fixtures and Fittings

At the forecastle bulkhead is a belfry, with an original bell carved from wood and painted green to resemble bronze patination. The model also features gunports, chainplates, channels, deadeyes, and riding bits. The model is fitted with 'piss-dales'.

Decoration

A noticeable feature is the rather restrained carved decoration brought about by the order of 1703, with the rounded and plainer gunport decoration on the quarter deck in evidence. The bow is fitted with a standard lion figurehead. The stern galleries, however, are surmounted by a very detailed taffrail. Carved in high relief, it shows two male figures either side of a crowned rose and thistle surmounted. One figure, on the port side, is shown in armour, seated above a shield, holding a sword in one hand and an olive branch in the other. The other, to the starboard side, is shown in classical dress holding a staff and leaning on an anchor stock.

Centrally, there is a shield bearing the royal monogram of Queen Anne, 'AR'. On the upper counter is a frieze carved in relief, depicting a central wreath with foliage either side. The lower counter is painted with a mythical nautical scene depicting Neptune with trident accompanied by other figures. The quarter figures are male, in classical dress, each standing on top of a dog. The quarter galleries are glazed with mica and surmounted with the monogram of Queen Anne.

Chichester (1706), 80 guns

NMM NUMBER: SLR0391

SCALE: 1:72

DATE MADE: *c.*1706

Dimensions	Model (scaled up)	*Chichester* (1706)
Length of Gun Deck	155ft	155ft 6in
Breadth	43ft	43ft 5in
Number of Guns	80	80
Length of Keel	122ft (touch)	127ft 6in
Depth (of hold)	18ft	17ft 10in
Tons (burden)	1271	1298

Introduction

In 1706, when the *Chichester* was rebuilt at Woolwich from an earlier two-decker of the same name, the 80-gun armament was rearranged on three decks, with the upper-deck guns still disposed as they had been on the quarter deck and forecastle of the earlier two-deckers (see the *Boyne*, SLR0006). The *Chichester* had a fairly uneventful career, taking part in the battle of Toulon in 1744 and later, in 1753, it was rebuilt as a 74-gun two-decker.

Identification

The dimensions match very closely with the known dimensions of the ship as rebuilt in 1706. In addition the royal monogram 'AR', of Queen Anne, is inscribed in the decoration on the stern galleries, which confirms the date.

Provenance

Previously in the collection of Sir Henry Wellcome. Purchased by Sir James Caird in 1938.

Construction and Materials

Although made with standard frames, and left unplanked below the double main wale, the lower hull has been planked from the keel to just below the heads of the floor timbers. The decks are largely unplanked to show the deck beams and internal construction. The model has suffered some damage over time, with the decking and bulwark rails restored in 1971.

Fixtures and Fittings

The model includes limited fittings, but bitts can be found on the quarter deck, foredeck, and in the waist. Roundhouses are built in to the beakhead bulkhead. Although missing on the port side, some remaining gunport lids can be found on the starboard side. Both sides include an entry port amidships at main gun-deck level.

Rigging

The channels are notably absent, although some marks around the middle wale amidships and forward, as well as upper wale aft, indicate that they were once fitted in the usual positions.

Decoration

The hull is varnished in a dark brown finish, the wales are painted black, and there are frieze panels along the top strakes and bulwarks of trophies and filigree decoration in gold paint on a black ground. The stern has suffered some damage, the upper one being open and with later repairs to the top section and two-deck quarter galleries. The plain black taffrail is a modern replacement, but the ornately carved quarter figures give an idea of how it was once decorated.

Bolton (1709), 6 guns

NMM NUMBER: SLR0395

SCALE: 1:32

DATE MADE: *c.*1763

Dimensions	Model (scaled up)	*Bolton* (1709)
Length of Gun Deck	53ft	53ft 2in
Breadth	14ft	14ft
Number of Guns	6	6 x 2pdr
Length of Keel	44ft (touch)	38ft
Depth (of hold)	8ft	7ft 6in
Tons (burden)	42	42

Introduction

The *Bolton* yacht was launched at Portsmouth in 1709 and used by the Governor of the Isle of Wight until 1763, when it was found to be 'entirely decayed'. The style and workmanship of this model would suggest that it was made at a considerably later than the building of the actual vessel in 1709, possibly in 1763, when the yacht was extensively rebuilt. As a secondary yacht, the *Bolton* was allocated to officers of state, rather than the personal use of the monarch. Later, in 1773, the *Bolton* was fitted for the use of the 'Young Gentlemen' of the Naval Academy at Portsmouth Dockyard to replace the *Portsmouth II* yacht (see SLR0390). The *Bolton* was eventually broken up in 1817.

Identification

The model fits the dimensions of the *Bolton* yacht closely, with the same number of guns. The model can be dated to the Georgian period owing to the inclusion of the 'GR' monograms on the stern and quarter badges.

Provenance

Previously at the Royal Naval Museum, Greenwich, and transferred to the NMM in 1934.

Construction and Materials

The framing is standard, with individual planks above the main wale. The hull shape differs from vessels of the seventeenth century in that the sheer line is very flat.

Fixtures and Fittings

The model is decked and includes a variety of fittings such as guns on wooden carriages and a large wooden windlass in the bow.

Rigging

The model is shown with single channels on either side of the hull, just aft a single cut-off mast. The vessel would have been rigged as a single-masted cutter.

Decoration

The model is typical of the eighteenth century in that the decorations are not painted gold; this mirrors the practice of the decoration on the ships themselves during this period. Despite the lack of gold

paint, the model is embellished with some wonderful Georgian carving. At the stern, the taffrail is carved in high relief; in the centre is a draped bust of a young man, possibly representing George III. To the starboard is a winged putto blowing a trumpet in his right hand, with his left resting on a badge with the 'GR' monogram for 'Georgius Rex'. To the port side is a clothed, childlike figure with left arm resting on a gun barrel and right on a close helmet and cuirass. In the centre, between two square-pane leaded windows glazed with glass, is a high-relief carving of a warrior figure. Helmeted, with shield portraying the Union flag in left hand, the right hand holds a stick to beat the drum depicted below. A flag and long poleaxe are shown behind.

The quarter figures carved in high relief show putti holding a stylised fish by the tail, supported in turn by carved mermen below. The quarter badges are comprised of two putti carved in high relief holding staffs, and raising a crown above a square glass window. Below are two escutcheons, one with the 'GR' monogram, and the other with the Union flag. Along sides of the hull are low-relief carvings depicting trophies of arms, shown in natural finish in contrast to the black-painted bulwarks, and gunports are wreathed with unusual decorative ivory carvings.

Sixth Rate, 30 guns (*c.*1710)

NMM NUMBER: SLR0397

SCALE: 1:72/1:64

DATE MADE: *c.*1710

Dimensions	Model (scaled up 1:72/1:64)	*Deal Castle* (1706)
Length of Gun Deck	111ft/98ft	98ft 2in
Breadth	30ft/26ft	26ft 2½in
Number of Guns	30	24
Length of Keel	99ft/88ft (touch)	74ft 6in
Depth	9ft 9in/8ft 7in (of hold)	11ft
Tons (burden)	445/296	301

Introduction

This model of a 30-gun Sixth Rate is unusual in that it has a flush upper deck, where there is no separate forecastle or quarter deck. In effect, the waist between the forecastle and quarter deck is decked over to provide a single continuous upper deck. This provided protection for the crew on the gun deck against the weather or, during battle, the enemy.

Identification

Its general appearance, simplified circular wreathed gunports on the quarter deck, and limited carved work suggest a date some time after 1703, when decoration was ordered to be limited. However, the model cannot be identified as a particular ship. At a scale of 1:72 the dimensions are close to those of the 30-gun ships of 1698–1711, but there is no record of a flush-deck vessel of this class being built. The scale of 1:72 is not uncommon for some models built in the early part of the eighteenth century. However, if the model is measured at a scale of 1:64, the dimensions match closely to the *Deal Castle*, launched at a private shipyard at Rotherhithe in 1706. The *Deal Castle* only had twenty-four guns, but it is not unknown for vessels of this period to have included more gunports than guns.

Provenance

The model was donated by Dr R.C. Anderson in 1949.

Construction and Materials

The framing is standard, but the model is unusual in that it represents a flush-decked ship. Planking above the main wale is a single panel of veneer secured by wooden treenails. Some of the gunport hinges are missing, and the gunports have simply been fixed closed.

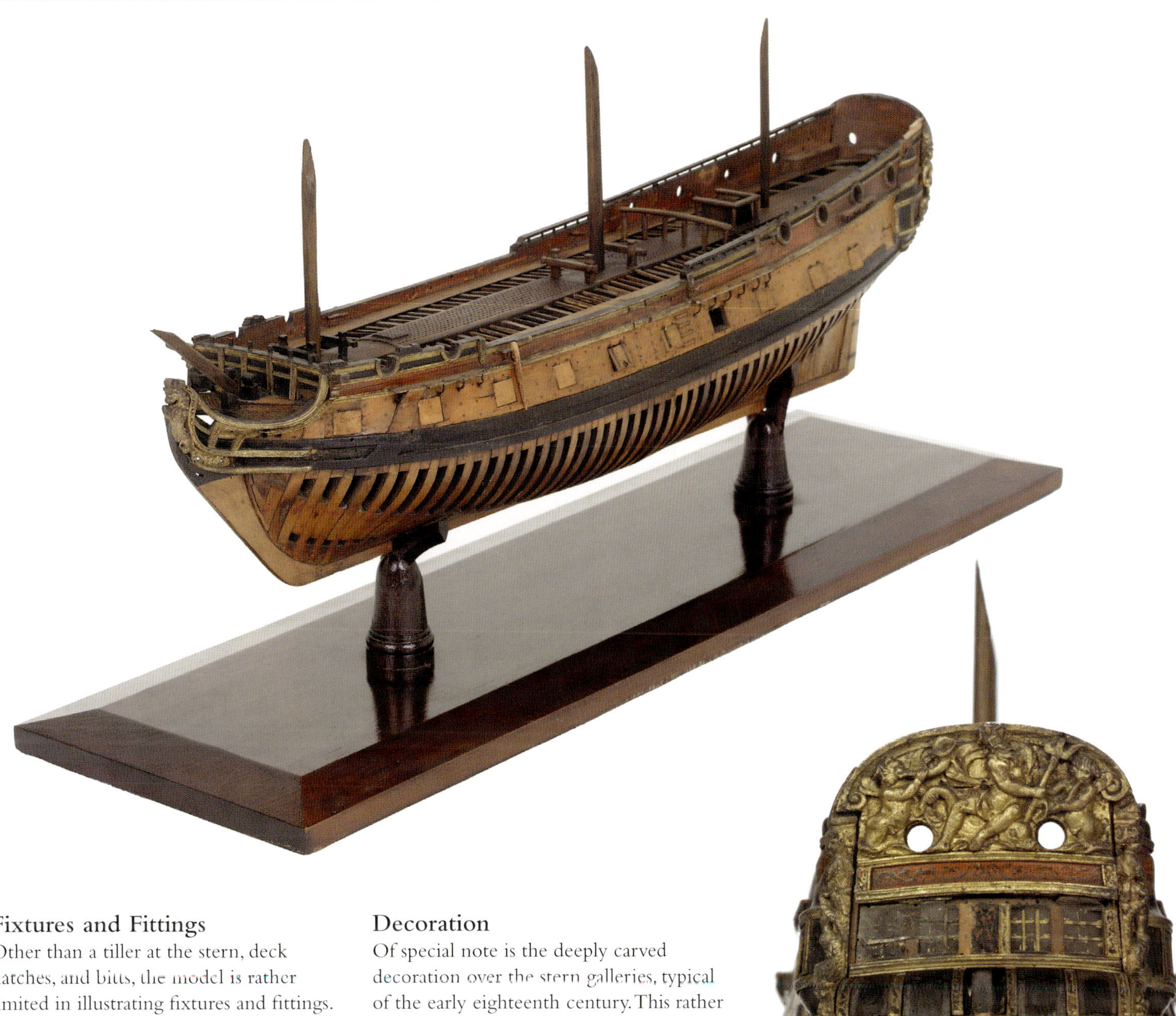

Fixtures and Fittings

Other than a tiller at the stern, deck hatches, and bitts, the model is rather limited in illustrating fixtures and fittings. The crosspieces consisted of a heavy frame of two strong oak pillars forward and aft of the fore- and mainmasts. Fixed securely to the deck beams, they were very important for the operation of the ship and were used for securing parts of the running rigging.

Rigging

The model is unrigged, but complete with three stump masts and a bowsprit (modern), as well as three sets of channels on each side, although there are no deadeyes.

Decoration

Of special note is the deeply carved decoration over the stern galleries, typical of the early eighteenth century. This rather rounded and gilded finish was soon to be replaced by the much crisper finish of the early Georgian period, with the improvement in tools and use of different woods playing a major part. The large taffrail is adorned with high-relief carvings depicting the god of the sea, Neptune, trident in hand, riding a stylised dolphin. To either side are trumpeting putti, and the quarter figures are carved putti above stylised dolphins. All are shown in high-relief carving and painted gold.

Royal Barge (*c.*1710)

NMM NUMBER: SLR0399

SCALE: 1:24

DATE MADE: *c.*1710

Dimensions	Model (scaled up)	Queen Mary's shallop (1689)
Length (overall)	36ft	41ft 7in
Breadth	7ft	6ft 7in
Length of Keel	31ft (touch)	36ft
Depth	2ft	2ft 11in

Introduction

This type of barge, known as a shallop, was commonly used for taking royalty to and from warships in anchorage and along the River Thames. Built in clinker fashion, it measured 36ft in length by 7ft in the beam. Remarkably, two full-size examples of these boats still survive: Queen Mary's shallop of 1689 (BAE0039) at the NMM, and the carvel-built barge of Charles II, at the Royal Naval Museum, Portsmouth.

Identification

The model was identified as a royal barge and dated to around 1710 owing to an original carved figure of Queen Anne positioned in the stern. Sadly, this original figure was lost, and the present replacement was carved by Mr R.A. Lightley and presented to the Museum in 1975.

Provenance

Purchased from A. Fleming, antique dealers in Southsea, by Sir James Caird, and presented to the National Maritime Museum on 12 December 1935.

Construction and Materials

The model is made entirely in wood, largely from boxwood and built plank-on-frame in the Navy Board style, in frame below the waterline and planked above. The model is clinker built, where plank edges are secured to each other in an overlapping construction, giving the hull extra longitudinal strength. The lower hull has been left unplanked to expose the hull frames, which in clinker construction are usually added after the 'shell' of planking is complete. This model differs from other Navy Board-style models in that the framing is not stylised or simplified, but shows the framing pattern as it was on the full-sized vessel.

Fixtures and Fittings

The model is partially decked and planked, and is complete with ten oarsmen. The model has metal fittings and the planks are secured with brass pins. Fittings include a tall ensign staff at the bow, but the flag is missing. At the stern, the rudder is a modern replacement, complete with a yoke for steering. It is unlikely that this method of steering was used, and due to the lack of space behind the seatback, a short wooden tiller would have been more practical.

Figures

As well as the modern carved figure of Queen Anne, the barge also includes ten rowing figures. They are all original, and clad in the uniform of the Royal Watermen. The figures are painted in realistic colours and finished with a high level of detail. These figures give a wonderful illustration of the dress of the Royal Watermen, whose full regalia consisted of a red wool coat and breeches with red stockings and black cap and shoes. On the model, they are shown with their coats off in white shirts, which was normal practice during the hard work of rowing.

Decoration

The exterior of the hull is left with a natural finish and the interior is largely painted red and the panels along the inboard bulwarks are royal blue. The staggered thwarts, where the oarsmen sit, are unpainted wood. The carved decoration along the gunwales is of the highest quality, with a floral motif towards the bow, and a mythological nautical scene at the aft end. At the bow, the top of the stem post is a blue and red shield, a later addition, quartered by a cross, supported by a carved lion on the starboard and a unicorn on the port side. Behind each, a carved, decorative fish-tailed putto, and a bearded merman are shown.

Rose (1712), 24 guns

NMM NUMBER: SLR0393

SCALE: 1:48

DATE MADE: *c.*1706

Dimensions	Model (scaled up)	*Rose* (1712)
Length of Gun Deck	89ft	94ft 3in
Breadth	23ft	26ft
Number of Guns	24	20
Length of Keel	77ft (touch)	76ft
Depth (of hold)	11ft	11ft 6in
Tons (burden)	212	273

Introduction

This is one of only a handful of models where the model maker may be identified. The ornamental dolphin crutches include the monogram 'BR', as well as the date '1706'. It is probable that the 'BR' stands for Benjamin Rosewell, who was the Master Shipwright at Chatham. Of the Master Shipwrights active in the Royal Dockyards in this period, Benjamin Rosewell is the only one with the initials 'BR'.

Identification

The model has been tentatively identified as the *Rose*, a 24-gun Sixth Rate sloop, launched at Chatham in 1712. The *Rose* was one of only three 20- or 24-gun ships built by Benjamin Rosewell. Taking into account the monogram and date on the crutches, which are thought to be original, it is logical to think that the model represents the *Rose*. The only other two ships of this size built by Rosewell were launched in 1727. The dimensions of this model do not exactly agree with the known measurements of any class, but are similar to the *Rose*, which was one of a number of 20- to 24-gun Sixth Rate vessels not built to an Establishment.

Provenance

The model was donated to the Royal United Services Institution on 21 July 1936 by Major A.E. Palmer and was acquired by the NMM in 1963.

Construction and Materials

The framing is the standard pattern in fine-grained wood, and the planking above the main wale is secured by wooden treenails.

Fixtures and Fittings

The model is partially equipped; however, the capstan, the tiller, two beakhead brackets, three stern roses, and the baseboard were made by the National Maritime Museum's model technician J Reg Varrall in 1965.

Rigging

Sixth Rates were the smallest rate of vessel in the Royal Navy, and performed a variety of duties. They were collectively referred to as 'sloops-of-war', but would have had a variety of rigs. Although unrigged, the presence of three sets of channels indicates that this model shows a sloop intended to be 'ship-rigged' with a fore-, a main- and a mizzen mast.

Decoration

Normally, ships of this period had painted frieze work along the bulwark; however, on this model it has been painted black. Along the upper wale and bulwark, the paintwork in gold and black is not of the same high standard as most of the Navy Board models of this period. It is possible that some of the present paintwork has been carried out at a later date, either to follow fashions or to cover damage. The quarter badges depict two carved putti holding a crown. At the bow, the figurehead is the standard lion, with mouth and crown picked out in red paint. The head rails and beakhead bulkhead are slightly old-fashioned in that they include gold-painted, carved figures more common in the seventeenth century. The stern decoration consists of a large taffrail with a central crowned escutcheon bearing the 'AR' monogram of Queen Anne, supported on either side by putti, all carved in relief and painted gold. Below the glazed mica windows are carved roses painted gold, and two chase-ports.

Sloop, 20 guns (*c.*1712)

NMM NUMBER: SLR0400

SCALE: 1:48

DATE MADE: *c.*1712

Dimensions	Model (scaled up)	*Success* (1712)
Length of Gun Deck	94ft	94ft
Breadth	26ft	26ft 6in
Number of Guns	20	20
Length of Keel	84ft (touch)	76ft 6in
Depth (of hold)	10ft 6in	11ft 10in
Tons (burden)	282	275

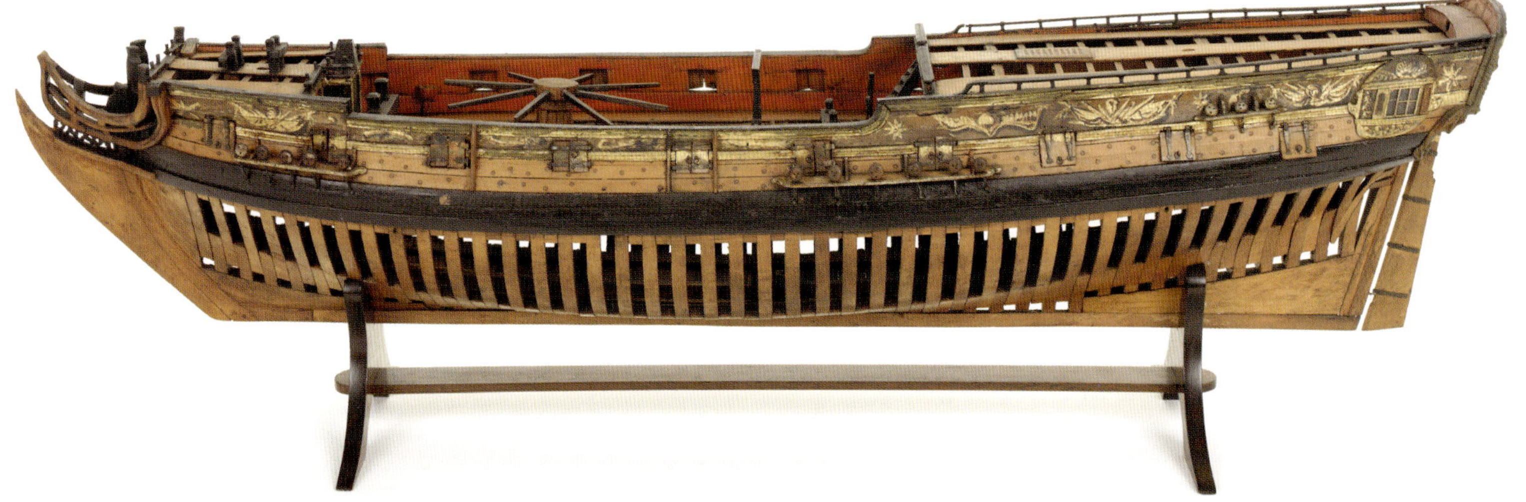

Introduction

This is a model of a 20-gun sloop of about 1712. Sloops were a class of small vessels rated as Sixth Rates or below. These vessels could be two- or three-masted, and were mainly employed on coastal escort work in the face of increased French privateering.

Identification

The model cannot be identified with a specific ship, but it illustrates a typical 20-gun sloop of the early eighteenth century, a large number of which were built between 1711 and 1713. The size and layout of the hull is typical of the sloop or 'cruiser' of the early eighteenth century, with the long quarter deck and no poop.

It has similar dimensions and layout to the *Success* (1712).

Provenance

Donated in 1949 by Dr R. C. Anderson.

Construction and Materials

The model is constructed with the standard framing, but at the bow some later reconstruction has been carried out. The stem post is possibly a replacement. The double main wale is painted black and planking above is secured with treenails.

Fixtures and Fittings

The model is decked and partially equipped with a capstan in the waist and galley chimney in the forecastle, and at the stern the model is fitted for a tiller. An unusual feature of this model is the fitting of the gunport lids to the ports in the waist. Normally, these ports were devoid of any doors or lids, and this model includes the normal type that hinged upwards, as well as the more unusual that opened sideways.

Rigging

The model is unrigged, but shows an arrangement of channels and deadeyes for a three-masted vessel.

Decoration

As expected for a ship of the early eighteenth century, the decoration is rather low-key compared to that of the seventeenth century. Unfortunately, the figurehead is missing, but there is still some gold-painted carved work at the stern, and some painted decoration along the bulwark screens. At the stern, in the centre of the taffrail is a carved bust of Queen Anne, flanked by two winged putti, who hold a crown above her head and trumpets to their mouths. At each side is a carved bird holding a fish in its talons. All the carved work, and the window frames below are painted gold.

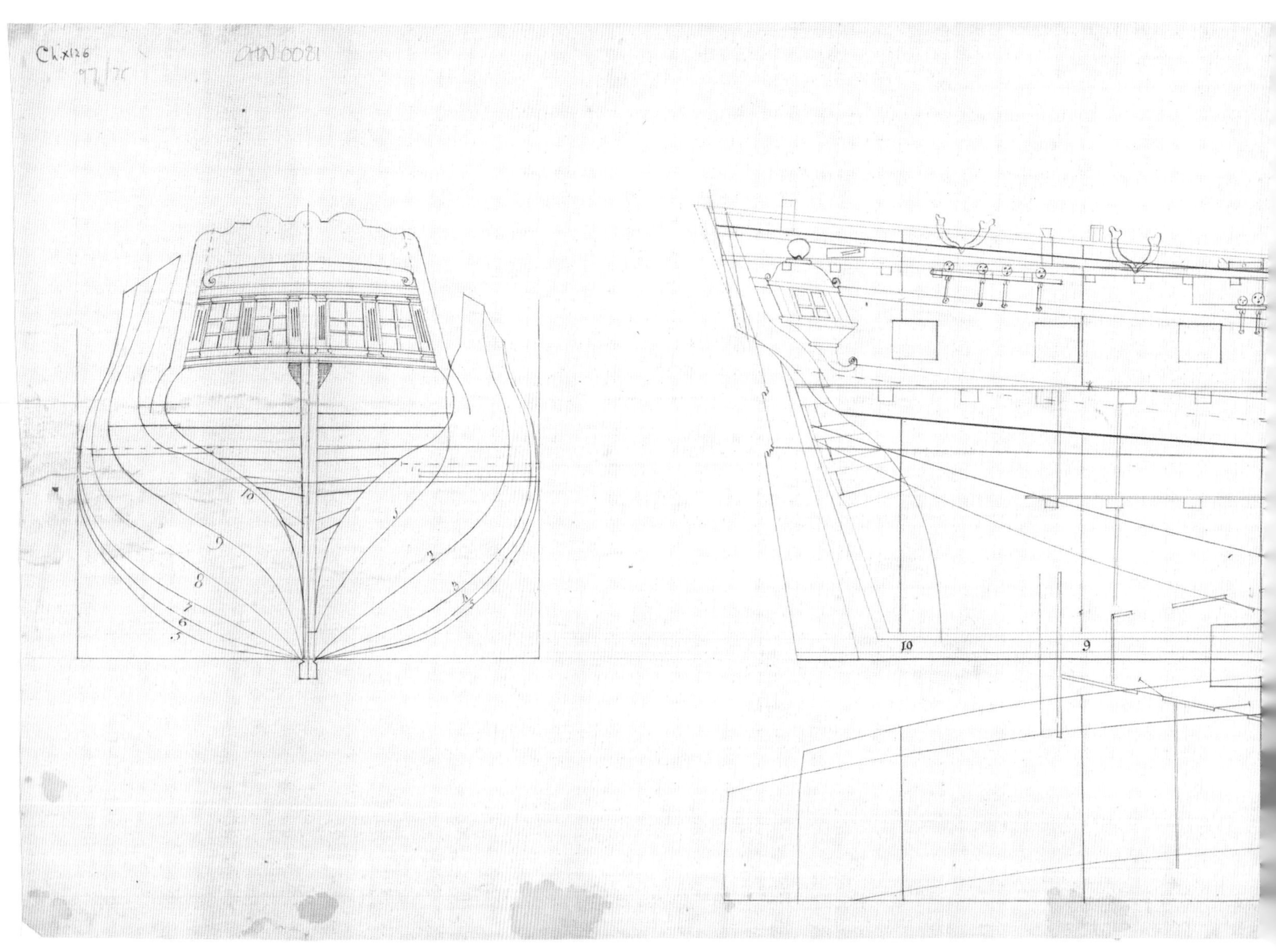

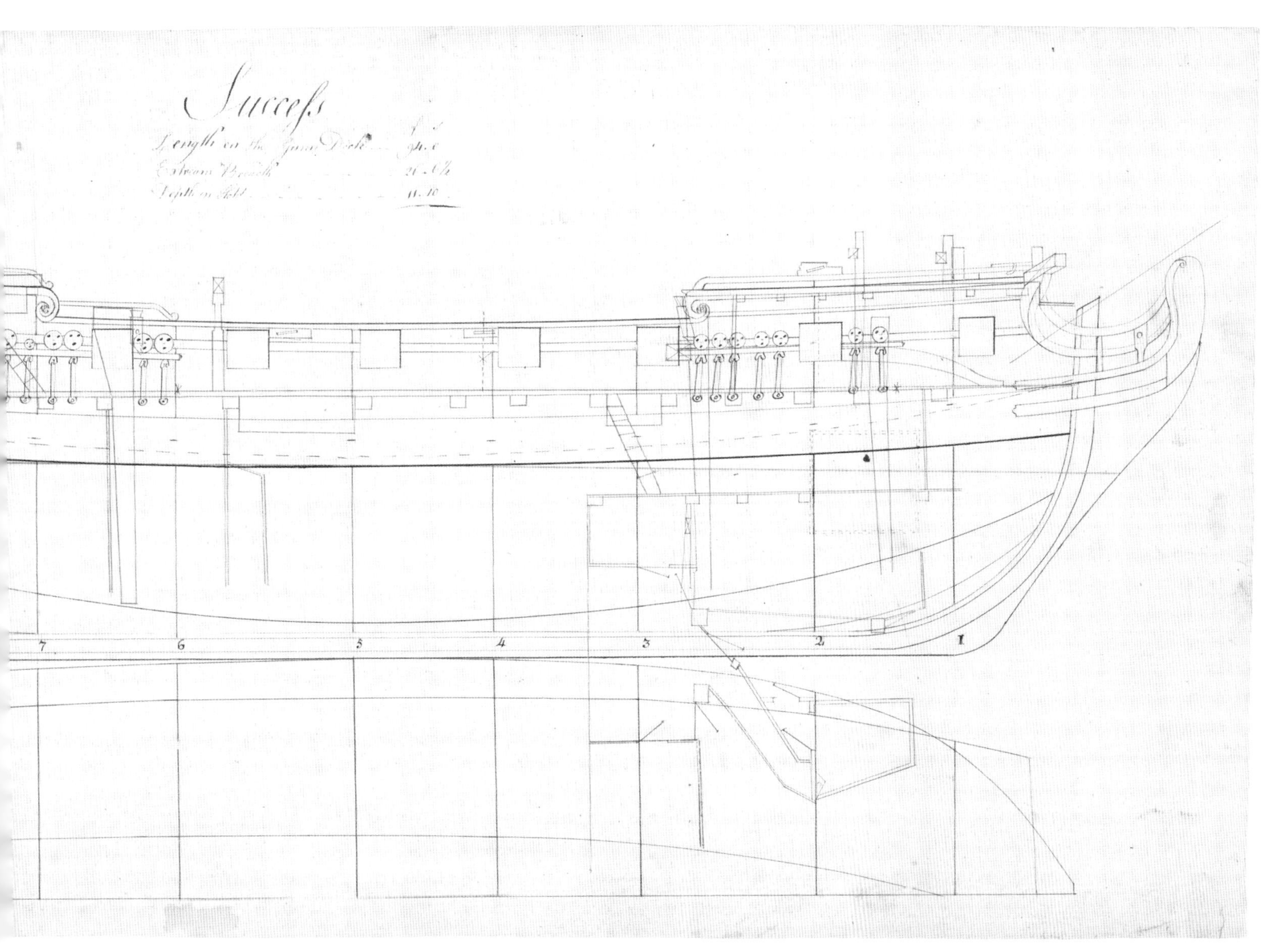

Scale 1:48 plan showing the body plan, sheer lines with some inboard detail, and longitudinal half-breadth for the *Success* (1712). (CHN0081)

Fourth Rate, 50 guns (*c.*1714)

NMM NUMBER: SLR0396

SCALE: 1:60

DATE MADE: *c.*1714

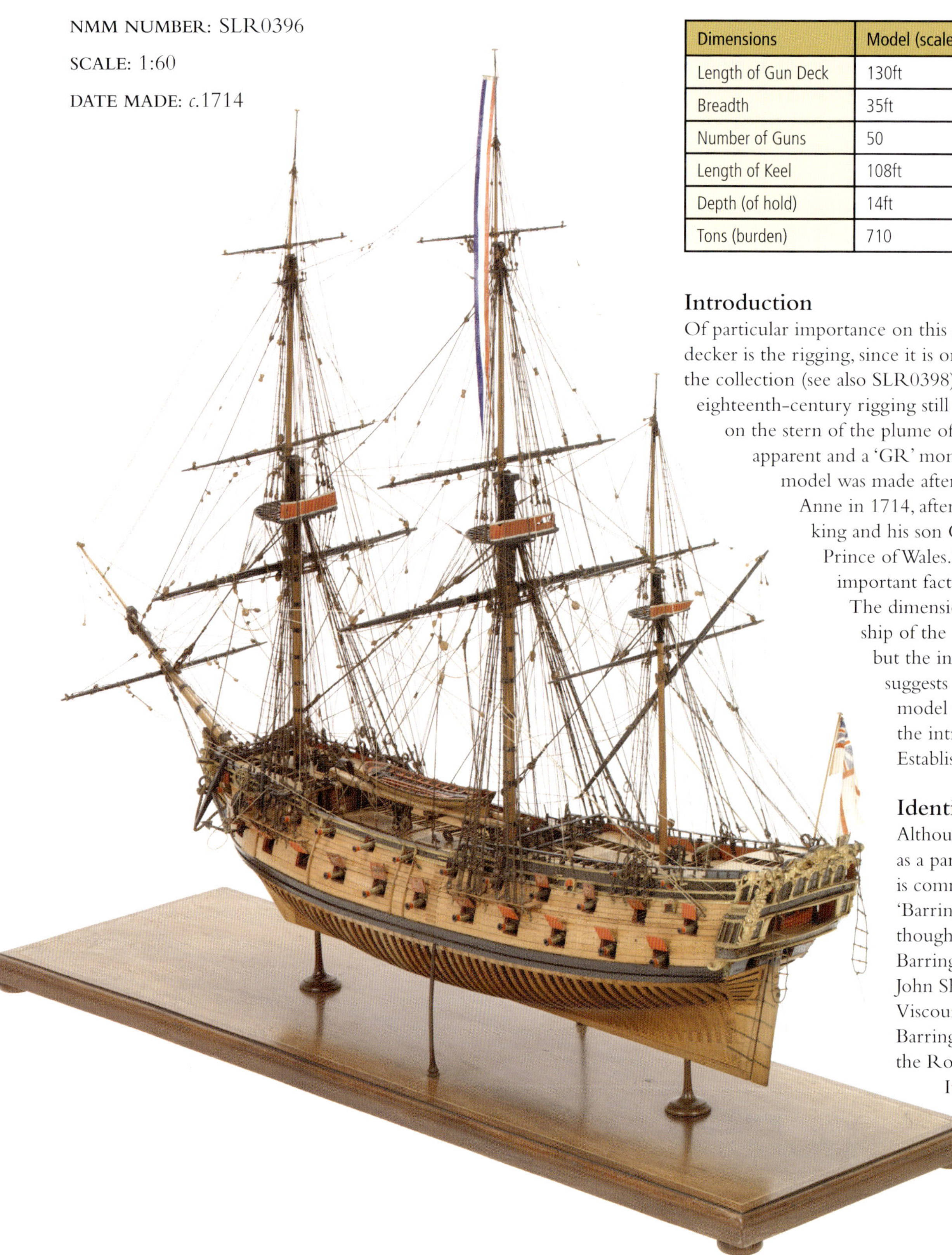

Dimensions	Model (scaled up)	*Norwich* (1718)
Length of Gun Deck	130ft	130ft
Breadth	35ft	35ft
Number of Guns	50	50
Length of Keel	108ft	108ft
Depth (of hold)	14ft	14ft 4in
Tons (burden)	710	704

Introduction

Of particular importance on this model of a small two-decker is the rigging, since it is one of two models in the collection (see also SLR0398) with its original early eighteenth-century rigging still intact. The presence on the stern of the plume of feathers of the heir apparent and a 'GR' monogram suggest that this model was made after the death of Queen Anne in 1714, after which George I became king and his son George became heir and Prince of Wales. The rigging was also an important factor in dating this model. The dimensions fit that of a 50-gun ship of the 1706 Establishment, but the inclusion of a jibboom suggests that if this is original, the model was possibly made after the introduction of the 1711 Establishment of Masts.

Identification

Although it cannot be identified as a particular ship, the model is commonly known as the 'Barrington model' because it is thought to be linked to Samuel Barrington, the fourth son of John Shute Barrington, 1st Viscount Barrington. Samuel Barrington was an admiral in the Royal Navy, born in 1729. It was once thought to represent the only 50-gun ship which Barrington commanded – the *Norwich*, launched in 1745. However, it depicts a ship of a much earlier date and, in fact, it fits the dimensions of the 50-gun Fourth Rates built to the 1706 Establishment, including an earlier *Norwich*, launched in 1718. The 1718 *Norwich* was renamed in 1744 as the *Enterprise* and bears no relation to the 1745 *Norwich* commanded by Barrington.

Provenance

Originally loaned to the NMM in 1940 by Walter Bulkeley Barrington, 9th Viscount Barrington (1848–1933), in 1993 the model was accepted by HM Government in lieu of inheritance tax and allocated to the Museum's permanent collection.

Construction and Materials

Constructed in the standard Navy Board framing, this model is an exceptionally fine example of craftsmanship at 1:60 scale. Planking of individual strakes is fixed above the black main wale with regularly spaced treenails.

Fixtures and Fittings

The model is partially decked and equipped to an astonishing level of detail. Fittings include guns turned in brass and mounted on fully rigged wooden carriages, a full set of anchors with all their gear, and a pair of Jacob's ladders slung over the stern. The model illustrates the practice of stowing a boat on the spare topmasts in the waist. Suitable for a pinnace or barge, this method was not suitable for the heavier longboats, which were normally towed astern. The commissioning pennant and the white ensign are modern additions.

Rigging

The rigging, which is almost entirely original, includes some features such as the extension of the bowsprit with a jibboom and the squaring-off of the fighting tops. The presence of the jibboom, used to extend the bowsprit, can be used to date this model to the first decades of the eighteenth century at the earliest.

Decoration

The effect of the order of 1703 limiting decoration is evident, this following the more staid forms typical of the eighteenth century. It has a standard carved lion figurehead at the bow, an absence of wreaths around the gunports, and carved work limited largely to the taffrail. In the centre of the taffrail is the plume of feathers of the heir apparent with the motto 'ICH DIEN' (German for 'I Serve'), supported by two winged putti. The quarter pieces are formed of carved floral motifs above scaled dolphin. The upper counter includes floral painted decoration with a central 'GR' monogram for 'Georgius Rex', which dates the model to after 1714.

Pair of Fourth Rates, 50 guns (*c.*1715)

NMM NUMBER: SLR0404
SLR0219

SCALE: 1:48

DATE MADE: *c.*1715

Dimensions	Models (scaled up) SLR0404	SLR0219	1719 Establishment
Length of Gun Deck	132	130ft	134ft
Breadth	34ft	35ft	36ft
Number of Guns	50	50	50
Length of Keel	108ft (touch)	108ft (touch)	109ft 8in (for tonnage)
Depth (of hold)	14ft (approx.)	14ft	15ft 2in
Tons (burden)	686	710	756

SLR0404

SLR0219

Introduction

These two models are a rare example of a pair of Navy Board models that are identical in almost every respect. As such, it is worth including them together in a single catalogue entry. Small two-deckers like these undertook a variety of roles, including cruising on a given station, gathering intelligence, and also convoy and fleet escort duties. In the early eighteenth century there was an emphasis on building smaller ships for trade defence, and there were no major fleet actions in this period.

Identification

They cannot be identified as particular ships, but probably represent a vessel built just prior to 1719. It will be noticed that there is only a slight increase in size over earlier 50-gun ships and the general appearance is much the same. SLR0219 has a very clear 'GR' monogram painted on the stern, which indicates that it is likely that both models were made after King George I came to the throne in 1714.

Provenance

SLR0404 was transferred from the Royal Naval Museum, Greenwich, in 1934. SLR0219 was donated to the Museum by Dr R.C. Anderson in 1949.

Construction and Materials

Like all Navy Board models, these two are partially planked to the main wales, leaving the exposed frames below. An unusual feature common to both of these models are the original baseboards, where each model is supported the entire length of its keel by a veneer and inlay 'keel block'.

Fixtures and Fittings

Both models are equipped with a jeer capstan in the waist, used for raising and lowering the yards and boats. The main capstan is located further aft on the deck below and would have been used when hauling the anchor and its cable. SLR0219 is fitted with three mica-glazed stern lanterns fixed to the top of the taffrail. From the early eighteenth century, these hexagonal-shaped stern lanterns replaced the oval or spherical lanterns common in the seventeenth century.

Rigging

The models are unrigged, but have channels fitted for three masts and would have had a full ship-rig, with square sails on the fore- and mainmasts, and a topsail and lateen sail on the mizzen.

Decoration

The carved decorations and painted frieze are typical of the early Georgian Fourth Rates. The amount of gilding and carved work on the full-sized ships had been substantially reduced by this date, on the grounds of production costs and maintenance, and this is reflected on these models. Both are decorated in the same manner but, noticeably, SLR0404 has been varnished, which adds a much darker colour to both the wood and painted decoration.

SLR0404

SLR0219

Third Rate, 70 guns (*c.*1717)

NMM NUMBER: SLR0220

SCALE: 1:48

DATE MADE: *c.*1717

Introduction

Apart from the newly introduced 80-gun ships of the 1690s, the 70-gun Third Rates remained the most prolific during the first half of the eighteenth century up until 1756 with the introduction of the new 74-gun ship. Many of the 70-gun two-deckers were built under the Establishments of 1706 and 1719.

Dimensions	Model (scaled up)	Third Rate, 1719 Establishment (70-gun Third Rates)
Length of Gun Deck	151ft	151ft
Breadth	41ft	41ft 6in
Number of Guns	70	70
Length of Keel	124ft (touch)	123ft 2in
Depth (of hold)	14ft 6in	17ft 4in
Tons (burden)	1130	1128

Identification

Previously, it was thought that this model was built as an aid for discussions for the proposed changes of the 1719 Establishment, although the size and quality of this model would surely cast doubt over this on the grounds of time and costs of construction. The hull dimensions are of those of the 1719 Establishment, but the open stern walk extending around the quarter galleries and the 'crow's feet' rigged to the topmast stays reflect an earlier period. The model's dimensions (within 2–3ft) would fit with most of the nineteen ships of this class built from 1703–15.

Provenance

Presented by Lord Sherborne, 1971.

Construction and Materials

The clean and sharp finish to the model, together with the reduction in carved decoration, certainly shows the early eighteenth-century construction, with most parts manufactured in box and English fruitwoods. Not surprisingly, these woods are prone to worm damage and, as such, a large part of the stem, forefoot, and

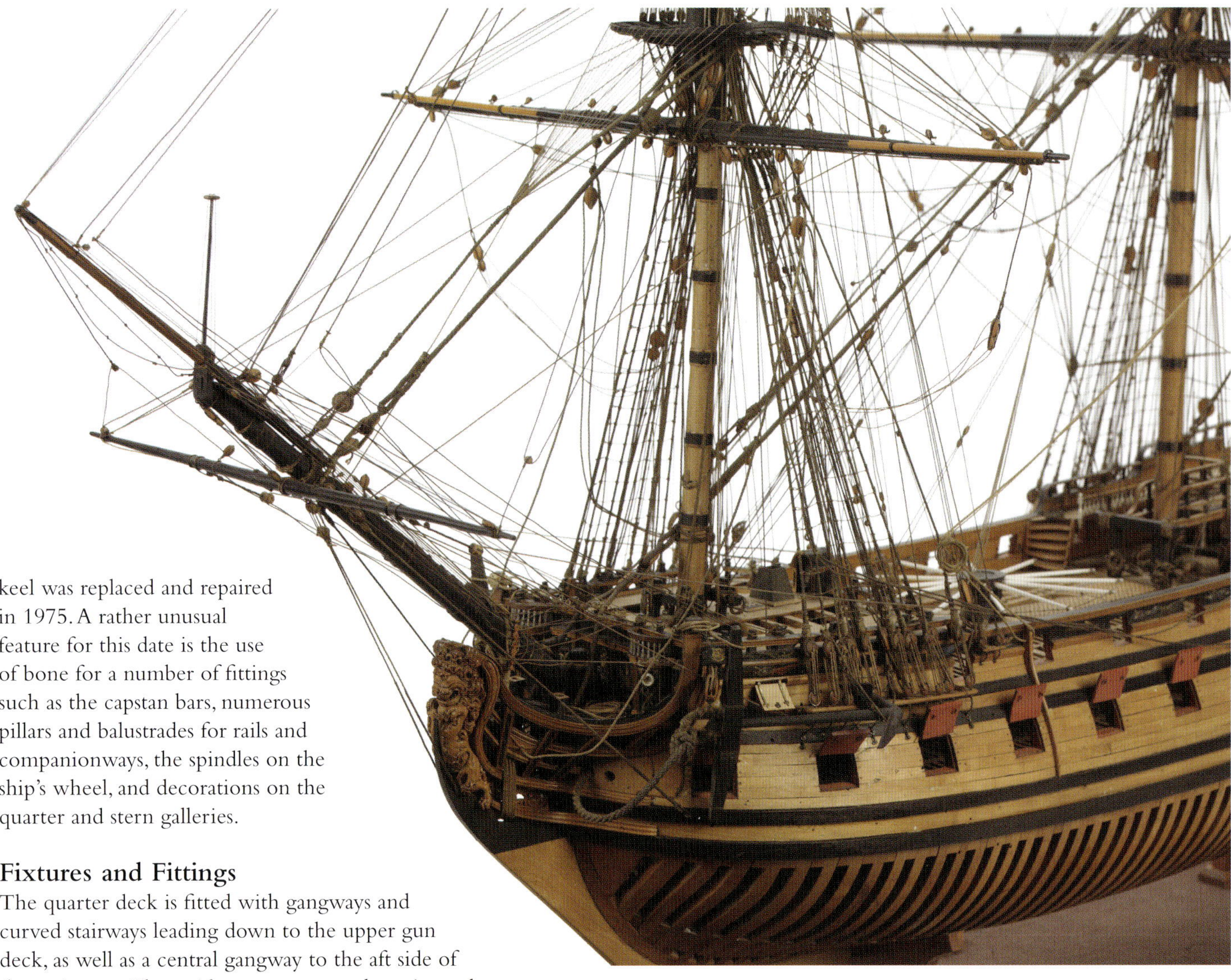

keel was replaced and repaired in 1975. A rather unusual feature for this date is the use of bone for a number of fittings such as the capstan bars, numerous pillars and balustrades for rails and companionways, the spindles on the ship's wheel, and decorations on the quarter and stern galleries.

Fixtures and Fittings

The quarter deck is fitted with gangways and curved stairways leading down to the upper gun deck, as well as a central gangway to the aft side of the mainmast. These side gangways are also mirrored on the poop deck, with balustrades and kingposts turned in bone. There is also a belfry mounted on the forecastle bulkhead, complete with a turned bell in brass. Above the taffrail is a complete set of stern lanterns made from individual parts and complete with glass lights. The whole model is mounted on its original carved wooden crutches.

Rigging

Largely in original condition, with minor repairs with some replacement to the running rigging. It is one of only a couple of models with mostly contemporary masts and spars that illustrates the introduction of the jibboom to the bowsprit and supporting bobstay. The fighting tops are also in the transitional stage from the earlier circular platforms to the slightly squarer version with the rounded corners and flat after side. The lower yards are also rigged with the heavy yard tackles which were used for working the anchors, as well as raising and lowering the ship's boats stored in the waist.

Decoration

Of particular note is the more restrained decoration as a result of the order issued in 1715. The only trace of the earlier wreathed gunports of the seventeenth century are on the quarter-deck bulwark screens and are a more simplified, square, moulded type. There is a very finely carved lion figurehead at the bow, with painted decoration on the beakhead bulkhead on a blue ground. This style of decoration carries on along the upper bulwark screens through to the quarter deck and around under the stern.

Fourth Rate, 50 guns (*c.*1719)

NMM NUMBER: SLR0354

SCALE: 1:64

DATE MADE: *c.*1719

Dimensions	Model (scaled up)	1719 Establishment
Length of Gun Deck	137ft	134ft
Breadth	36ft	36ft
Number of Guns	50–52	50
Length of Keel	120 (touch)	109ft 8in (for tonnage)
Depth (of hold)	13ft	15ft 2in
Tons (burden)	795	756

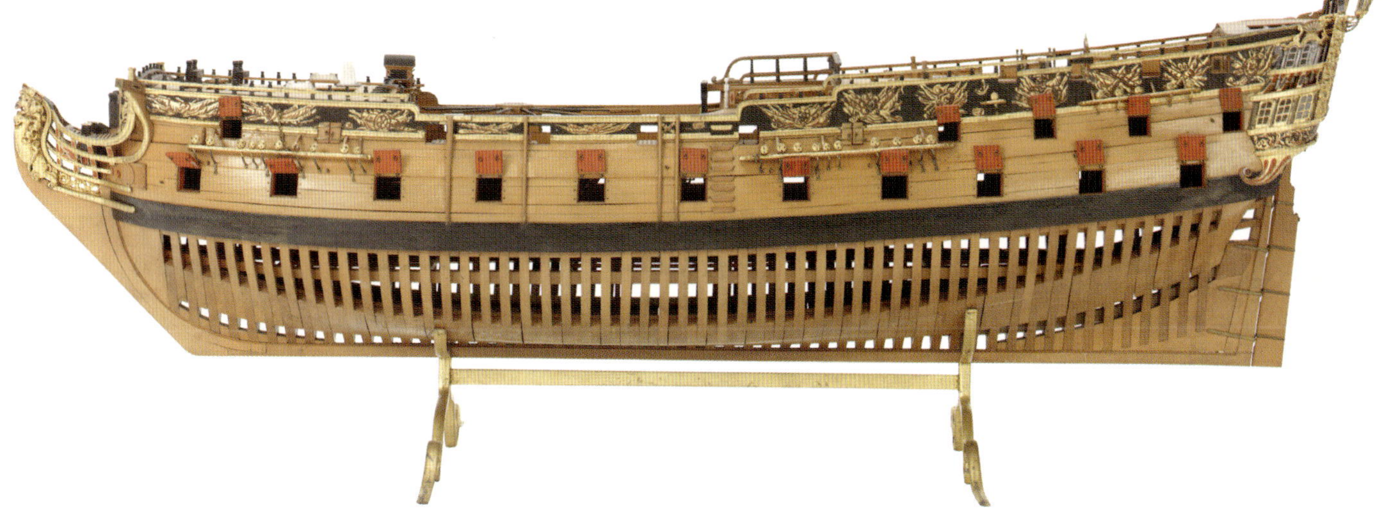

Introduction

This model depicts a 50-gun, small two-decker of between 1719 and 1733. Even at the rather unusually small scale of 1:64, the model is highly detailed and complete with both carved and gold-painted decoration.

The 50-gun ship originated from the pre-Commonwealth frigates of the seventeenth century. During the eighteenth century, these small two-deckers gradually moved away from the line-of-battle role to the heavy cruiser role.

Identification

The model's dimensions conflict with the two establishments of 1719 and 1733. The model is slightly longer than the 1719 Establishment set out for 50-gun ships.

Provenance

The model was purchased by Sir James Caird, via the agent Spink, from the trustees of Hugh, 6th Marquess of Hertford, Ragley Hall, Warwickshire. It was known in that family as a model of *Leviathan* – the ship commanded by the fifth son of the 1st Marquess of Hertford, Hugh Seymour, at the Battle of the Glorious First of June, 1794. The model had been at Ragley since his day, but it is certainly not the 74-gun *Leviathan*, launched in 1790: in actual fact, the model is considerably earlier.

Construction and Materials

The model follows the standard framing, but with longitudinal stringers fixed to the inside of the frames. Above a solid black wale, the hull is planked with individual strakes fixed with brass pins at the edges of the gunports, which in the waist have no lids, as was common during the reign of Queen Anne.

Fixtures and Fittings

The fixtures and fittings are of particularly fine quality, often constructed with both wood and bone elements. The model is partially decked and complete with hatches and stairways. Details such as hatch combings, drift rails, and bitts are picked out in matt black paint. At the forward end of the waist is a wooden capstan complete with bars, with the chocks and top of the spindle elegantly carved from bone. At the break of the forecastle, there is a simple arched belfry painted black, complete with bone bell. Forward of this is a pyramidal-shaped galley chimney carved from bone,

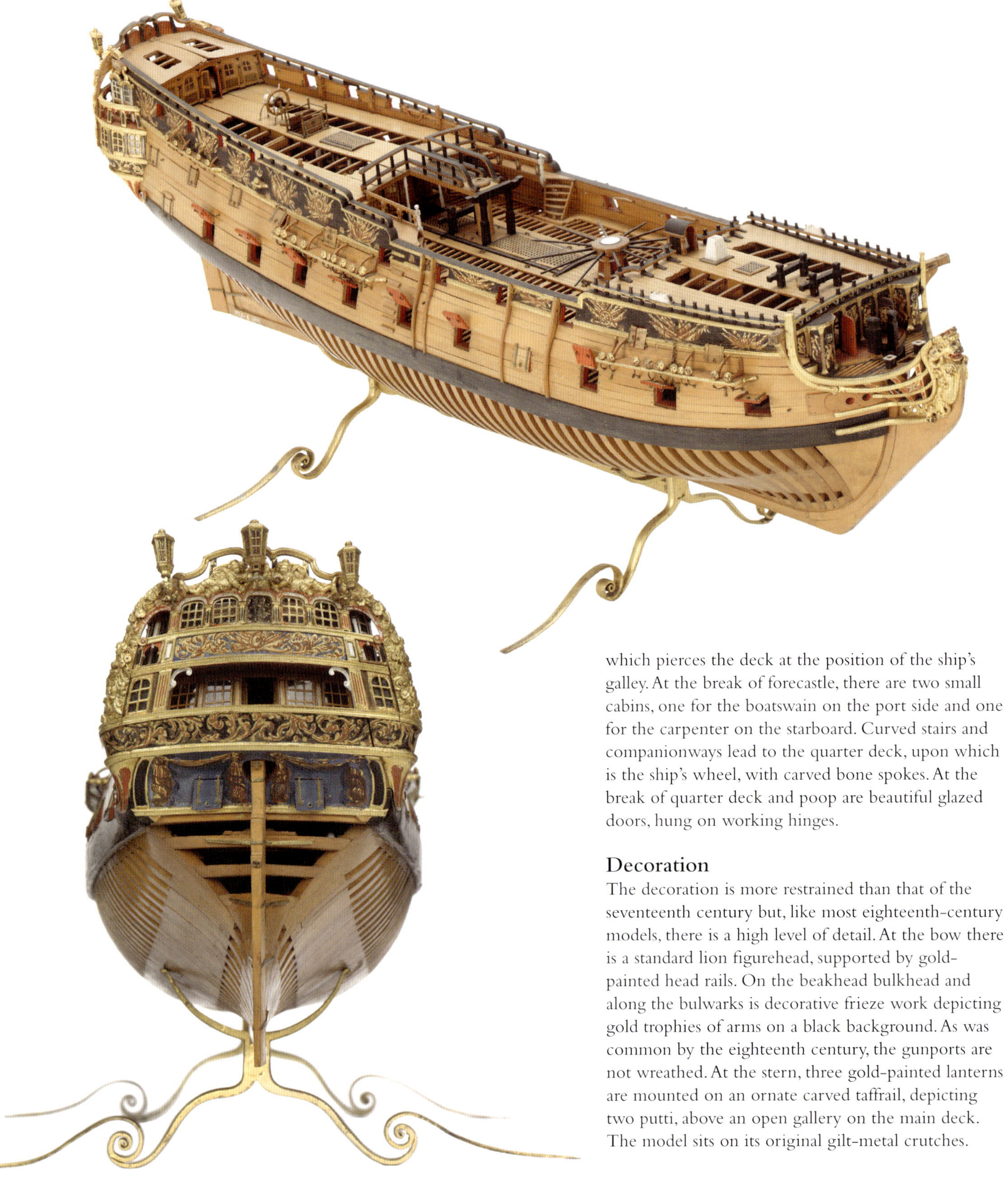

which pierces the deck at the position of the ship's galley. At the break of forecastle, there are two small cabins, one for the boatswain on the port side and one for the carpenter on the starboard. Curved stairs and companionways lead to the quarter deck, upon which is the ship's wheel, with carved bone spokes. At the break of quarter deck and poop are beautiful glazed doors, hung on working hinges.

Decoration

The decoration is more restrained than that of the seventeenth century but, like most eighteenth-century models, there is a high level of detail. At the bow there is a standard lion figurehead, supported by gold-painted head rails. On the beakhead bulkhead and along the bulwarks is decorative frieze work depicting gold trophies of arms on a black background. As was common by the eighteenth century, the gunports are not wreathed. At the stern, three gold-painted lanterns are mounted on an ornate carved taffrail, depicting two putti, above an open gallery on the main deck. The model sits on its original gilt-metal crutches.

Royal William (1719), 100 guns

NMM NUMBER: SLR0408

SCALE: 1:60

DATE MADE: *c.*1719

Dimensions	Model (scaled up)	*Royal William* (1719)
Length of Gun Deck	175ft	175ft 4in
Breadth	50ft	50ft 3½in
Number of Guns	100	100
Length of Keel	142ft 6in (touch)	142ft 7in
Depth (of hold)	20ft	20ft 1in
Tons (burden)	1928	1918

Introduction

A stunning model of the First Rate *Royal William* (1719), a 100-gun three-decker ship of the line, built plank-on-frame in the Navy Board style. This model is one of three full-hull models of this vessel in the NMM collection, two of which were made in the Navy Board style (see also SLR0222 and SLR0409).

The *Royal William* was an early eighteenth-century three-decker, one of six First Rates in the class of the largest warships. She was launched at Portsmouth in September 1719. The *Royal William* was never fitted out for sea as a 100-gunner, however, and her active life began when she was reduced to a Second Rate of 84 guns in 1756. The ship saw service during the Seven Years War as part of Admiral Edward Hawke's fleet in 1757, took part in the expedition to Quebec, and carried home the body of General James Wolfe in 1759. The *Royal William* was reduced to a Third Rate of 80 guns in 1771. During the American Revolutionary War, she was involved in the relief of Gibraltar, before becoming a receiving ship at Portsmouth in 1790 and, from 1801, a guardship at Sheerness. Not broken up until 1813, her longevity is sometimes ascribed to George III's particular fondness for her. A more likely explanation is that she was constructed from charred winter-felled oak.

Identification

The model can be identified by comparison with the surviving plan, as well as the figurehead, which includes a crowned 'ЯWR' monogram of William III. It was possibly made before the vessel was completed, as there are some slight differences in design, notably that the beam of the model is about 1½ft (on the scale) too narrow.

Provenance

Royal Naval Museum, transferred to the NMM in 1934.

Construction and Materials

The model is constructed with standard Navy Board framing. It is mounted on a baseboard with a modern mirror, enabling the viewer to see clearly the underside of the hull.

Fixtures and Fittings

The model is shown equipped with turned brass guns and stern lanterns, as well as anchor and tackle.

Rigging

It was re-rigged in 1925 at the Royal Naval Museum, but is fairly accurate for the period. The masts and spars are original. The rigging on the bowsprit allows for both a spritsail topsail and a jib to be carried. This arrangement would hardly have been practicable, and the former was soon to disappear.

Decoration

The large First Rates often had an elaborate figurehead carved specifically for the ship, as opposed to the lion figurehead as was common for the smaller rates. This model displays a wonderful example of a Georgian figurehead, which, left ungilt, allows the definition of the carving to stand out. In the centre is a crowned monogram 'ЯWR', flanked on either side by King William III on horseback, wearing Greco-Roman dress, laurel-wreathed with commander's baton in hand, which draws flattering comparisons to the classical past. The horse is shown trampling a chained figure representing enslavement, which symbolises William's rejection of absolutism to uphold the liberty of England. Between the cheek mouldings, the trailboard has intricately carved putti, scaly dolphins, and goose-like birds. On the taffrail, situated above the open stern galleries, is a bust of William III, supported by a variety of figures from ancient mythology, as well as a wealth of foliage and putti. Immediately to port is a female personification of Justice, with scales and sword, and to starboard is female figure personifying Fortitude, holding a decorative column.

The quarter figures consist of female figures with shield and spear, possibly representing Athena, the goddess of wisdom. Below on the starboard side is a carving of Hercules, club in hand, battling the many-headed Hydra. The port side is a depiction of Samson, the mythical biblical figure who slayed an army of Philistines armed only with a jawbone.

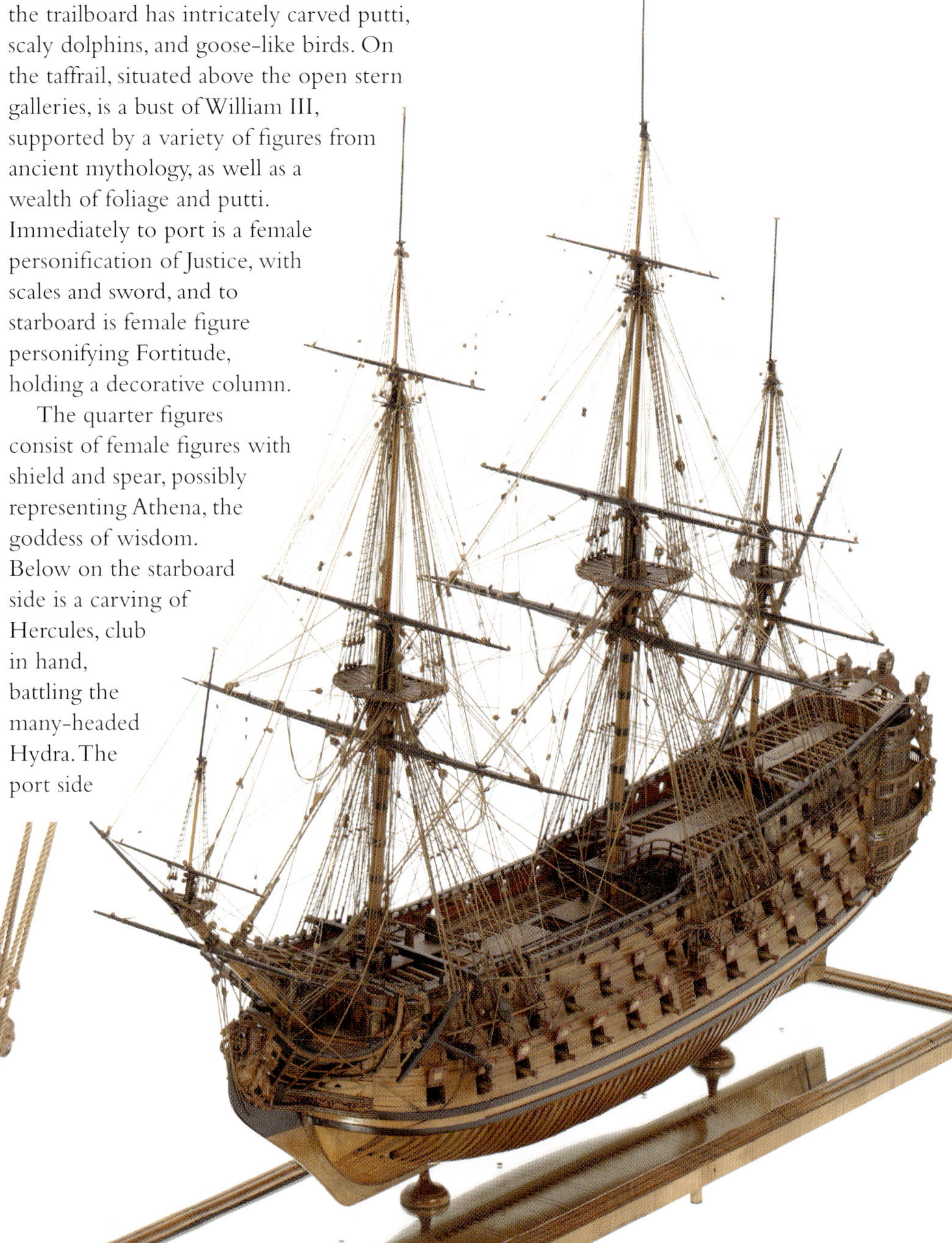

Royal William (1719), 100 guns

NMM NUMBER: SLR0409

SCALE: 1:60

DATE MADE: *c.*1719

Dimensions	Model (scaled up)	*Royal William* (1719)
Length of Gun Deck	175ft	175ft 4in
Breadth	50ft	50ft 3½in
Number of Guns	100	100
Length of Keel	158ft 9in (touch)	142ft 7in
Depth (of hold)	19ft	20ft 1in
Tons (burden)	1928	1918

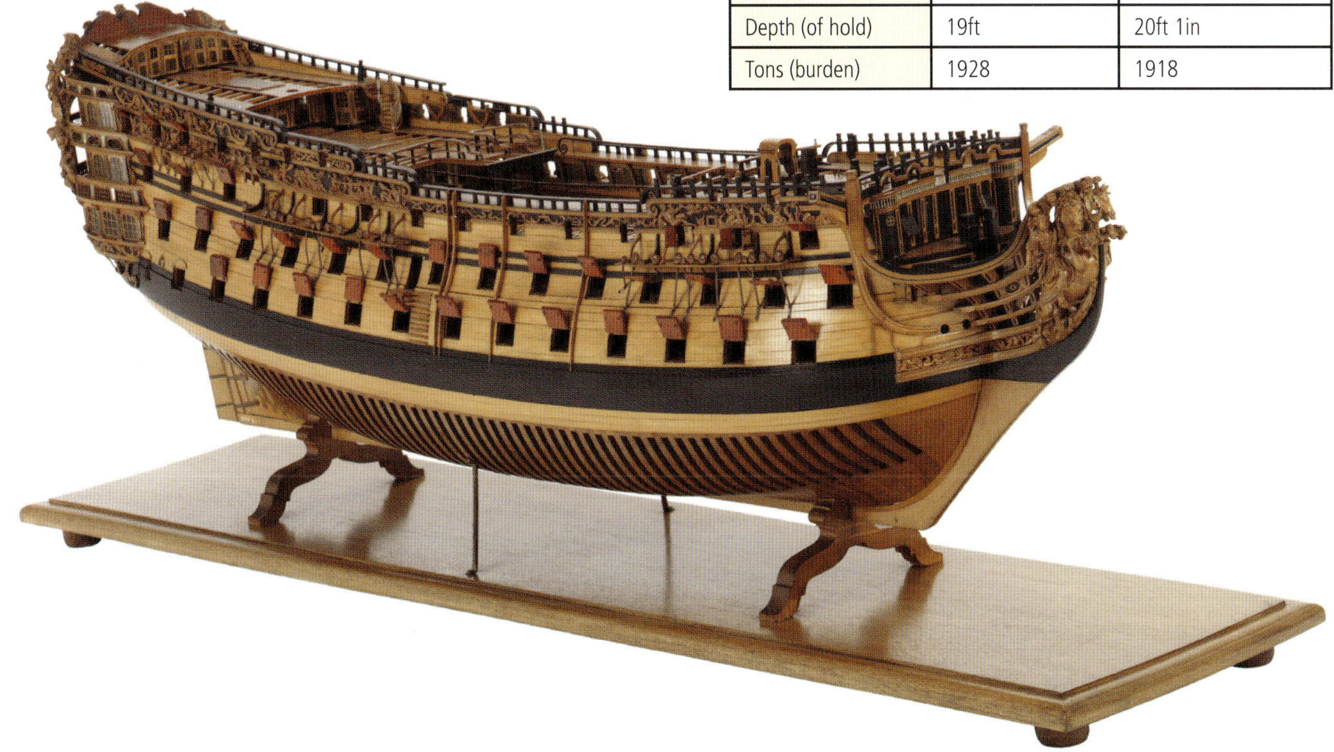

Introduction

This superb model, unlike SLR0408, depicts the ship as built: not only do measurements fit, but also contemporary drawings of the *Royal William* afloat show the lower wales 'closed', or made solid as in the model. The *Royal William* was an early-eighteenth century three-decker, one of six First Rates in the class of the largest warships. (See SLR0408 for a brief history of the ship itself).

Identification

The model, much like SLR0408, can be identified by comparison with the surviving plan, as well as the figurehead which includes the crowned 'ЯWR' monogram of William III.

Provenance

Royal Naval Museum, transferred to the NMM in 1934.

Construction and Materials

This model is among those that set the standard for later ship modellers. Typical of the first half of the eighteenth century, this model shows the quality achieved by the model makers in this period. Plank-on-frame in construction, the *Royal William* demonstrates a high standard of craftsmanship, not only in its technical construction, but also in the fittings, and particularly the decoration. The framing is of the standard Navy Board type and the planking is individually laid planks secured with glue, with three planks included below the black 'closed' main wale. Unusually for a Navy Board model, the entire model splits horizontally, on the waterline, just below the main wale. This exposes the partially planked deck beams of the lower gun deck, as well as further exposing the construction of the lower transom, and framing, which forms a solid run of floors and futtocks at the height of the main wale. On the upper deck the partially planked deck is fitted with hatch gratings.

Fixtures and Fittings

The model includes a number of detailed fixtures and fittings. In the waist, a large drumhead capstan, with bars, is shown towards the break of the forecastle. On

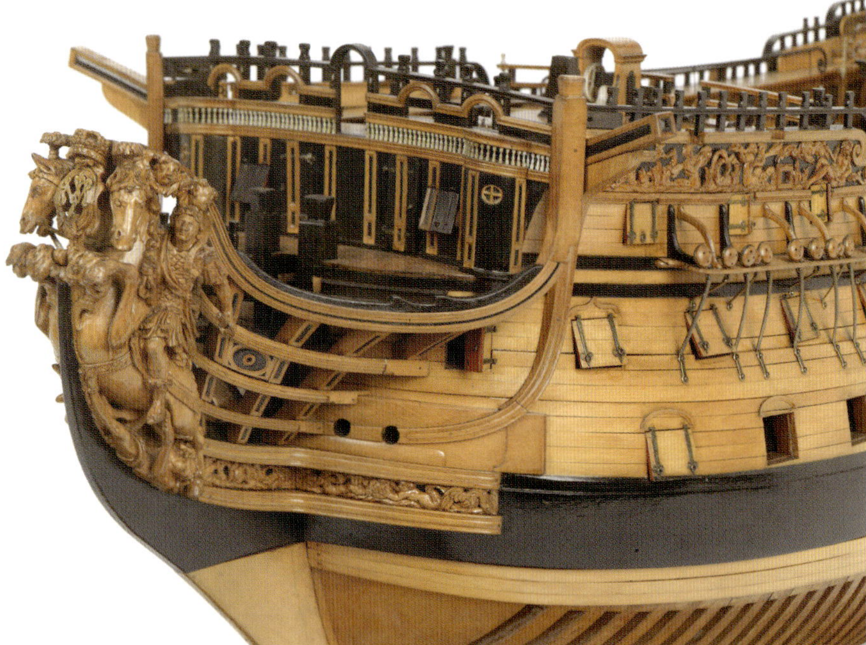

the foredeck, an ivory bell and bell wheel is housed in an elegant arched belfry. The black chimney of the galley stove pierces the foredeck just forward of this.

The quarter deck is linked to the foredeck via narrow gangways which run along the sides of the waist – a feature which would become mandatory for Royal Navy ships by 1782. In addition, the centre of the fore edge quarter deck is extended to the mainmast by a central gangway, which allowed easier operation of the rigging. Under the quarter deck, the main companionway linking the upper deck with the middle gun deck is fitted with fine ivory balustrades. The quarter deck is similarly linked to the poop deck by a curved stairway. A small coach house is fitted at the aft end of the poop deck. At the bow, the roundhouses, with round glazed windows, are fitted neatly into the scheme of the black beakhead bulkhead, which is topped with short ivory balustrades.

Rigging

The model is unrigged, but channels, chainplates, and deadeyes are fitted along the sides for three masts. To allow for the reduction in tumblehome, the channels have been raised to the level of the upper wales, which means the chainplates are elongated in comparison to earlier vessels.

Decoration

The model shows a particularly elaborate figurehead, comprising of an equestrian group with the Royal Arms positioned centrally. Almost identical to SLR0408, the carving is only finished with a light lacquer. In the centre is a crowned monogram 'ЯWR', flanked on either side by King William III on horseback, wearing Greco-Roman dress, laurel-wreathed with commander's baton in hand, which draws flattering comparisons to the classical past. The horse is shown trampling a chained figure representing enslavement, which symbolises William's rejection of absolutism to uphold the liberty of England. It differs from SLR0408 in that two winged putti heads are positioned above the figure of William.

Along the sides, the gunports are the plain, unwreathed type typical of this period. The sides of the hull are plain, except for elegant, light-relief carvings along the bulwark screens, which include George crosses, interspersed with floral motifs and mythological nautical scenes in wood on a black-painted background. The quarter figures consist of female figures with shield and spear, the port side possibly representing Athena, who mounted the severed head of a gorgon on her shield, and the starboard is likely to be Britannia, with a Union flag shield. Below on the starboard side is Hercules, club in hand, battling the many-headed Hydra. The port side is a depiction of Samson, the mythical biblical figure who slayed an army of Philistines armed only with a jawbone. Together these figures represent the kingly attributes of wisdom and strength. Following the same scheme as SLR0408, on the taffrail is the bust of William III supported by a variety of figures from ancient mythology, as well as a wealth of foliage and putti. Immediately to port is a female personification of Justice, with scales and sword, and to starboard is a female figure personifying Fortitude, holding a decorative column. The fretwork on the upper gallery includes the interlocking 'ЯWR' monogram.

Fourth Rate, 50 guns (*c.*1720)

NMM NUMBER: SLR0415

SCALE: 1:60

DATE MADE: *c.*1720

Dimensions	Model (scaled up)	1719 Establishment (50-gun Fourth Rates)
Length of Gun Deck	134ft	134ft
Breadth	36ft	36ft
Number of Guns	50	50
Length of Keel	117ft (touch)	109ft 9in
Depth (of hold)	15ft (approx.)	15ft 2in
Tons (burden)	774	756

Introduction

Fourth Rate 50-gun ships were the smallest to feature in the line of battle. In addition to this, they undertook a variety of duties, including escorting and protecting commerce, as well as remaining on a station, or patrolling large areas to protect British interests around the world. However, by the early 1730s, they were considered to be too weak to take the line and were slower than a frigate, and so were subsequently replaced by the 60-gun Fourth Rates.

Identification

Based upon the length of the gun deck and maximum beam measurements, this model represents one of twenty-two 50-gun Fourth Rates built to the Establishments of 1719. This is further confirmed by the dimensions of the masts and spars.

Provenance

Royal Naval Museum, transferred to NMM in 1934.

Construction and Materials

The unusually small scale of this model, and the fact it is fully rigged, would suggest that it was commissioned by a wealthy individual with an interest in or association with this class of ship. It is made largely from boxwood and is a fine example of craftsmanship, even at this unusually small scale. A number of pillars and rails inboard, as well as the balustrades on the open stern gallery, have been turned in bone. As well as the specific measurements of the model, the draught marks are scored and painted on the cutwater of the stem and are ⅗in apart, which has helped determine the scale of the model.

Fixtures and Fittings

In the waist, just aft of the forecastle, is a pair of piss-dales, which is unusual to find on a model of this date, since they had all but disappeared by the early eighteenth century. The gratings running along the centreline are made up, as opposed to the punched style, and supported by flush and raised combings. The jeer capstan is of the drumhead type and is fitted with ten wooden bars. Either side of the mainmast are side gangways, which lead down

from the quarter deck to the upper deck and are complete with balustrades turned in bone.

Rigging

The masts and spars on this model are original, but the rigging is a modern replacement. It clearly illustrates the development of the sailing rig in several areas. First, the replacement of the sprit topmast with the jibboom extended the bowsprit to enable more fore and aft sails to be set. These sails, called jibs, were used primarily to help turn the ship's head through the wind when tacking. The addition of these sails meant that the bowsprit needed extra support, so the rope bobstay was developed and was secured to the cutwater just below the figurehead. Secondly, the shape of the main tops changed from being circular to a square shape with rounded corners. On the mizzen, the long lateen yard was still in use with a single topsail above. By the middle of the eighteenth century, this long yard was only partially used, as the newer driver or spanker sail was introduced and was laced to the mizzen mast, and only required the after and upper part of the yard.

Decoration

At the bow is a finely carved lion figurehead supported by the standard drift rails and trailboards. There is also painted decoration along the bulwark screens, which consists of a mixture of trophies of war, figures, animals, and mixed foliage. This almost 'chinoiserie' style of decoration continues around the stern onto the upper counter and includes male figures in classical dress holding shields and spears. The carved decoration on the quarter galleries consists of a pair of figures, one of which is holding a trident, which lead to crouching lions on the taffrail. There is a crown in the centre, which is supported by a male and female figure in classical dress.

Spy (1721), 12–14 guns

NMM NUMBER: SLR0416

SCALE: 1:48

DATE MADE: *c.*1721

Dimensions	Model (scaled up)	*Spy* (1721)
Length of Gun Deck	61ft	62ft 1in
Breadth	19ft	20ft
Number of Guns	12–14	12
Length of Keel	47ft 6in (touch)	48ft 6in
Depth (of hold)	8ft 6in	9ft
Tons (burden)	95	103

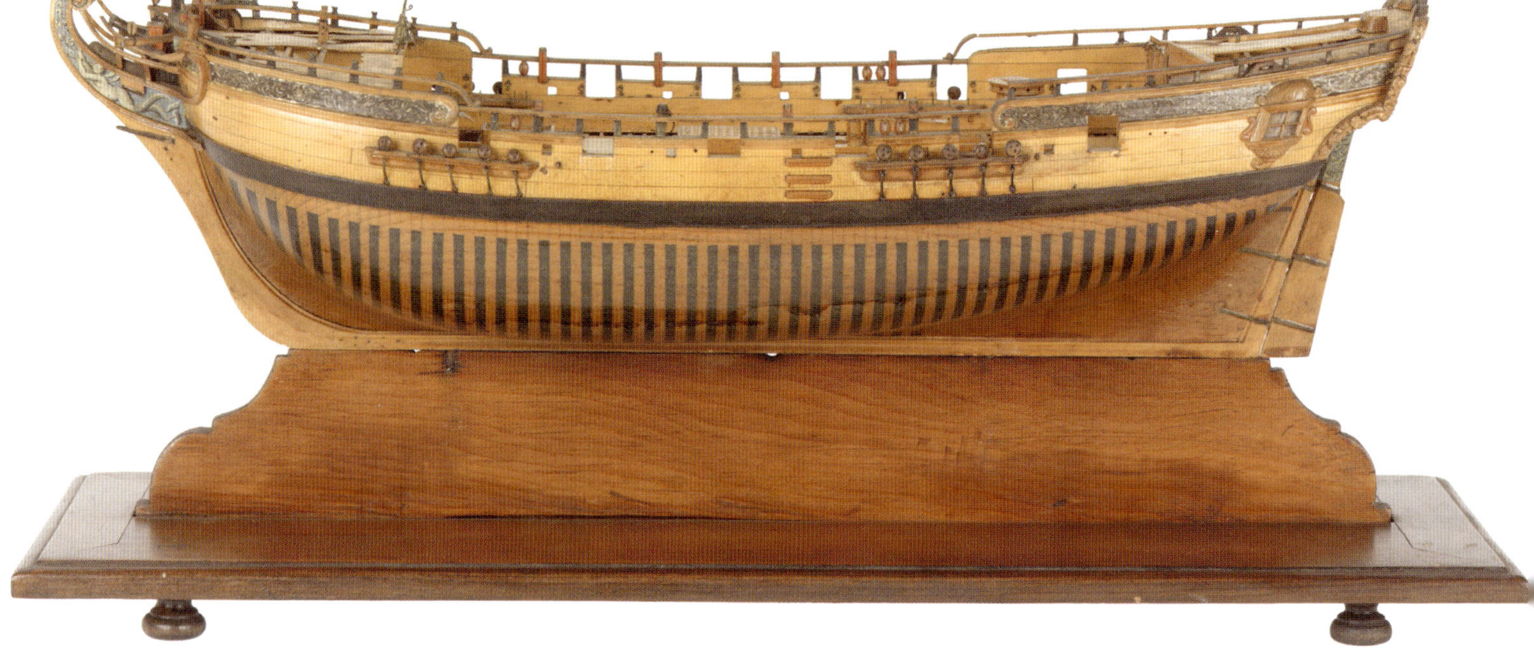

Introduction

These sloops were rated below 20-gun Sixth Rates and predominately played a cruising role around the British coast, with such duties as fishery protection, surveying, anti-smuggling, and communications. They were also employed in foreign waters to protect British interests against piracy and privateering.

Identification

Historically, this model has been linked to the *Cruizer* class of sloops launched in 1721, with the gun-deck dimension particularly close to the *Swift*. However, the dimensions are similar to two classes of four sloops ordered and also launched in 1721. Recent research would now suggest that this model represents the *Spy*, especially upon closer examination of the decoration on both the billet head of the bow and the stern counter (see decoration section below). This is supported by the similarity in dimensions to the *Spy*.

Provenance

Caird Collection, 1935.

Construction and Materials

The lower portion of the hull from just below the main wale is carved from a solid piece of wood (the grain pattern is evident beneath the varnish layer) which has then been carved out internally to produce a shell. The Navy Board-style framing has been inked and painted on below the main wale to mimic the construction. In terms of the style and finish, the decoration on this model is very similar to the two identical models of 50-gun ships of *c.*1715 (SLR0219 and SLR0404). Its construction is exactly the same method as the model of the *Lowestoft* (SLR0420). All four of these models are mounted on the same type of baseboard, with a central keel support with fashioned mouldings at the bow and stern. The upper works and planking have then been applied and built up from the carved hull shell.

Fixtures and Fittings

The upper deck is fully framed with beams, carling, and ledges, with a central portion of planking in the waist supporting the hatches, elm tree pumps, and a single capstan and a run of three planks inside the bulwarks. There is a small cabin aft for the captain and open forecastle in the bow protecting the riding bitts. On the deck above, this cabin is fitted with a diamond-shaped wooden frame rigged with blocks. The steering rope connected to the end of the tiller would then be led either side through two large sheaves in the bulwark rails and back to this frame and sent down to the drum of the steering wheel below.

In the waist are a number of timber heads on which the swivel guns were mounted. At the break of the small forecastle deck is a bell mounted in a twisted wire belfry set off-centre and connected to a wooden deck rail.

Rigging

The rig for this class of sloops varied, but the presence of two sets of channels, together with the number of deadeyes, suggests that this vessel was probably rigged as a brig, brigantine, or two-masted schooner.

Decoration

On the counter of the stern there is a very fine and detailed painted scene, depicting a winged Neptune holding a trident in the left hand and holding a spyglass or telescope to his eye with his right. He is standing on a scalloped-type chariot, drawn by two hippocampi with scaled and forked tails, with another winged putto holding a floral wreath over their heads. On the bow is an inwardly curving scroll, known as a 'billet head', which is decorated with a similar winged Triton with twin scaled fish tails and also holding the same instrument to his eye. This depiction would suggest that the model represents the sloop *Spy*, one of the four *Cruizer* class launched in 1721.

Lowestoft (1723), 20 guns

NMM NUMBER: SLR0420

SCALE: 1:48

DATE MADE: *c.*1723

Dimensions	Model (scaled up)	*Lowestoft* (1723)
Length of Gun Deck	106ft	106ft 3in
Breadth	28ft	28ft 5in
Number of Guns	20	20
Length of Keel	92ft 6in (touch)	88ft
Depth (of hold)	15ft	9ft 2in
Tons (burden)	371	383

Introduction

Ships of this size and complement of guns were built in large numbers during the latter seventeenth and early eighteenth centuries. From 1715 to the early 1730s, it was a relatively peaceful time and, as such, ships of this configuration tended to be deployed in a whole range of duties, especially in a cruising role protecting the British overseas interests. A number of these operations were in shallow waters against fleets of specialised craft powered by oars. Therefore, it could be argued that this brought about the revival of the use of sweeps to combat the threat posed by these ships.

Identification

This model has been identified in the past as representing the *Lowestoft*, launched in 1723, based upon the gunport arrangements on the original draught (ZAZ3799). It represents one of a class of twenty-one 20–24-gun Sixth Rates built to the 1719 Establishment. However, the presence of a ballast port amidships and the sweeps on the lower deck to avoid interference with the guns illustrate the change from single-decked to a two-decked 20-gun ship which was introduced in the 1733 Establishment proposals. This model is very similar in many respects to the model of the unidentified Sixth Rate *c.*1725 (SLR0012), with the main difference being the shorter quarter deck and the lightly constructed bulwark rails above and between the gunports.

Provenance

Purchased from Gay's Antiques, Cheshire, 1979.

Construction and Materials

The hull is carved from a wooden core which consists of horizontal layers of planks in 'bread-and-butter' fashion, which is then gouged out internally to produce a thin wooden shell. The frames and dark spaces have been scored and painted onto the wooden shell to give the impression of the Navy Board style of framing. Both this finish and the raised hull support along the keel and baseboard are identical to the small sloop model *c.*1720 (SLR0416). The topsides from the main wale above are constructed plank-on-frame in the traditional method to the solid bulwark to the middle of the gunports, above which are fitted the lighter rails, which have been painted black.

Fixtures and Fittings

Sadly, this model has suffered from damage in the past and a large part of the fixtures and fittings are missing. That aside, the hull is complete with a keel with a scarph joint at the touch and a square tuck at the stern. The lack of forecastle provides a detailed view of the gun deck with scored planking along the ship's side, and gratings, which are punched as opposed to made-up, are located in hatch combings along the centreline. The deck beams are also visible and are complete with the smaller carlings and ledges. Again, the incomplete stern galleries reveal the construction and materials used, the windows consist of small pieces of glass with the wooden frames glued on.

Rigging

The presence and some remains of the three sets of channels with deadeyes illustrate the standard three-masted ship rig.

Decoration

Unlike the other, almost-identical model of this class of ship – SLR0012 – the decoration is painted on the bulwark screens, quarter galleries, and the upper and lower counters at the stern. The finely executed paintwork consists of a variety of animals, figures, and foliage painted in white on a red ground. The lower counter has a pair of winged figures holding back drapes with rope tassels on a blue background.

First Rate, 100 guns (*c.*1725)

NMM NUMBER: SLR0422

SCALE: 1:48

DATE MADE: *c.*1725

Dimensions	Model (scaled up)	*Royal George* (1715)
Length of Gun Deck	174ft	171ft 9in
Breadth	50ft	49ft 3in
Number of Guns	100	100
Length of Keel	145ft (touch)	139ft 7in
Depth (of hold)	17ft	19ft 6in
Tons (burden)	1915	1801

Introduction

From 1714 it was decided that the overall size of the Navy was to be maintained at 124 ships, of which seven were First Rates. It was also common practice during the late seventeenth and early eighteenth centuries for the large First and Second Rates to be taken to pieces and later rebuilt. Therefore, it is not surprising that there are a number of contemporary models, draughts, and illustrations of First Rates that survive from the early eighteenth century.

Identification

The finely carved group figurehead with the 'GR' monogram suggests that the model should demand a 'Royal' name. There are points of resemblance to the *Royal George* of 1715 and the *Royal William* of 1719, but the model possibly represents a type rather than an actual ship.

Provenance

Royal Naval Museum, transferred to NMM in 1934.

Construction and Materials

The framed hull is complete with individually laid planks, as well as partial decking for potential accommodation of the guns and gratings along the centreline. The most noticeable feature of this model is the exuberant use of bone for carved decoration, as well as certain structural features. The whole model is mounted on a pair of moulded keel blocks, four turned wooden pillars supporting the turn of the bilges, all of which are secured to its original wooden and varnished softwood baseboard.

Fixtures and Fittings

Some of the inboard fittings for rigging are carved from bone, as well as internal cabin furnishings such as bulkheads and doors. There is also a semicircular serving table with 'barley-twist' legs located centrally under the forecastle deck in front of the galley stove. Internally, most of the main structural fittings are included, such as the pumps, riding bitts, and stairs between the three gun decks.

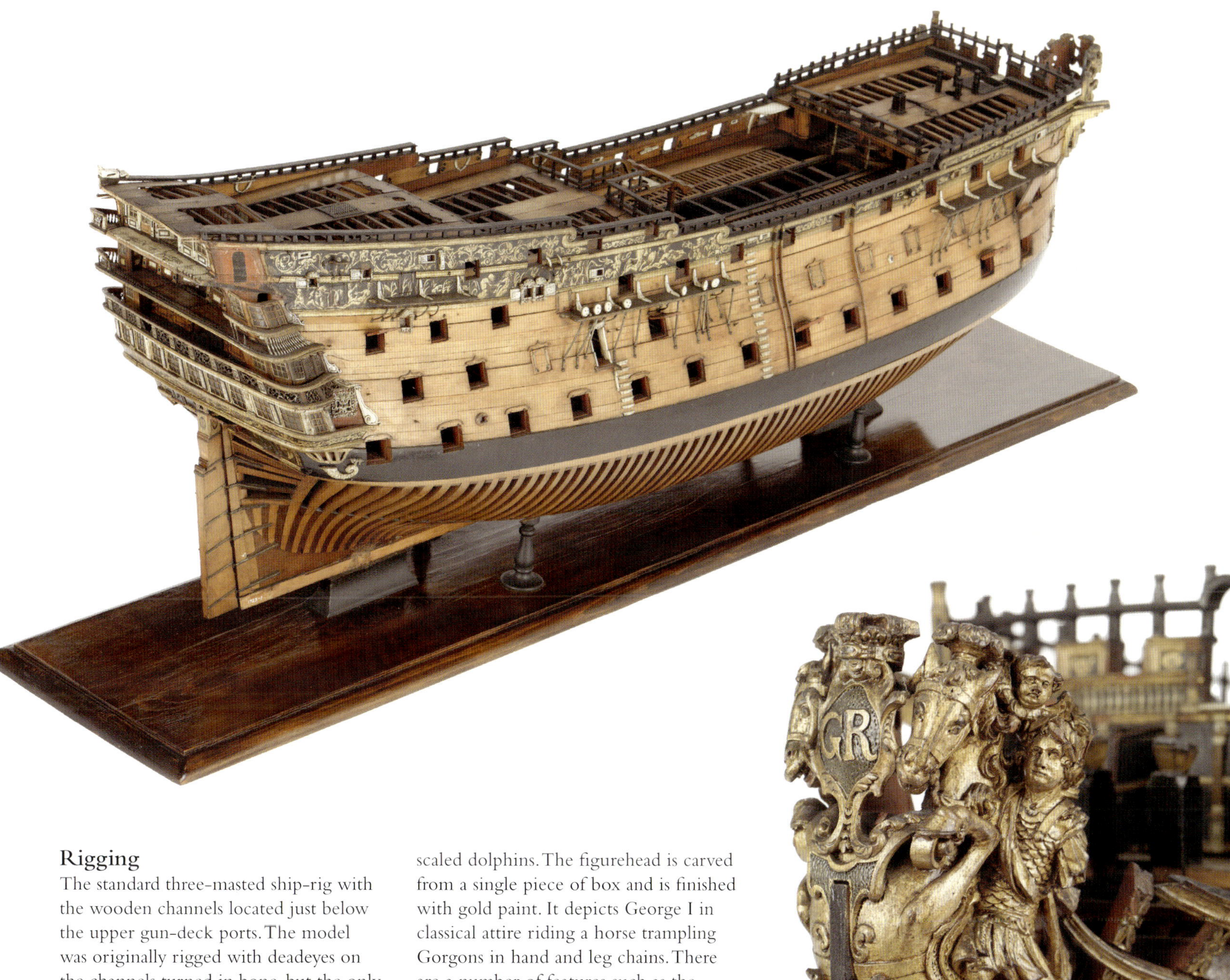

Rigging

The standard three-masted ship-rig with the wooden channels located just below the upper gun-deck ports. The model was originally rigged with deadeyes on the channels turned in bone, but the only remaining examples are on the starboard side for the mainmast.

Decoration

The painted decoration on the bulwark friezes and around the stern galleries is particularly fine. Painted in gold on a black background, it includes a variety of reclining and standing male classical figures amongst water and foliage with scaled dolphins. The figurehead is carved from a single piece of box and is finished with gold paint. It depicts George I in classical attire riding a horse trampling Gorgons in hand and leg chains. There are a number of features such as the finishing pieces, entry port, boarding steps, and quarter-gallery moulding carved in bone. Other details in bone include structural items such as the channel knees, mouldings around the ventilation and cabin windows, balustrades, and pilasters on the stern galleries. Brass wire has been used to produce delicate patterned rails around the stern gallery as well.

Sixth Rate, 20–24 guns (*c.*1725)

NMM NUMBER: SLR0012

SCALE: 1:48

DATE MADE: *c.*1725

Dimensions	Model (scaled up)	1719 Establishment (20-gun Sixth Rates)
Length of Gun Deck	107ft	106ft
Breadth	29ft	28ft 4in
Number of Guns	20–24	20
Length of Keel	90ft (touch)	87ft 9in
Depth (of hold)	10ft	9ft 2in
Tons (burden)	400	374

Introduction

Ships of this size and complement of guns were built in large numbers during the late seventeenth and early eighteenth centuries. From 1715 to the early 1730s, it was a relatively peaceful time, and as such, ships of this configuration tended to be deployed in a whole range of duties, especially in a cruising role protecting British overseas interests. A number of these operations were in shallow waters against fleets of specialised craft powered by oars. Therefore it could be argued that this brought about the revival of the use of sweeps to combat the threat posed by these ships.

Identification

This model at this scale probably represents a class of twenty-one 20-24-gun Sixth Rates built to the 1719 Establishment. However, the presence of a ballast port amidships, the sweeps on the lower deck to avoid interference with the guns, together with the extended quarter deck, illustrates the change from single-decked to a two-decked 20-gun ship which was introduced in the 1733 Establishment proposals. It is almost identical to the model of the *Lowestoft* (SLR0420), except for the difference in the length of the quarter deck.

Provenance

Presented by Sir Kenneth Anderson, Bart, 1935.

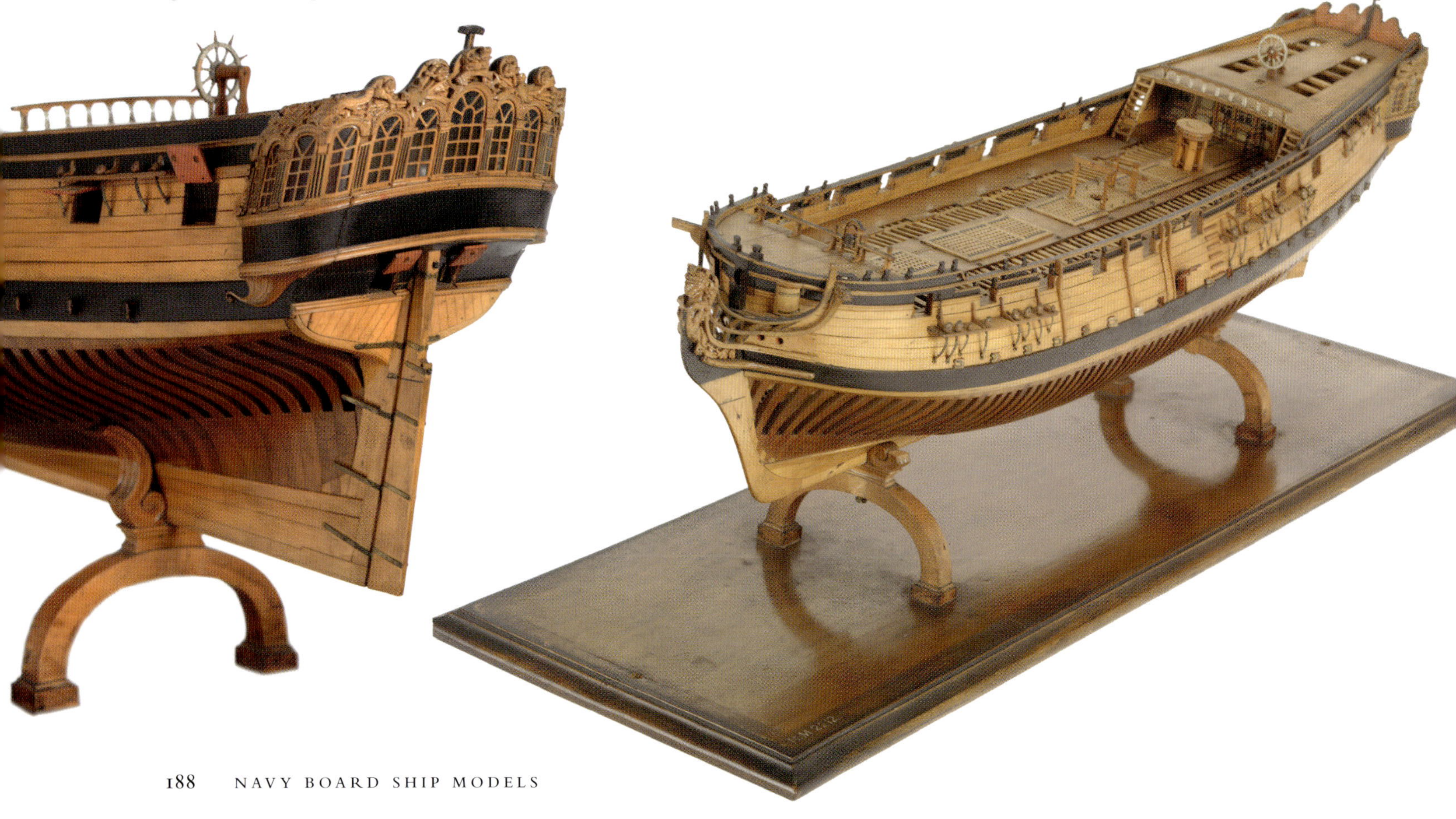

Construction and Materials

The hull frames are made from an unusually darker wood than the surrounding planking, and possibly highlights the underwater shape better against the lighter woods. It is fitted with a square tuck stern with the garboard and an additional two planks fitted along the keel, which in itself includes a detailed scarph joint at the touch. The deck planking is a mixture of individually laid as well as scored with butt joints. Bone has been used in several cases, in particular for the ship's wheel, decorative features on the quarter-deck bulkhead screens and rails, as well as a number of sheaves in the cathead, clevels, and sheet blocks. A waterline has been marked on the hull in ink at the stem and stern post and the whole model is mounted on a pair of original and ornately carved wooden crutches secured to a baseboard.

Fixtures and Fittings

Forward of the rounded forecastle beakhead are a pair of small roundhouses, which are hinged for access and fitted with waste pipes made in bone. The forecastle deck is open towards the waist and acts more like a shelter deck for sail handling and other uses. It is fitted with a small but elaborate belfry mounted just off the centreline and is complete with a bell and clapper turned in wood. In the waist, all of the gratings are of the made-up variety, with some longitudinal members made of a dark wood, possibly ebony. Both the gunport lids and sweeports are fitted with finely made hinges in brass, as are the chainplates and deadeye strops. The longer quarter deck extending beyond the mizzen mast allows the placing of a single steering wheel, which gave a better site to the sails and way ahead to the helmsman. Internally, the main cabin at the stern is fitted with bulkheads, painted with a red decoration and black fleur de lis, and a diamond floor covering.

Rigging

The presence of the three sets of channels with deadeyes illustrates the standard three-masted ship-rig.

Decoration

Externally, the only decoration is carved with a small-scale lion figurehead on the bow and on the wrap-around stern galleries, consisting of a mixture of trophies of arms and a centrally placed crown on the taffrail. The quarter galleries are supported by finishing pieces, whilst on the roof is a finely carved set of plume of feathers. The bulwark screens and the stern counter are finished in black and made in ebony. The windows or lights around the stern are complete with carved frames and are interspaced with columns inlaid with strips of ebony and connected by rounded arches.

Third Rate, 70 guns (*c.*1725)

NMM NUMBER: SLR0424

SCALE: 1:48

DATE MADE: *c.*1725

Dimensions	Model (scaled up)	1719 Establishment (70-gun Third Rate)
Length of Gun Deck	151ft	151ft
Breadth	41ft	41ft 6in
Number of Guns	70	70
Length of Keel	124ft (touch)	123ft 6in
Depth (of hold)	18ft	17ft 4in
Tons (burden)	1130	1128

Introduction

Large numbers of these 70-gun ships were built to the 1719 Establishment between 1721–33. It was these, and the later 74-gun ships, that were the backbone of the line, taking part in all major fleet actions for the next seventy years.

Identification

Although this model cannot be identified to any particular ship, the dimensions represent a 70-gun ship built to the 1719 Establishment, but before the revised 1733 proposals. However, the raised channels above the upper gun-deck ports suggest a later date of 1745.

Provenance

Purchased by Sir James Caird in 1926, and subsequently presented in 1934.

Construction and Material

The hull frames are of the standard pattern, except that the futtocks extend all the way to the keel. The hull and deck planking consists of both scored and individually laid planks. The hull planking is secured with wooden treenails and is complete with the solid main wales as well as the open upper wales. The deck planking has an odd patination in terms of the colour and finish overall, and suggests that it may be a later restoration. There is also some use of bone with the decorated columns on the poop bulkhead.

Fixtures and Fittings

The deck is fitted with scored planking, together with gratings fitted in combings running along the centreline. There are a pair of short gangways leading from the quarter deck down to the upper gun deck, finishing in a curved set of stairs. The jeer capstan is situated in the waist, together with a wooden belfry, fitted with a turned bell, mounted on the forecastle bulkhead. Directly aft of the carved lion figurehead are a pair of roundhouses with a decorated semicircular top with turned wooden balustrades.

Rigging

The wooden channels have been raised above the upper gun deck, which was a feature introduced after 1745. They are complete with wooden deadeyes secured with brass strops and chainplates.

Decoration

The decoration is painted directly onto the bulwark screens and is largely in original condition and consists mainly of foliage and trophies of war, and carved and gold-painted decoration on figurehead, quarter, and open stern galleries. The taffrail has a large eagle resting on a crown with its wings spread above the monogram 'GR'. It is supported by winged putti either side, with a scaled dolphin leading down the bracket, and connecting with the screen of the open stern gallery below. The turned wooden balusters on the open stern gallery are painted gold on a red ground to match to cabin bulkheads inside.

Fourth Rate, 50 guns (*c.*1725)

NMM NUMBER: SLR0431

SCALE: 1:48

DATE MADE: *c.*1725

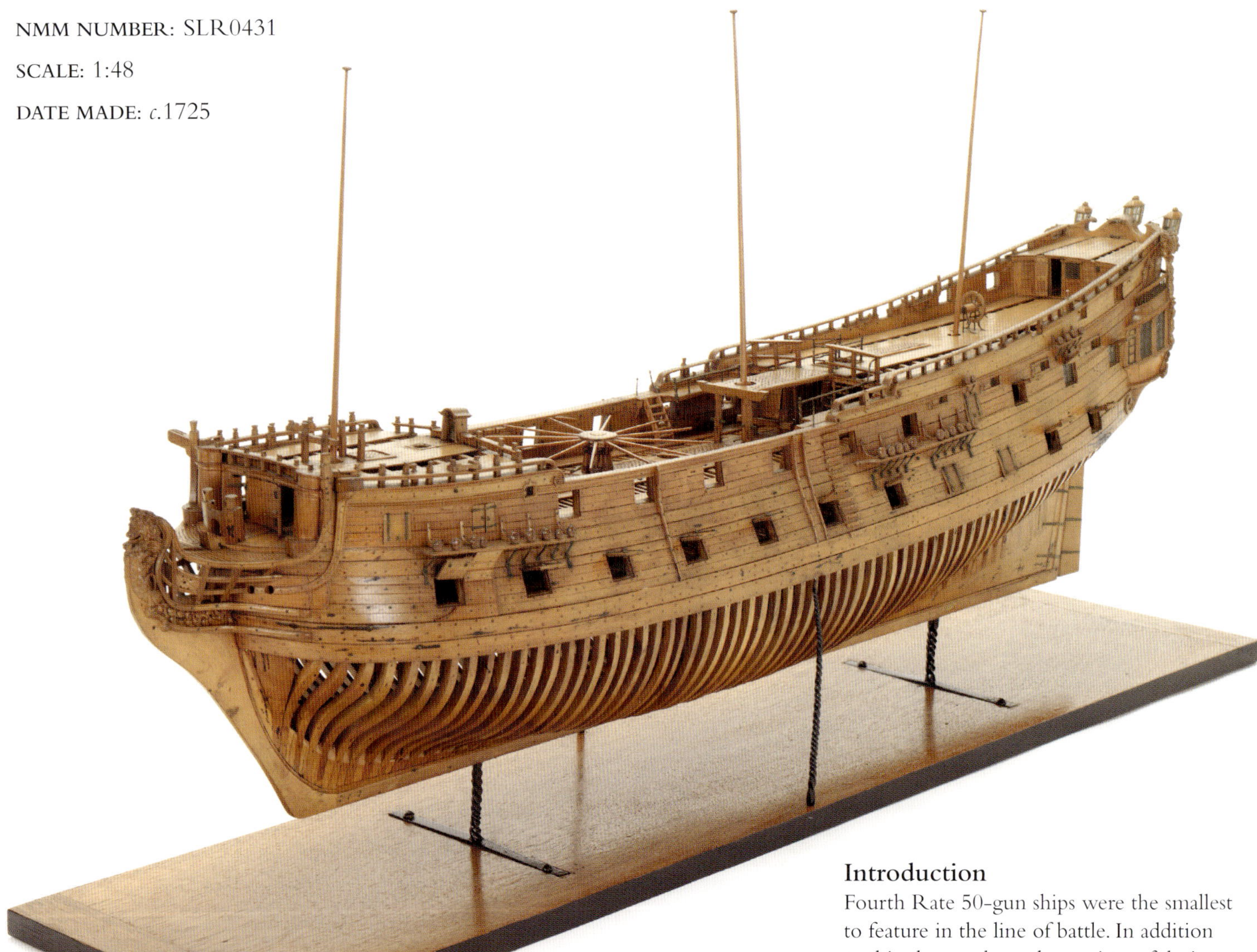

Introduction

Fourth Rate 50-gun ships were the smallest to feature in the line of battle. In addition to this, they undertook a variety of duties, including escorting and protecting the merchant fleets, as well as remaining on a station or patrolling large areas to protect British interests around the world.

Dimensions	Model (scaled up)	Fourth Rate 50-gun, 1719 Establishment
Length of Gun Deck	136ft	134ft
Breadth	36ft	36ft
Number of Guns	50	50
Length of Keel	120ft (touch)	109ft 8in (for tonnage)
Depth (of hold)	16ft	15ft 2in
Tons (burden)	789	756

Identification

Although the beam is correct for the 1719 Establishment, the length of the gun deck is 2ft in excess.

Provenance

Purchased by Sir James Caird from Montague Marcussen Ltd, 98 Crawford Street, London W1, 1955.

Construction and Materials

A striking feature of this model is the representation of the single piece frames and the lack of the floors rising from the keel. The individual planking above the main wales has been applied and fastened with wooden treenails, albeit over-scaled. The whole model has been left in the natural wooden finish with a protective layer of varnish and no evidence of paint. This rather unusual finish would suggest that the model was made in one of the many private dockyards, where a large number of these Forth Rates were built. This suggestion is further strengthened by the unusual choice of beech wood for construction rather than the standard fruitwoods and box. The other prominent feature is a, rather unusually, frequent use of brass for a number of fittings and decorative features, such as the 'barley twist' in the rails for the companionways and architectural structures for stern.

Fixtures and Fittings

A prominent feature seen at the break of the forecastle is the ornamented belfry, in which was hung the ship's bell. It is turned in brass and fitted with a knotted bell rope. In the waist is the jeer capstan, of the drumhead type and fitted with ten wooden bars. The deck gratings are a mixture of punched with scored joints and the 'made-up' variety, set in jointed hatch combings. There is a single wheel mounted on brass spindles directly aft of the mizzen mast. Of particular note are the rare inclusion of launching poles, and also the complete set of stern lanterns mounted on brass supports on the taffrail. They are a fine example of craftsmanship with sharp joints, the finials on the roof for ventilation, as well as the glass panels overlaid with brass frames. The model is mounted on a two pairs of 'barley-twist' iron supports under the keel and amidships, all of which are secured to the original wooden baseboard.

Rigging

The hull is complete with a full set of wooden channels typical of the three-masted ship-rig. They are fitted with wooden deadeyes, supported by the metal strops and chainplates. It is also quite rare that the original launching poles have survived, since these can often become detached, as well as being susceptible to damage if the model was originally displayed in a case. There is no evidence to suggest that they were rigged with flags.

Decoration

The carved decoration on this model is of a very high-quality, sharp finish and depth, and only a light varnish finish has been applied. This allows a close inspection of the detailed design, which normally can be obscured by over-varnishing or layers of gold and other paints. At the bow is a beautifully carved example of the standard lion figurehead, complete with a decorated trailboard. This quality of craftsmanship is continued on the stern and quarter galleries. The taffrail consists of a pair of reclining putti, either side of a larger figure in Roman dress, with spear and shield, standing on a platform with trophies of arms on the upper counter. Either side of this figure are the lion and unicorn supporting coats of arms.

Centurion (1732), 60 guns

NMM NUMBER: SLR0227

SCALE: 1:48

DATE MADE: *c.*1729

Dimensions	Model (scaled up)	*Centurion* (1732)
Length of Gun Deck	151ft	144ft
Breadth	34ft (moulded)	40ft 1in (extreme)
Number of Guns	60–62	60
Length of Keel	125ft 6in (touch)	117ft 5in
Depth (of hold)		16ft 5in
Tons (burden)	847	1021

Introduction

This model of the Third Rate 60-gun ship *Centurion*, launched in 1732, is quite rare because it has the open frames painted below the waterline to emulate a Navy Board-style model. In most cases of this style of model, these solid blocks were normally painted white below the waterline. These models were a quick and robust way of producing a three-dimensional hull form, which could then be sent by the master shipwrights of the various yards to accompany their drawings to London for discussion by the Navy Board. In fact, it could be said that these block models were the real 'Navy Board models'! Although block models are not as elaborate as the plank-on-frame variety, they are still a valuable source of reference in terms of hull shape, colour scheme, layout of fittings and, in some cases, elaborate decoration.

Identification

The dimensions and gunport arrangement match closely with the original plan of *Centurion*. Even taking into account that the block model shows the moulded (to the outside of the frame), rather than extreme breadth (to the outside of the planking), the dimensions still work out slightly larger than those of the ship. It is possible that this model was originally the shipwright's block model of the *Centurion* produced for the ship's design in 1729 (see p.23). If this is true, it is likely that this model was upgraded to make it more visually appealing after the Navy Board had finished with it.

Provenance

Normally, block models were not sent back to the dockyard, but were initially kept at the Navy Office as 'a Record for the Board'.[13] It is possible that some were later dispersed into private hands. This model was given to Greenwich Hospital by Captain William Browell, a former lieutenant-governor there. Browell's father had been a midshipman aboard *Centurion* during Admiral George Anson's epic circumnavigation of the globe in 1740–44. Along with the rest of the Greenwich Hospital Collection, it has been on long-term loan to the National Maritime Museum since 1936.

Construction and Materials

It was once thought that that this model is made from the wood of the ship's davit, a large beam mounted on the forecastle for retrieving and stowing the anchors. However, this is highly unlikely – ship's davits were made of oak, and the model is made from a much finer-grained wood. To make a bread-and-butter model, the shipwright would first design the ship on

paper in the form of a lines plan. Next, a series of horizontal layers of wood (called 'lifts') were cut to shape, determined by the waterline shape of the hull at different heights above the keel taken from the lines plan. These lifts were then glued together one on top of the other and, finally, this 'stepped' model was then planed and sanded, with reference to the lines plan, to produce a fair hull shape.

Fixtures and Fittings

Apart from the head rails and catheads for the anchor at the bow, the model is devoid of most physical fittings, but it is painted with numerous fittings and details. A painted *trompe l'œil*, or optical illusion, shows gunport lids either open or partly open; channels for all three masts are shown with their deadeyes; and stern and quarter gallery balusters are all rendered realistically in paint.

Decoration

Compared to most block models, this one is quite elaborately decorated to mimic the Navy Board style. The model has elaborate frieze work of trophies of arms painted along the bulwarks. At the bow, the typical Royal Navy figurehead is painted, rather than carved. On the stern, a central male bust is flanked by flags and arms, and further male figures are painted carefully to mimic the usual carved work.

Two-decker, 60 guns (*c.*1734)

NMM NUMBER: SLR0436

SCALE: 1:48

DATE MADE: *c.*1734

Dimensions	Model (scaled up)	*Nueva España* (1734)
Length of Gun Deck	142ft	140ft
Breadth	40ft	40ft
Number of Guns	60	60
Length of Keel	128ft (touch)	
Depth (of hold)	16ft	
Tons (burden)	1004	950

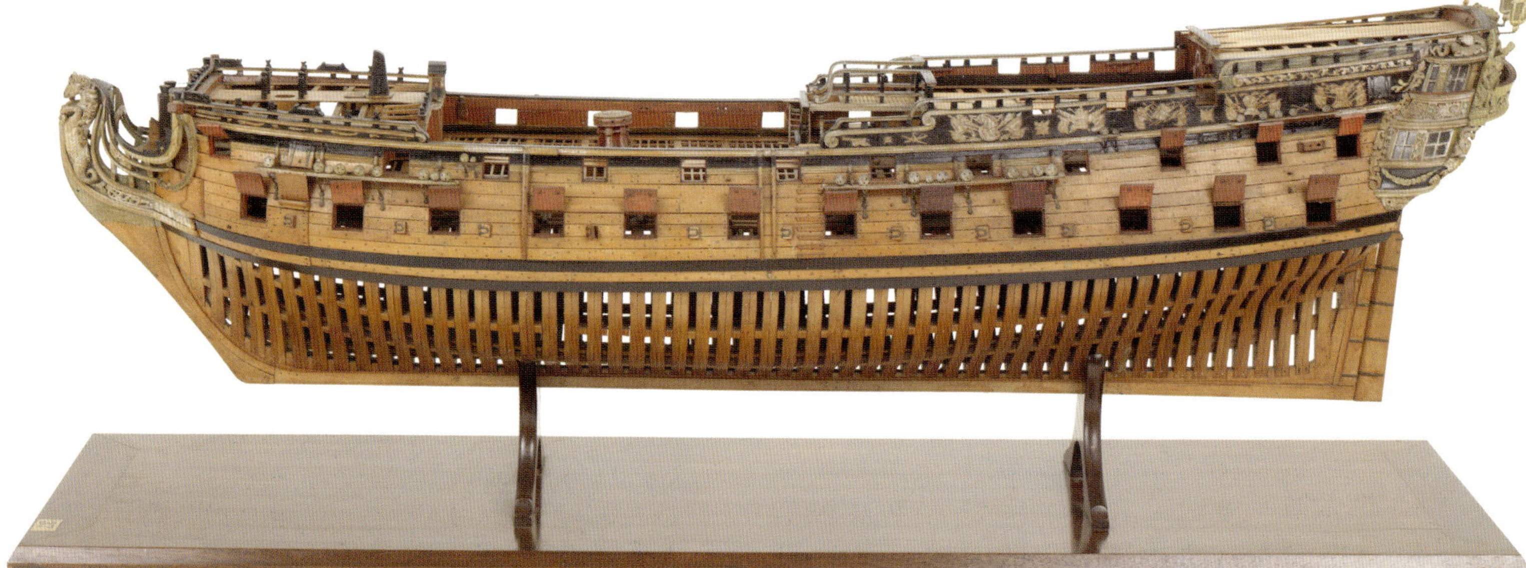

Introduction
The date and nationality of this model of a 60-gun two-decker ship are both uncertain. The method of construction and the finish are unlike any other British models. Oar ports would not be found on a British ship of this size and the decoration is somewhat different.

Identification
Although similar in size to the British 60-gun ships of the 1719 Establishment, owing to the inclusion of an eagle and snake carving, a symbol of Mexico, it has been tentatively identified as the Spanish 60-gun *Nueva España*, built at Havana, Cuba, around 1734, and which roughly matches the dimensions.

Provenance
Mercury Collection.

Construction and Materials
The framing, although stylised, is made up of a pair of floors, futtocks, and top timbers. This bears a very close resemblance to existing surviving eighteenth-century Spanish ship models at the Museo Naval in Madrid.[13] Above the main wale, the planking is made up of individual strakes secured by treenails. The keel is made up in four sections.

Fixtures and Fittings
The model is partially decked and fitted with capstan, belfry with bell, a galley chimney can be seen on the foredeck, and a wheel is fitted on the quarter deck. At the stern, three hexagonal stern lanterns are fitted. Between the gunports, small oar ports are included, which would have allowed the ship to be propelled with long oars called sweeps during calm weather.

Rigging
Along the sides, channels, chainplates, and deadeyes are fitted for three masts. Gunport lids are shown painted red on the inside, but are absent in the waist of the ship on the upper decks.

Decoration
At the stern, in the centre of the taffrail, is a carved eagle clutching a snake supported on either side by winged putti.

It is probable that this represents an Aztec legend, according to which the gods told the people to found a city where an eagle, eating a snake, was perched on a prickly pear cactus. After finding such a bird in 1325, the city of Tenochtitlan was founded, which later became Mexico City after being conquered by the Spanish in 1521. The eagle and snake continued to be used as a symbol of Mexico throughout the Spanish colonial period (1521–1821) before being adopted as the coat of arms of a newly independent Mexico in 1821. South America, and in particular the Aztec Empire of Mexico, had been a source of much of Spain's wealth for over 300 years via their famous 'treasure fleets', and much of the Spanish navy had been devoted to protecting this convoy system. The inclusion of the eagle and the snake supports the idea that the model represents a Spanish ship and, in particular, one launched in an Americas port such as Havana, which was a major Spanish dockyard. The quarter figures, carved in high relief, depict warriors in classical dress with shields and spears, above which are finely carved dragons with forked tongues. Along the bulwarks are finely carved low-relief trophies of arms on a black background. At the bow, the carved figurehead depicts a mythical sea horse, with a horse's head and the scaled lower body of a fish.

In Focus: Medical Technology – X-ray, CT Scanning and Endoscopy

Introduction

Advances in medical technology have had unintended positive consequences on the study of ship models. X-ray, endoscopy and CT scanning each have their unique role to play in broadening our understanding of the complex construction of these models. The benefit of these procedures is that they are mainly a non-invasive way of seeing inside a model that would otherwise be a closed world to curators, conservators and researchers. The result of exploring the models from the 'inside out' includes a better understanding of the sequence of assembly, the fastening methods and materials used, and the different types and layers of wood used. In most cases, these woods are still in their natural state without staining or other finishes. Overall, the results produced by this range of medical equipment provide an important insight into these models, which can support or add to our knowledge from written or illustrative sources.

X-ray

X-raying a ship model shows it in a more 'transparent' form. It can be used to reveal the grains of the woods used in the model construction, as well as to highlight the different types of fastenings, such as brass pins or wooden pegs (treenails). The X-ray also gives an insight into the glues used to hold the complex framework together, as well as the ghostly outline of deck beams and other more substantial structures inside the model. For ships of the later periods, such as 'Georgian' models, the X-ray can also show where fittings have become loose, for whatever reason, and are now hidden in the model. However, X-rays also have their limitations. For example, they create a 2D image of a 3D object and require knowledge of the layout, construction, and fitting of ship models to tease the results out from the images.

Endoscopy

Video and digital recording has revolutionised the study of the inside of ship models. The borescope and flexible endoscope are hand-held optical devices which allow a close examination of the models' internal structure that, recorded, can be studied in more detail to help understand how a model was made and the techniques and materials used.

These two pieces of equipment have revealed an amazing breadth of detail about the models. For instance, there are clues about the craftsmanship from the surviving pencil marks on the frames and the underside of the decks. Moreover, on some models there are numerous tool marks left by saws, scrapers, and chisels, a feature removed from the external finished surfaces. In some cases, these marks, coupled with glue and paint runs, throw light on the sequence of construction.

In a couple of cases, there is evidence that the model was modified, either during, or slightly after, construction. A good example of this is the *Royal Oak* (SLR0230), in which a pair of gunports close to the quarter galleries have been filled in and are now hidden from view by the external finishes. Similarly, the results

RIGHT

Of interest in this example is the remarkable amount of detail hidden by the external coatings. The multitude of small white dots indicates conservation as a result of damage by woodworm. (SLR0217)

BELOW

Model being examined using a flexible endoscope with viewing screen. (SLR0453)

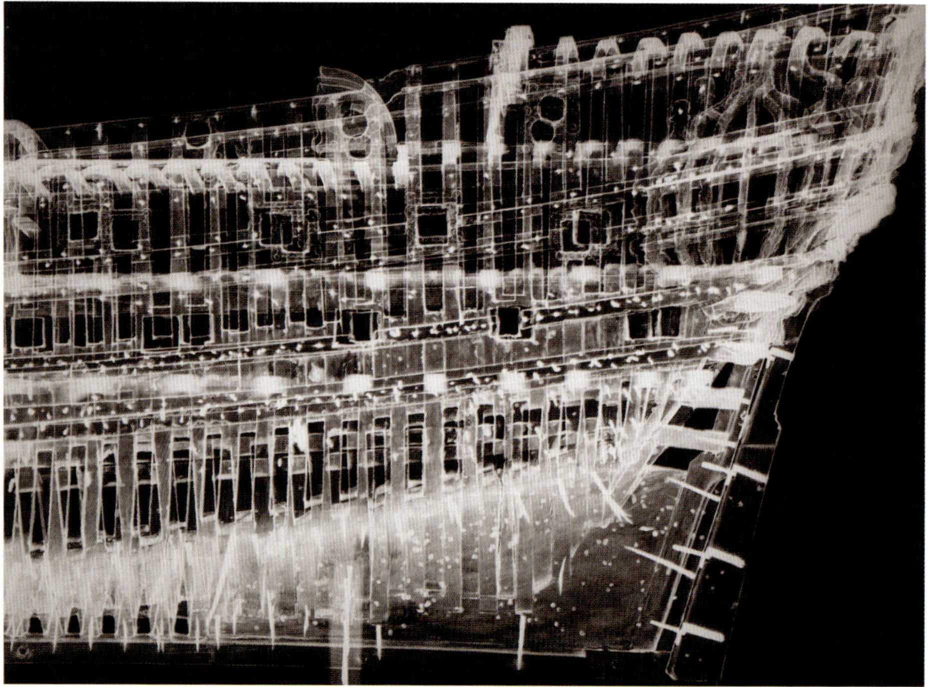

can show later restoration or alteration work, which has been hidden by the external finish. Further research into this will hopefully reveal interesting facts about why the model was altered and what restoration work had been done.

In addition to gaining a better understanding of the physical model, there have been occasional exciting discoveries within the model that help us understand who made the models. Unlike paintings, which are generally signed and dated by the artist, information on specific model makers is very rare, so the discovery of signatures or hidden notes from model makers is very significant. These have been found on the undersides of decking, or the notes are loose or pinned to the inside of the hull. This has now opened up fresh avenues of research on the social history of these craftsmen.

The exploration of the model interiors has revealed a level of craftsmanship that is unexpected. For instance, in some cases, despite being hidden from view, there can be a significant amount of internal fixtures and fittings that show a high level of detail. This does raise questions about why the model maker would spend so much time on well-crafted details in areas of the ship that would not be seen by people viewing the model. What it does reveal is skill and eye for detail, whether it was visible or invisible on the model. Examples of this include the rigging for a proposed steering arrangement, and the miniature paintings in the stern cabin of an unnamed 90-gun ship (SLR0386).

CT scanner

The shared use of a medical CT (computed tomography) scanner, which combines multiple X-ray images taken at different angles to create a three-dimensional image, has taken the understanding of these models to another level. The two main advantages of this system are that it is completely non-invasive and it creates a three-dimensional digital reconstruction of the model that can be manipulated in a variety of ways. However, because of the shape and size of the scanner, it is restricted to scanning unrigged models. By creating digital slices through the model, it generates extremely fine, multiple cross-sections that provide an amazing level of detail about the model's construction. These sections then can be built up to create the finished three-dimensional image.

In addition to learning about the model, the digital reconstruction has potential for other possible uses, including online and gallery display to help guide people through a model and create additional layers of interpretation. There is also the opportunity to recreate lines plans from the models to match against existing contemporary plans, exploring correlations between the plans and the models. These newly created plans would be of interest to current model makers, who want to make models of ships for which no lines plan survives.

TOP
Royal Oak (SLR0230), interior of the stern cabin on gun-deck level showing later modifications – indicated by the old blue paint, blocked up gunports, and quarter-gallery openings.

ABOVE
A handwritten note found glued to the hull underneath the gun deck on the model of the *Bellona*: 'Wm Thompson & Thos Burkett fecit – Chatham 1759'. (SLR0503)

BELOW
The Navy Board model of the 90-gun three-decked warship *c.*1703 (SLR0386) being scanned at the City University Hospital, London.

Royal Oak (1741), 70 guns

NMM NUMBER: SLR0230

SCALE: 1:48

DATE MADE: *c.*1741

Introduction

Apart from the newly introduced 80-gun ships of the 1690s, the 70-gun Third Rates remained the most prolific during the first half of the eighteenth century up until 1756 with the introduction of the new 74-gun ship.

Identification

The measurements of the model agree closely with the contemporary plans of the ship as rebuilt in 1741. However, there are a number of contradictory features which put the date of this model into question: in particular, the lack of two open stern galleries,

Dimensions	Model (scaled up)	*Royal Oak* (1741)
Length of Gun Deck	150ft 3in	151ft
Breadth	40ft 10in	43ft 5in
Number of Guns	70	70
Length of Keel	128ft (touch)	122ft 2in
Depth (of hold)	16ft 8in	17ft 9in
Tons (burden)	1117	1223

a common practice up until the 1730s. It is clear from internal examination that the model has been modified at a later date (see below).

Provenance

The model is said to have been passed from the Navy Board and/or from King George II to Prince Frederick, Duke of York and Albany (1763–1827).[14] It was subsequently purchased by Mr Andrew Wadell of Restalrig, Edinburgh, at the sale of the duke's effects in London. In 1853, it was presented to John Smith of Trinity House, Leith, remaining there until 1974, when it was purchased by the NMM at auction from Christie's, London.

Construction and Materials

The hull is largely constructed from boxwood, with the planking above the main wales and on deck fashioned from large pieces of veneer with the plank lines and butt joints scored on. They have been attached with a mixture of brass pins and wooden treenails, as well as a number of fastenings stamped on. Both close examination externally, as well as internal inspection with an endoscope, have revealed that the stern of this model has been modified. It was originally fitted with an open lower gallery and several smaller gunports near the quarter and stern galleries. This has now been glazed with two dummy windows at each side. A large amount of gold paint has been used to highlight the carved decoration and also cover the ornate and original metal crutches that support the hull. A thin, and now faint, waterline running from bow to stern has been scored and then marked on with white paint.

Fixtures and Fittings

The large wooden beam known as the fish davit is rigged across the forecastle deck (for explanation see SLR0454), while in the waist is the jeer capstan of the drumhead type, painted red and turned with rigging from the anchor handling

A close-up of the steering wheel with the original rope on the drum rigged. It is mounted above the helmsman's companion, which would throw light to the deck below.

gear. There are also long, narrow gangways leading from both the poop and quarter decks for access between the decks, as well as the single central gangway enclosing the mainmast. Another rare and interesting feature is that the single wheel located just aft of the mizzen mast is rigged with an original steering rope through a glazed companion, which throws light to the deck below.

Rigging

Largely in original condition with some minor repairs to the running rigging carried out in 1974–75. Of particular interest is the wooden lantern fitted to the main top, which was used for signalling when in convoy with the rest of the fleet.

Decoration

The elaborately carved decoration at the bow, quarter galleries, and stern is covered in a layer of gold paint. There are numerous examples of oak leaves and acorns appearing, putting the identification of the model beyond doubt. The quarter pieces at the stern are figures of Neptune with a trident and Hercules holding a club. The taffrail includes a large central bust of Charles II, surrounded by oak leaves and acorns – referencing the story of the Boscobel Oak in which the future king hid to escape the Parliamentarian forces following the Battle of Worcester in 1651. At either side are winged trumpeting putti and two crowned medallions, one containing a monogram 'CR', and the other an Admiralty fouled anchor. The name 'Royal Oak' has been painted on paper and then glued to the lower gallery in the style and format of the order issued in 1772.

'*Medway*'s Longboat' (*c.*1742)

NMM NUMBER: SLR0329

SCALE: 1:48

DATE MADE: *c.*1742

Dimensions	Model (scaled up)	Georgian model longboat (SLR0330)
Length (stem to stern)	28ft	28ft
Breadth	8ft	8ft
Length of Keel	27ft 6in	27ft 6in
Depth (of hold)	2ft 6in	2ft 6in

Introduction

The longboat was the heavy work boat used by most of the warships during the seventeenth and eighteenth centuries. Depending upon its size, it was either towed astern or stowed in the waist on the spare topmasts and chocks held up from the deck by the forecastle bulkhead and stag horns.

Identification

This model, together with a fully-rigged example (SLR0330), are said to have been made (or are part of a group) along with the contemporary Georgian-style model of the 60-gun ship *Medway* (SLR0328), launched in 1742. As such, it has historically been known as the '*Medway*'s longboat'. The dimensions and layout fit the known designs for this craft of the period and as part of a suite of boats carried by this class of ship.

Provenance

Acquired from the Royal United Services Museum, 1963, together with the fully rigged longboat and fully rigged model of the *Medway* itself.

Construction and Materials

A well-crafted model made entirely from boxwood. While having aspects of the Navy Board style, strictly speaking, the framing of this model depicts the construction accurately rather than stylised. The top three strakes of planking are attached clinker-fashion to the frames

(SLR0330)

with minute fastenings, too small to tell if made of brass or wood. The remaining joints along the keel, which is scarphed, and frames are fastened with brass pins and glued. A number of fittings such as the tiller, gudgeons and pintles, bowsprit clamp, mast clamp, and belaying pins are made in brass. The hull is varnished overall, except for the gunwale capping seating in the stern, which is finished in red. It is mounted on a pair of turned wooden pillars and inlaid baseboard with stylised square feet.

Fixtures and Fittings

The windlass amidships is removable via a pair of slotted cheeks inboard. It was used for towing and working the ship's anchors and cables. The central thwart is fitted with mast clamp and belaying pins, whilst the stem head has a brass ring for securing a running bowsprit. The three layers of clinker planking below the gunwale are secured to the frames with small brass pins. Inboard, there is a set of floorboards resting on the keel and frames, whilst a pair of metal rollers on the portside of the stem head and on top of the transom allowed the use of ropes over the side without chafing, especially when working the anchors.

Rigging

Even though most of the fittings are present, the model is not rigged. It consisted of a single-masted cutter with a running bowsprit through the bow as can be seen on its Georgian counterpart.

Decoration

There is a foliage decoration painted directly on the blue ground of the rubbing strake which has been enlarged on the transom.

Yarmouth (1745), 70 guns

NMM NUMBER: SLR0454

SCALE: 1:60

DATE MADE: *c.*1745

Dimensions	Model (scaled up)	*Yarmouth* (1745)
Length of Gun Deck	161ft 10in	160ft
Breadth	43ft 10in	44ft 3in
Number of Guns	70	64
Length of Keel	135ft 6in (touch))	135ft 6in
Depth (of hold)	16ft 9in	18ft 11in
Tons (burden)	1384	1355

Introduction

Apart from the newly introduced 80-gun ships of the 1690s, the 70-gun Third Rates remained the most prolific during the first half of the eighteenth century, up until 1756 with the introduction of the new 74-gun ship.

Identification

In the past, the dating of this model has ranged from before 1730, owing to the open wales, and after 1745, as the dimensions are greater than the 1745 Establishment. However, this is contradicted by the absence of side gangways in the waist and the position of the channels below the upper deck gunports, all of which were pre-1745. The dimensions and layout of the model compared against the draught of the ship agree almost exactly. Added to this, the coat of arms in the centre of the taffrail are of the town of Great Yarmouth in Norfolk, which puts the identification of this model beyond any doubt.

Provenance

Caird Collection, 1945.

Construction and Materials

The hull is constructed in the traditional method, with the form and dimensions

agreeing perfectly with the draught of the *Yarmouth* dated 1745. Internally, there are square deck pillars fitted to every other deck beam in the hold and set on top of the keelson. All of the guns are turned in brass, and are complete with bone tompions and mounted on wooden and wheeled carriages. A number of the architectural-type features such as the balusters and pilasters are made from bone, as well as a number of internal fittings, such as the deck pillars and spokes on the ship's wheel.

Fixtures and Fittings

This model is one of the few where the large wooden fish davit is rigged horizontally across the forecastle. The inboard end is located in a large square metal ring on deck, known as a span shackle, with the outer end rigged with a large single block for raising and lowering the lower part of the anchor, whilst the large ring above the wooden stock is hooked on the cat block rigged to the catheads. The black conical-shaped float is stowed in the shrouds with a line rigged to the anchors and is used to indicate the position on the seabed. The whole model is mounted on a pair of turned metal pillars, together with two metal rods amidships, all of which are secured to the original veneered wooden baseboard.

Rigging

Largely original standing, but a fair proportion of the running rigging has been repaired or replaced. There is also a wooden lantern fitted to the main top, which was used for signalling when in convoy with the rest of the fleet.

Decoration

There is a very finely carved lion figurehead with a trailboard on the bow. The decoration along the bulwark screens is painted onto paper, then applied onto the model, and consists of a mixture of figures in water with a variety of animals and foliage. The stern is a particularly fine example of miniature carving, with the coat of arms of *Yarmouth* placed centrally on the taffrail, and supported either side by a large triton blowing a conch shell (see page 48). Both the upper open and lower enclosed galleries' structural features are picked out in bone with the lights (windows) fitted with wooden frames over thin sheets of glass. The upper counter is painted in the same theme as the bulwarks, whilst the lower counter has the drapes tied with tasselled ropes on a blue ground.

Fourth Rate, 50 guns (*c.*1747)

NMM NUMBER: SLR0479

SCALE: 1:48

DATE MADE: *c.*1747

Dimensions	Model (scaled up)	*Assistance* (1747), *Tavistock* (1747) and *Greenwich* (1748)
Length of Gun Deck	144ft	144ft
Breadth	41ft	41ft
Number of Guns	50	50
Length of Keel	123ft (touch)	117ft 8½in
Depth (of hold)	20	17ft 8in
Tons (burden)	1068	1068

Introduction

In terms of style and constructional details, this model of a 50-gun ship bears a very close resemblance to the NMM's model of the East Indiaman *Somerset* (SLR0452), launched about 1738.

Identification

The dimensions of the model agree with the 50-gun ships of the 1745 Establishment. In fact, there are a number of plans in the museum that suggest it may represent one of three ships, the *Assistance*, *Tavistock*, and *Greenwich*. Of these ships, only four were built in the Royal Dockyards, with the remainder built to contract in the private yards. This, together with the execution and rather rustic finish, which is not to the same standard as the Royal Dockyards, would also suggest that this model was made in one of the private yards, as was the *Somerset*.

Provenance

Mercury Collection. Caird Collection, 1934.

Construction and Materials

The hull and deck planks are made individually and pinned to the beams and frames with wooden treenails. The frames themselves would appear to be made from a large-grained softwood, such as pine. The model includes two planks below the main wale and some more from the garboard strake up. The hull has been repainted and varnished in the past, as well as the roughly applied red paint inboard. The gudgeons and pintles on the stern post supporting the rudder have been made from lead and show signs of past oxidation, which has now been stabilised.

1:48 scale model of the *Somerset*, an East Indiaman launched about 1738. Although it has many similarities to SLR0479, this model differs from the Navy Board style with framing that accurately represents construction, rather than stylised. (SLR0452)

CURATOR
Regd. No. 1394
SHIP OR SUBJECT Assistance
Press Mark Box 24
ADMIRALTY, WHITEHALL
ZA21653

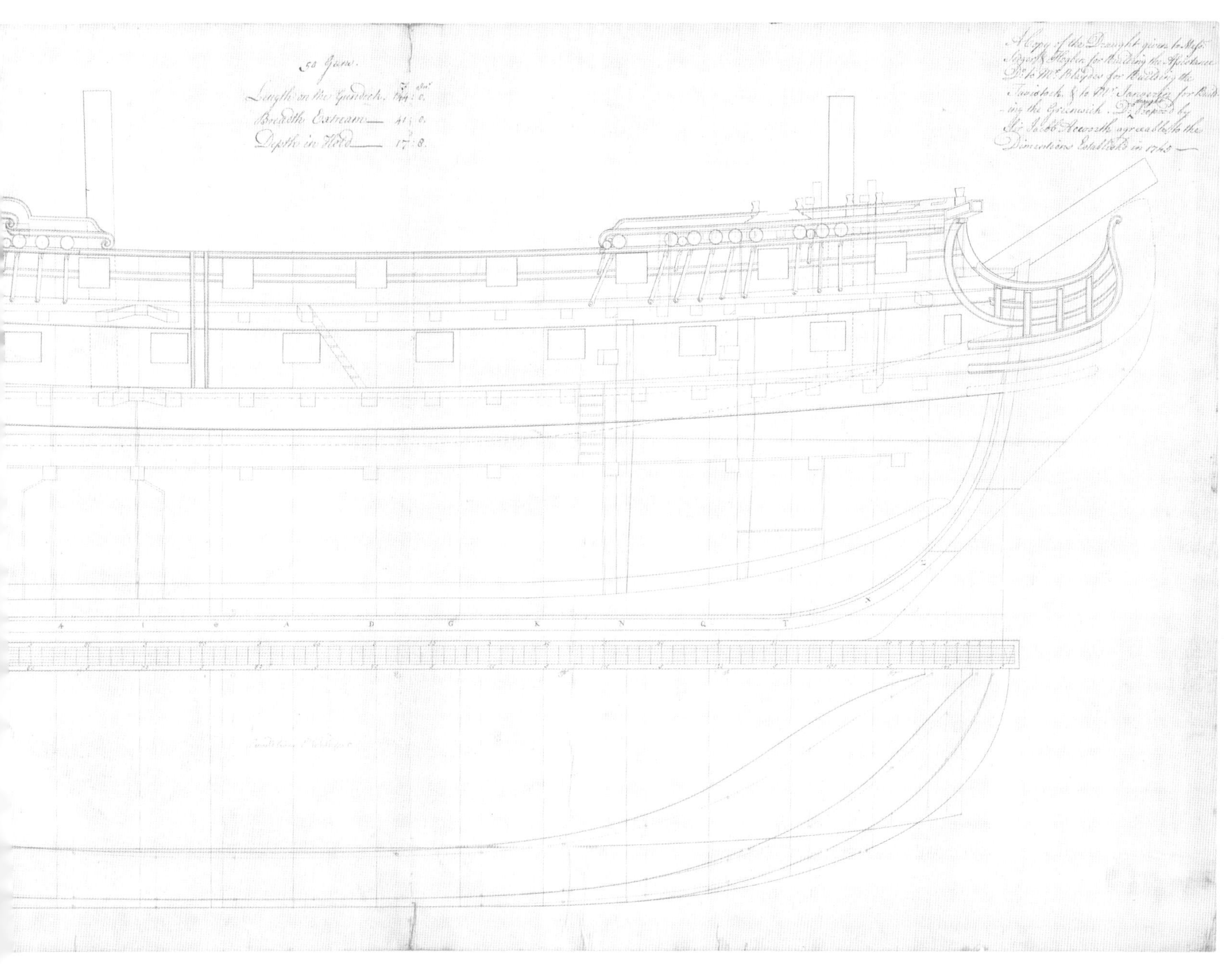

1:48 scale plan for *Assistance* (1747), *Greenwich* (1748), and *Tavistock* (1747), all 50-gun Fourth Rates. (ZAZ1653)

Fixtures and Fittings

Externally, the boarding steps are fitted together with wooden skids for handling both the ship's boats and barrels over the side. Of particular interest in the waist at the forecastle bulkhead is a wooden bench. It was used by the crew waiting for the food cooked in the galley and then taken aft for the officers in the stern. Just forward of the quarter deck is a large raised set of stag horns on which the spare topmast spars were stored, as well as the ship's longboat and cutters.

Rigging

The model is complete with the wooden channels, still located in the old position below the upper deck, with wooden deadeyes supported by metal strops and chainplates.

Decoration

The solid or block figurehead, which is part of a poor nineteenth-century restoration of the bow and later improved in 1944, is of a format in keeping with the existing contemporary plans, whereby a class of ship is represented rather than an individual. The bulwark friezes are painted black, as opposed to the decorative floral schemes found on most ships and models of this period. Inboard, nearly all of the vertical surfaces, including bulkheads, as well as most of the deck fittings, have been painted red. The stern and quarter galleries are quite plain, with minimal carved acanthus leaves around the extreme ends of the upper taffrail.

Barfleur, reduced to 80 guns (rebuilt 1755)

NMM NUMBER: SLR0453

SCALE: 1:48

DATE MADE: *c*.1755

Dimensions	Model (scaled up)	*Barfleur* (1755)
Length of Gun Deck	162ft	163ft
Breadth	45ft	47ft 3in
Number of Guns	80	80
Length of Keel	137ft 3in (touch)	131ft 9in
Depth (of hold)	19ft (approx.)	18ft 6in
Tons (burden)	1454	1565

Introduction

This model illustrates the development of the three-decked 80-gun ships from the 1690s through to the mid-eighteenth century with three complete decks of guns and a lightly armed quarter deck. The proportions of the high profile of the hull against the length would suggest that it would have problems of stability in certain weather conditions.

Identification

Even though the name 'Barfleur' has been painted on the counter, the dimensions of the model are far too small for the *Barfleur* launched in 1768. The measurements of the model suggest a date between the 1733 and 1741 Establishments. However, the layout of the gunports differs slightly, with the middle gun deck agreeing with both

Establishments; the upper and main gun deck are over-gunned by one on either side.

The dimensions are similar to the *Barfleur* launched in 1716 as a 90-gun Second Rate, which was then reduced to eighty guns in 1755. It is likely the model illustrates this *Barfleur* towards the end of her career, before being hulked in 1764. This is supported by the fact that the model includes a number of later features. It is likely that the name was painted on the model after an order introduced the practice on full-sized ships in 1772.

Provenance

Royal Naval Museum, and subsequently transferred in 1934.

Construction and Materials

A large amount of bone and some mother-of-pearl, inlaid on doors and bulkheads, have been used on this model to highlight certain features such as the entry ports decorated with turned bone spindles. A large proportion of the decorative as well as architectural features are also made from bone – in particular, the belfry, cabin window canopies, balustrades and pilasters around the stern galleries. The hull is of the standard framing with individual planks glued on, with no evidence of fastenings. The windows of the quarter and stern galleries are made from small pieces of glass, the frames of which are overlaid carved wood. A unique feature of this model is that the deck gratings are of the constructed and punched type, and consist of both wood and bone.

Fixtures and Fittings

The high quality and finish of this model includes a large amount of fittings. Of particular note is the double wheel of carved wood, fitted with bone spokes. It is mounted on a decorated and painted bone pair of spindles and located just forward of the mizzen mast on the quarter deck. The belfry has been beautifully constructed in wood with carved and bone inlaid panels. It has a turned brass bell with a working clapper and knotted bell rope. The rudder is hung on brass gudgeons and pintles, and

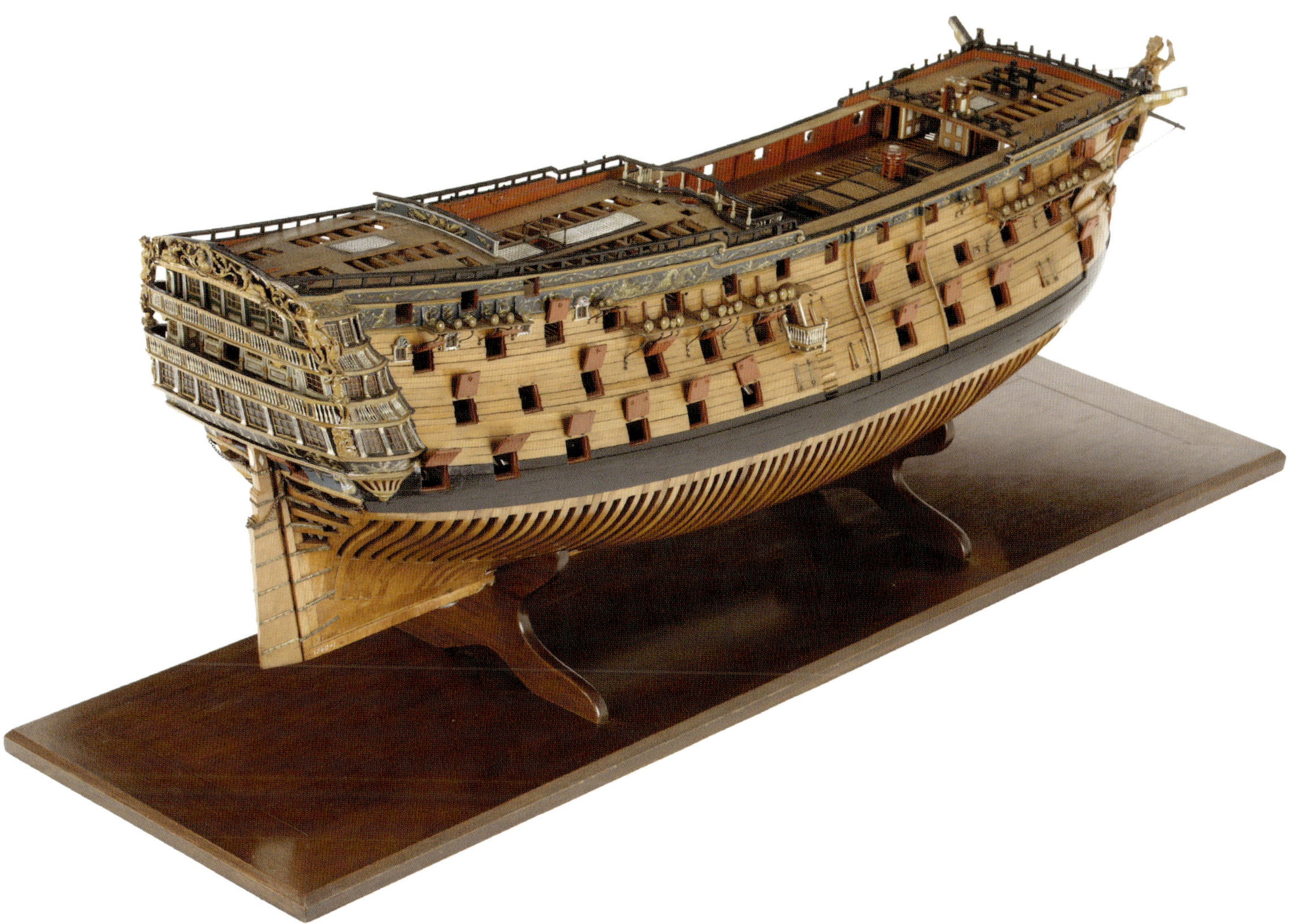

is complete with brass preventer chains fastened by ring bolts under the counter. Internally, there are two double capstans fitted, bilge pumps, riding bitts, and diagonal braces from the turn of the bilge to the deck beams of the lower gun deck. Again, there is a large amount of turned bone used for the spindles of the majority of the stairways, as well as the deck pillars on the quarter deck.

Rigging

There are three sets of wooden channels with turned wooden deadeyes, all supported with brass chainplates double-fastened to the hull. The fore and main channels, together with their stools, are mounted above the middle gun deck, whilst the mizzen channels are above the upper gun deck.

Decoration

The high quality and sharpness of the carved decoration is of particular note. The figurehead consists of a male figure in classical decorated armour with a flowing cloak, wearing a helmet with a plume of feathers on top, followed by a crouching, fire-breathing dragon on the trailboards either side. Carved decoration is left in its natural state with only a thin varnish finish. The bulwark friezes have been painted directly onto the hull and include a variety of water birds, fish, and foliage. On the starboard side is a caricature of Neptune in his seashell chariot being pulled by a pair of snorting hippocampi, surrounded by winged putti blowing horns and waving banners. The port side has a nude female in the same manner. The large quarter figures are of two women in classical dress with a staff and shields, the whole of which are supported with Hercules-like figures beneath. In the centre of the taffrail is a male bust with a helmet of a similar design to the type on the figurehead. It is surrounded by a pair of females in classical dress holding drapes of foliage. Both the poop and upper gun-deck stern cabins are decorated with inlaid parquetry floors and panelled bulkheads with bone and mother-of-pearl inlay.

Plymouth (*c.*1755)

NMM NUMBER: SLR0494

SCALE: 1:38.4

DATE MADE: *c.*1755

Dimensions	Model (scaled up)	*Plymouth* (1755)
Length of Gun Deck	65ft 6in	64ft 6in
Breadth	18ft 10in	18ft
Number of Guns	10	2 x 6pdrs
Length of Keel	53ft 7in (touch)	52ft 6in
Depth (of hold)	9ft 8in	10ft
Tons (burden)	102	89

Introduction

As opposed to the more well-known and recognisable Royal Yachts in use during the eighteenth century, there were a number of official yachts for the use of high-ranking naval officers and civil servants. This particular example was as the official yacht for the use of the Commissioners of Royal Dockyard Plymouth, to enable them to carry out their various duties, such as visiting other yards, attending meetings in London, and general survey work.

Identification

By careful measurements taken from the model and comparing these against the surviving contemporary ship's plans (see HIL0224 below, and NPD0741 and NPD0742 also in the NMM's collections) and known dimensions, it has been possible to positively identify this model as representing the yacht *Plymouth*, launched in 1755.

Provenance

By gift from Dr R.C. Anderson, 1949.

Construction and Materials

The hull frames are of the typical style with both the deck and hull planking comprising of a mixture of individually laid, as well as scored. Around the skylights of the main cabin bulkheads, and the quarter and stern galleries are a number of structural decorative features which have been made in bone, together with glass for the windows. Fittings in metal include the chainplates supporting the deadeyes on the channels, the capstan pawls, and the gudgeons and pintles for the rudder on the stern post. The poop decking, companionway at the break of the poop, and stump masts are modern replacements.

Fixtures and Fittings

A rather unusual feature shown here is the remains of three seats, with the upright back support now either missing or collapsible. They are located on the roof of the 'skylight', which throws light into the main cabin below, and they were presumably used by the passengers as a place to sit in favourable weather. There are two of these skylights located on bulkheads at either end of the cabin which have a detailed drawing on the original plans (HIL0224). Internally, the accommodation in the large cabin in the waist is fitted with two longitudinal screens denoting separate cabins around a larger central space. The stern cabins are complete with the standard chequered floor covering, which would have been painted canvas on the actual vessel.

Rigging

The model is complete with stump masts, and the presence and location of the channels indicate that it was rigged as a ketch. This rig, with the taller mainmast and smaller mizzen, was the preferred format for all official yachts during this period. The exceptions were the *Dorset* (1753) and the Royal Yacht *Royal Caroline* (1733), both of which had three-masted ship-rigs.

Decoration

As befitting a vessel of this status, the model also illustrates the ornate but measured amount of painted and carved decoration. Of particular note is the figurehead, which depicts the winged messenger Mercury mounted in an upright position holding a staff – caduceus – in his left hand. This may imply the symbolism associated with one of the many uses of these vessels such as the carrying of messages and communication. There is also an ornate trailboard just below the head rails adjoined to Mercury's feet and shows a winged dragon being chased by a scaled dolphin. The painted decoration along the bulwark friezes is the familiar trophies of war, foliage, and dolphins on a blue green ground. This style continues on and past the quarter and onto the stern galleries, with a larger counter decorated with tricoloured drapes and gold cordage. There is a male bust in the centre of the taffrail, with figures either side holding shields with heraldic carvings. Directly below this is a small, full male figure in classical dress, holding a sword and an oval-shaped shield. There are two large female quarter figures which support the taffrail and frame the stern galleries.

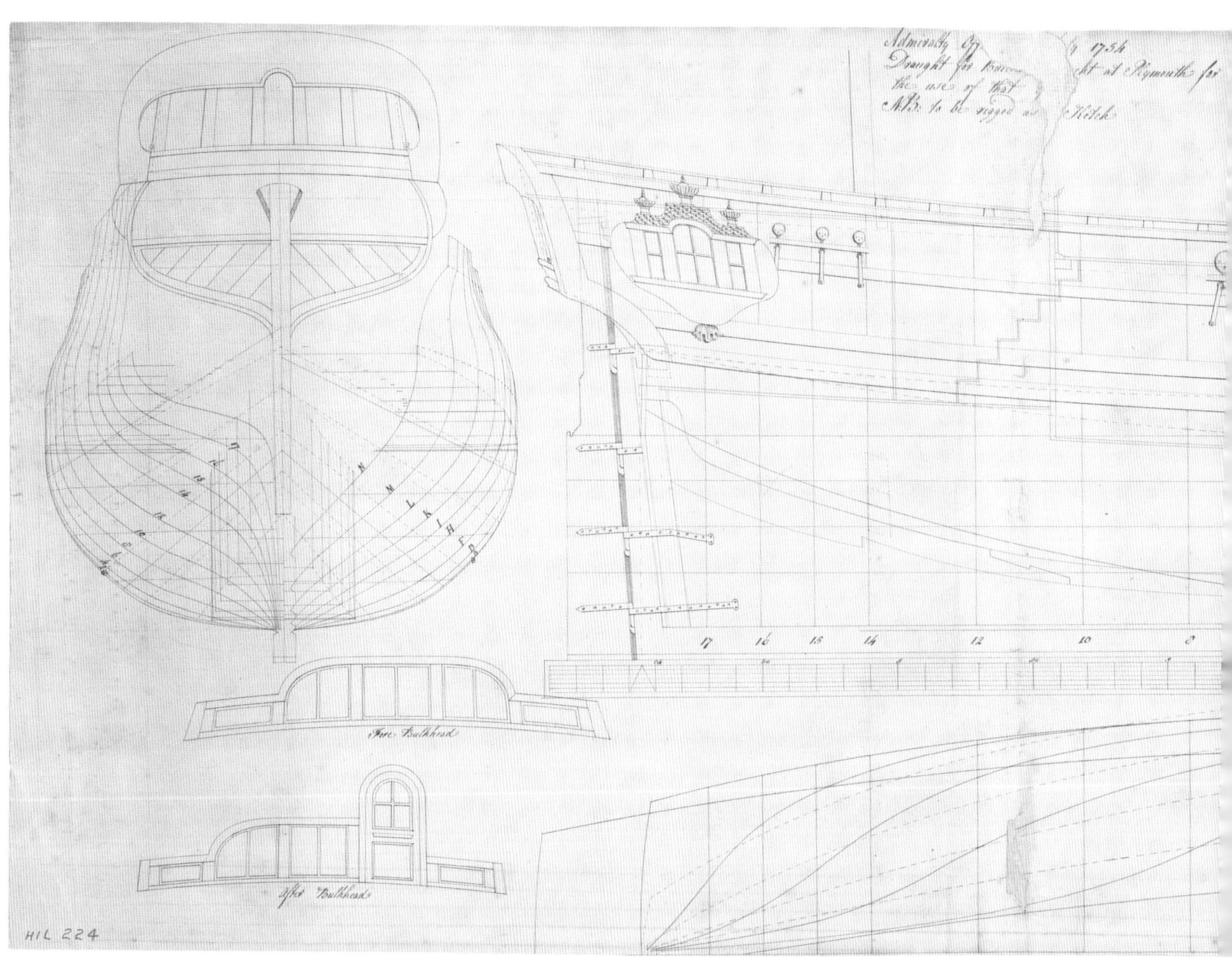
Fore Bulkhead
Aft Bulkhead
HIL 224

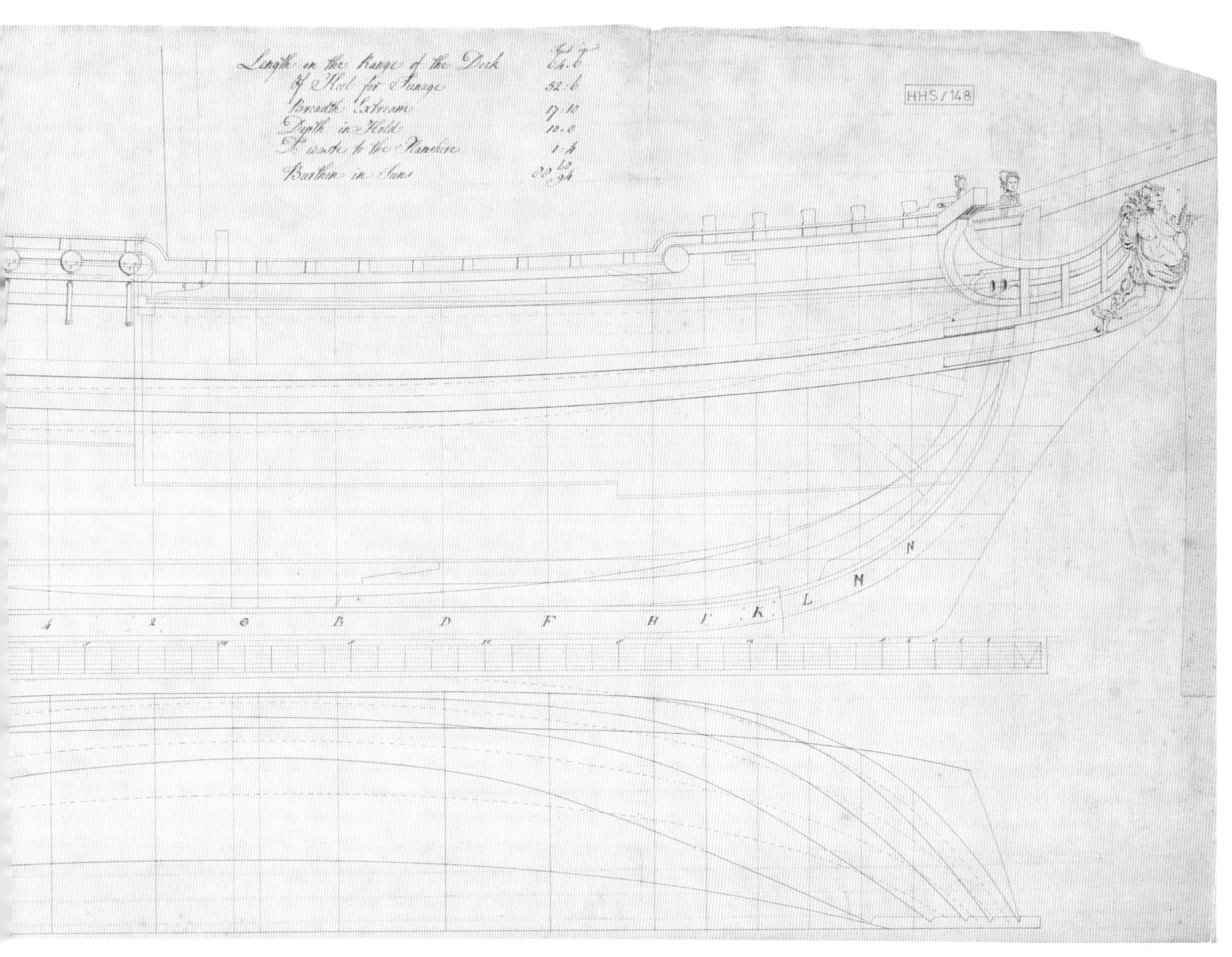

1:32 scale plan for the 64ft ketch-rigged Commissioner's Yacht *Plymouth* (1754) for use at Plymouth Dockyard, dated July 1754. (HIL0224)

Ajax (1767), Third Rate, 74 guns

NMM NUMBER: SLR0311

SCALE: 1:48

DATE MADE: *c.*1767

Dimensions	Model (scaled up)	*Ajax* (1767)
Length of Gun Deck	168ft	167 10in
Breadth	47ft	46ft 10in
Number of Guns	75	74
Length of Keel	136ft (touch)	138ft 9in
Depth (of hold)	20ft (approx.)	20ft 3in
Tons (burden)	1613	1615

Introduction

This model of the *Ajax* represents one of the many 74-gun Third Rates built during the latter half of the eighteenth century, which formed the backbone of the line of battle in most major actions under sail. This model illustrates the long quarter deck and forecastle and the comparatively short waist of the ship designed by Master Shipwright William Bateley.

Identification

There is a small cartouche with the name 'Ajax' painted on the stern counter. The model's dimensions also agree with the known dimensions of the actual ship.

Provenance

Caird Collection, 1933.

Construction and Materials

The framing is standard, except for the fact that the futtocks extend all the way down to the keel. This model is a very rare example of a type that has been constructed to split horizontally along the main wales at the lower gun deck, so as to reveal the complex internal construction and layout of the lower decks and hull. It is largely built of boxwood with a number of fittings in bone. Planking is individually laid over frames with very little deck planking on all decks, so as to show the construction throughout. The hull is complete with brass gunport hinges and metal chainplates fitted with wooden deadeyes.

The model includes some old-fashioned features, such as lack of gangways in the waist, and the style of the stern, which differs from the surviving plans of the *Ajax*. In particular, the plan (ZAZ0687) shows it with a full-width open stern gallery and the deck plans indicate the upper deck was enclosed for the guns, but no gangway provision on the bulwarks, which were not high enough (ZAZ1921 and ZAZ1922).

It is also complete with its original, ornate metal hull crutches and veneered

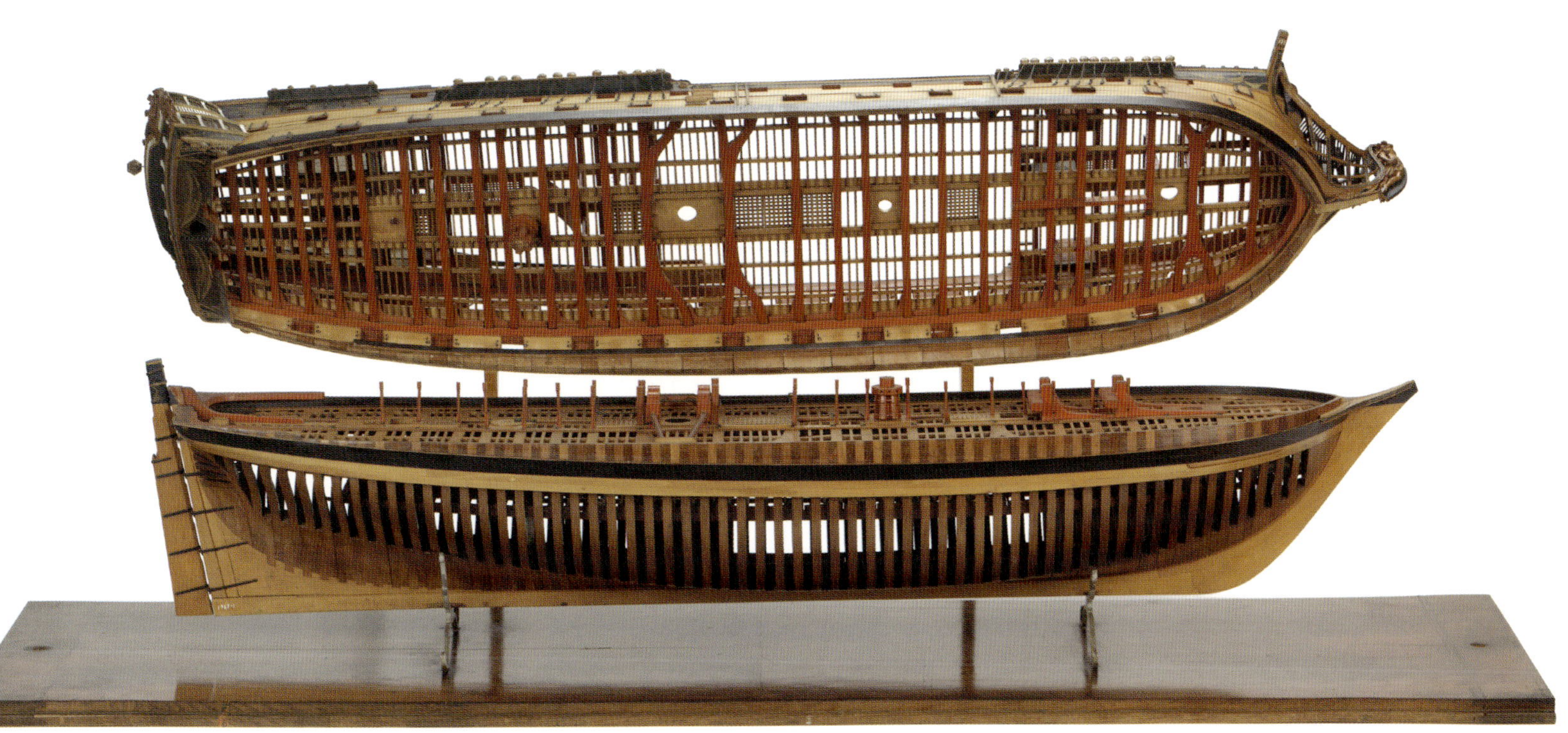

oak baseboard which has been designed to withdraw from a display case. The turned knobs for operating this are now missing.

Fixtures and Fittings

Because the model splits along the gun deck, it has highly detailed construction and fittings. All of the deck gratings are made up in the correct way and the forecastle is complete with galley stove and chimney. Below decks there are a number of cabins fitted throughout, whilst a detailed set of bilge pumps, together with the ventilated trunking, are located around the mainmast apertures. The glass windows are overlaid with metal and wood frames. The belfry is fitted with an original, turned bell with fixed clapper, mounted in a square, bone-pillared, wooden canopy.

Decoration

Even though the name appears on a small cartouche on the counter, it has been painted in a different style that probably predates the order of 1772, in which the size and style of the lettering was very precise. The figurehead is a carved figure of Ajax in classical dress. The frieze decoration along the bulwarks and around the stern has been painted directly onto the hull, and consists of a series of flora and fauna groupings, interspaced with classical human figures. Most of the architectural features on the stern galleries, such as pilasters, etc., have been carved in bone. The deck pillars, quarter-deck rails, and belfry canopy supports are also turned in bone. The taffrail has a pair of reclining female figures with a female bust centrally. Either side are a pair of lions adjoining the quarter carvings for the galleries with male figures in a classical dress supported by two putti.

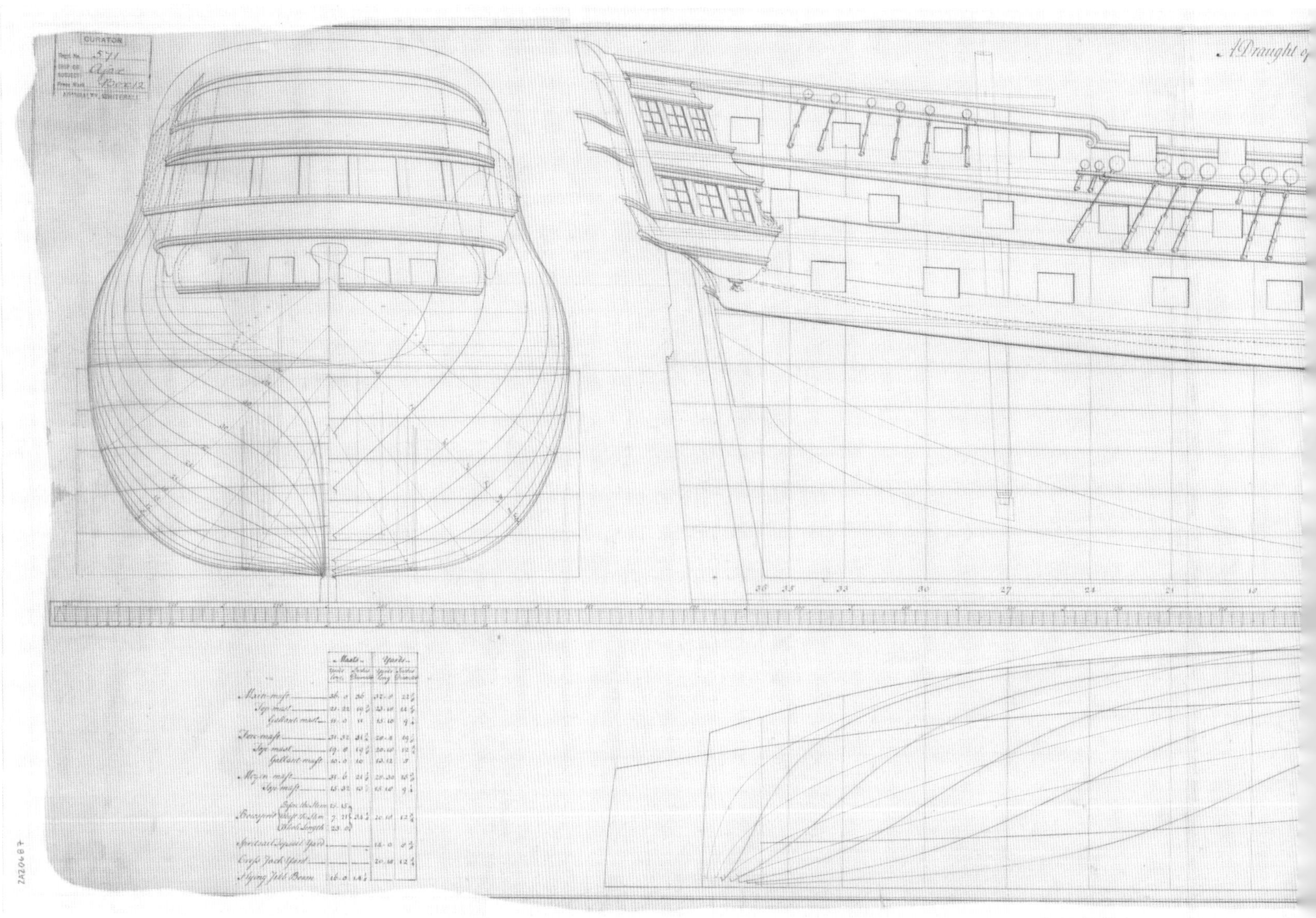
A Draught of
Masts
Yards
Main-mast
Fore-mast
Mizen-mast
Bowsprit
Flying Jibb Boom

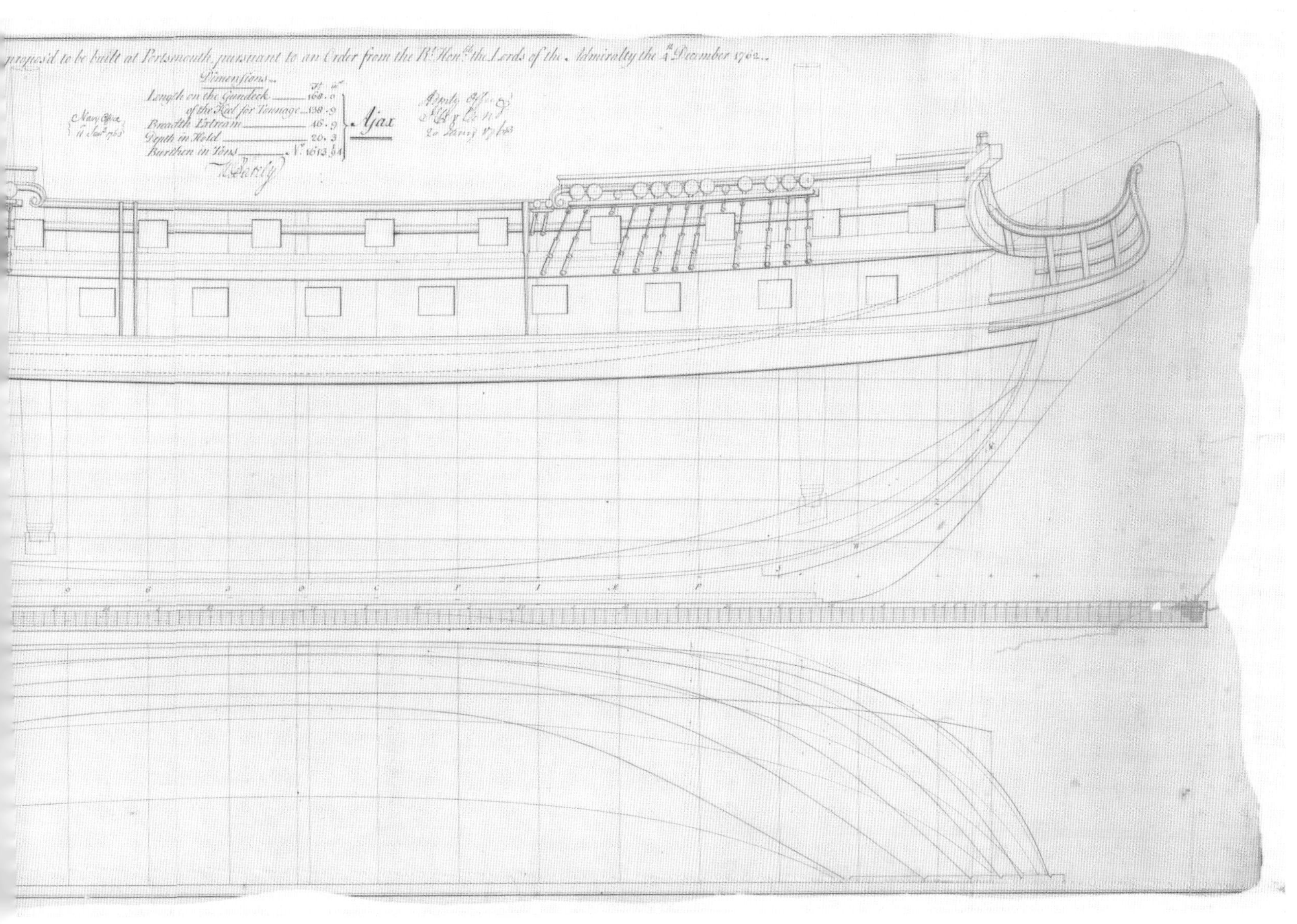

1:48 scale plan of *Ajax* (1767), dated to 11 January 1763. (ZAZ0687)

Third Rate, 64 guns (*c.*1775)

NMM NUMBER: SLR0313

SCALE: 1:48

DATE MADE: *c.*1775

Introduction

During the 1770s, the various confrontations would lead to the larger ships of the line becoming almost redundant, as most of the actions involved demanded smaller and faster ships to patrol the coast, protect commerce, and be able to land troops. These 64-gun ships were basically a cheaper version of the 74-gun Third Rates, and enjoyed some success during this period.

Identification

The measurements for this model closely agree with known dimensions of a group of contract-built Third Rate ships of 1782–85, such as the *Crown* built at Blackwall in the 1770s. However, these had slightly larger quarter decks and the channels for the mizzen mast were located higher, both of which indicate an earlier date. Measurements also match those of a class of Third Rates built about 1775 or slightly earlier.

Provenance

Presented by Dr R.C. Anderson, 1949.

Construction and Materials

The hull frames are constructed from the traditional lighter fruitwoods, together with the almost-black wood thought to be ebony. This wood has been used for the floor timbers, as well as the top timber below the main wale, and accentuates the light and dark contrast colours to show off the complex lines better, especially around the bow and stern. Of particular interest are the timbers around the bow, which are canted, a method of construction that proved stronger than the previous system of angled frames and filling pieces. The model is mounted on three turned wooden pillars along the keel, and supported by two metal rods amidships, all of which are secured to the original wooden baseboard.

Dimensions	Model (scaled up)	*Crown* (1782)
Length of Gun Deck	160ft	160ft
Breadth	44ft	44ft 7in
Number of Guns	64	64
Length of Keel	139ft (touch)	133ft 3in
Depth (of hold)	19ft 5in	19ft
Tons (burden)	1376	1409

Fixtures and Fittings

By this period, the quarter deck had been extended to just aft of the mainmast and the poop deck going beyond the mizzen mast. Notice also the gangways running between the quarter deck and forecastle, a feature that was later to increase in size, and eventually lead to a fully enclosed waist. Also, by this date, the decking on the models was becoming more rather than less of the earlier styles, especially when it was more common to include the guns mounted on wooden trucks for a model of this detail and size. The rudder is also fitted with preventer chains, which are made in brass. These prevented the rudder, if it became unshipped or damaged, from floating away, and thus rendering the ship vulnerable in bad weather or running onto rocks or ashore.

Rigging

The masts and spars are original, but the standing and running rigging is twentieth-century, added in 1930 and generally correct for the period. The long lateen yard rigged on the mizzen was still a prominent feature, but only the after portion was used. The fore and lower portion of this yard was later cut and 'jaws' were fitted to the remaining section to form a gaff. The luff or forward edge of the sail was then laced to the lower portion of the mizzen mast. Notice also that the fore and main course yards are fitted with stunsail booms which allowed a greater sail area to be set in fair weather.

Decoration

At the bow is the standard lion figurehead, which by this period had gone out of general use. The bulwark screens are painted directly onto the model and consist of a series of figures, animals, sea serpents, and mixed foliage, which continues round to the upper stern counter. Below this and around the rudder head are the familiar drapes painted red, secured with cord tassels on a blue ground. The quarter galleries include a pair of male and female figures in classical dress, with the remains of the lion and unicorn and putti on the taffrail.

Legacy of the Navy Board Ship Models

The legacy of the Navy Board models for ship model making cannot be overstated. Before the advent of Navy Board-style models, accurate scale models were rare and, in comparison, crude. However, by the late seventeenth century, Navy Board models elevated model making to a standard that amalgamated the beauty of a great work of art with the accuracy and detail of a technical record. They began to reflect a desire for a more technical understanding of the actual ship-building process, even if the construction of the model did not follow the same process exactly.

This tradition set a benchmark of quality and established many of the styles and construction features that were to continue with the more realistic 'Georgian' style, which followed from around the 1740s. Despite being superseded by the 'Georgian' model and then by the builders'-style models from the mid-nineteenth century, the Navy Board style was not completely abandoned, carrying on well beyond the eighteenth century. It is a recognised construction style that has been emulated in more recent times.

Academic interest in the Navy Board ship models in the early twentieth century was rekindled by Dr R.C. Anderson through regular publication in the Society for Nautical Research's (SNR) journal *Mariner's Mirror*. He had a deep interest in the seventeenth-century sailing navy – in particular the rigging aspect, which he must have developed further in his work on the Sergison collection. Publications about ship models continue today, including this one, with authors investigating many aspects of the model, its construction and history, and the history of the ship it represents.

In December 1922, the Cuckfield Park collection, previously owned by Pepys's successor Sir Charles Sergison, was sold to the wealthy American collector Colonel Henry Huddleston Rogers, now held at the US Naval Academy in Annapolis, Maryland. The loss of this highly important collection abroad further highlighted the need for a national museum dedicated to Britain's maritime heritage. It was this event together with the *Mercury* ship model collection potentially heading in the same direction that was to play a major influence on the subsequent founding of the National Maritime Museum in 1934. Thus the early twentieth century saw the models being elevated from being objects of desire for wealthy individuals to a status of national importance which deserved preservation for the public good. This is also true in other countries, where museums have important collections of Navy Board models, recognising their historic and technical significance.

As has been discussed earlier, the Navy Board models were known to be commissioned for rich patrons. This tradition of making models has continued today, with many model makers choosing to build high-quality ship models to order in a variety of styles, including the Navy Board. It seems that the aesthetic appreciation of this model style is still important for the client, and the technical aspects are perhaps relegated at its expense. The style has been emulated by a number of notable model makers over the twentieth century and a few of them are mentioned below to illustrate how the legacy of the models continues.

'Model Ship Builder' by Frederick William Elwell (1870–1958). It dates from *c.*1938 and shows Robert Spence in his studio, working on what is probably his model of the *Naseby* (SLR0001). On the left of the picture is another model of a two-decker, whilst there is a small model of a royal yacht on a table on the right. (Beverley Art Gallery)

Robert Spence (1871–1964)

One man who had a huge influence on both the understanding and appreciation of Navy Board models was Robert Spence. Born into a North Shields Quaker family in 1871, Spence later moved to London to become an artist. After serving in the First World War as an ambulance driver, Spence became well-known for his engravings depicting trench warfare. However, Spence can be counted among the few modern model makers who have worked in the Navy Board style in a way that truly rivals the quality of the original models.

Made in the 1940s, Spence's Navy Board-style models of the *Naseby* (SLR0001) and the *St Albans* (SLR0376) are of such high standard they have been included alongside the original models in this catalogue. Spence owned the original model of the *St Albans*, now at Trinity House, London, from which he made the copy in the National Maritime Museum (SLR0376). He also made a replacement model of the *Loyal London* for Trinity House, whose original model had been destroyed during the Blitz of the Second World War.

Aside from the main construction of the model, Spence's skill lay in his dexterity as a wood carver, which can be seen in the replacement stern carvings for the *St Michael* (SLR0002). Spence died in 1964 at the age of ninety-three, but his work remains as a testament to his skill as a model maker. In fact, one of the problems for the ship model researcher is the difficulty in spotting the difference between Spence's work and the seventeenth-century originals. For example, the markings, patination, and finish on the *Naseby* are very close to an original seventeenth century model.

Donald McNarry (1921–2010)

Another model maker heavily influenced by the style of the Navy Board models was Donald McNarry. Originally from London, McNarry worked as a freelance model maker from his home on the south coast of England, and regularly exhibited and won medals with his ship models at the annual Model Engineer competition between 1935 and 1953.

McNarry made a wide variety of ship models from the Ancient to the Modern period, but is perhaps best known for his Navy Board-style models. Working at a miniature scale ranging from 100ft to 16ft to the inch (1:1200 and 1:92), McNarry made numerous Navy Board-style models. He pioneered the method of producing the framed hulls at these small scales and his work was completed with an extraordinary level of detail, especially considering that some of his models measured only six inches long! He built over 350 models during his lifetime, fifty-eight of which were in the Navy Board style.

Donald McNarry at his work bench with his finished model of the Royal Yacht *Fubbs*. (Image courtesy of Michael Wall, American Marine Model Gallery, Inc., USA)

Philip Reed (born 1941)

Professional model maker Philip Reed was born in 1941 and latterly became a teacher in painting, ceramics and photography. Building models in his spare time and eventually professionally, he mentioned in his book *Building a Miniature Navy Board Model*:

> I would never have embarked on the building of a miniature Navy Board models had it not been for the inspiration received from the books and work by Donald McNarry. His models in general had a huge influence on me but it was particularly his miniature Navy Board work that had the greatest impact [...].[1]

In the foreword to Reed's book, written by Michael Wall, Director of the American Marine Model Gallery, the latter states:

> Among avid modellers there is a widely held consensus that the construction of a replica Navy Board style ship model is one of the most difficult endeavours that a modeller can undertake. I often call them the 'ship modeller's model'.

Model of the 55-gun *Prince Royal* (1610) made in the Navy Board style. (ZBA1462)

This is not surprising when the skills required to undertake such a daunting project include the woodworking of the complex hull structure, metal working, understanding and making up rigging, and the carved and painted decoration.

John Franklin (1930–2001)

John Franklin, a cabinet-maker by trade, was drawn to the Navy Board models by the quality of the craftsmanship. In his book *Navy Board Models*, Franklin highlighted many aspects of their construction and raised the profile of the Navy Board models, questioning many of the previously held assumptions about their construction and use. Published in 1989, Franklin's detailed book helped to ensure that the Navy Board style of model making continues today.

Basil Grenville Peter (1914–2007)

The open-framed construction of the Navy Board models has been used for modern models of historic ships. For example, a model of the 55-gun three-decker *Prince Royal* (1610), made by Basil Grenville Peter in 1991, has been constructed in a style that replicates the Navy Board style (see ZBA1462). Made entirely in wood, with some metal fittings, the 1:48 scale model has been left unplanked to show the stylised frames below the main wale. The upper works from just below the lower gun deck are planked and varnished.

Although no Navy Board-style models are known from 1610, it is a fitting celebration of the ship which was built by Phineas Pett. Decorative elements, mainly on a green ground with gold embellishments and an open stern gallery, are based on the fine contemporary painting of the *Prince* by the Dutch artist Adam Willaerts in the NMM collection (see BHC0266 and BHC0267).

Navy Board models around the world

The appreciation of Navy Board models mentioned above has spread worldwide thanks to some major collections of models being located overseas. The United States Naval Academy Museum in Annapolis, Maryland, has perhaps the best collection of Navy Board models outside Britain. Not only does it include one of the earliest rigged models in original condition, the *St George* of 1701, it also has a number of original late seventeenth-century display cases as well.

Navy Board models form an essential part of the collection presented to the Canadian nation by the late Lord Thomson of Fleet, and now forming the Thomson Collection at the Art Gallery of Ontario in Toronto. Thomson clearly had a passion for miniature carving and sculpture and it was not surprising that when on rare occasions these models came up for auction, he was often in the running for their acquisition.

By far the largest collection in private hands is owned by two brothers, Arnold and Henry Kriegstein in the United States of America. Between them they have amassed fourteen contemporary examples and have recently published an illustrated book on the provenance and in most cases identification of the models.[2]

The Russian Maritime Museum in St Petersburg holds Navy Board models that were taken back by Peter the Great when he returned to Russia after his stay studying shipbuilding in England in the late seventeenth century. The collection includes five English Navy Board models, as well as four models of Russian ships built in a similar style. The model made by Peter the Great himself in 1698, regarded as 'the most precious memorabilia of Russian naval history', was clearly influenced by the Navy Board style.[3]

Another legacy of the influence of both English shipbuilding and Navy Board models can be found in Scandinavia, where a model dated to around 1655 can be found at the Statens Sjöhistoriska Museum in Stockholm and the Danish Royal Yacht *Elefantan* at the Orlogsmuseet in Copenhagen. They are thought to have been made by English Master Shipwright Francis Sheldon when he went to work there in the late seventeenth century.

Surprisingly, a single English Navy Board model of a Third Rate dated to around 1684 is held at Vienna's Heeresgeschichtliches Museum in landlocked Austria, where the maritime collections span the period when Austria's borders stretched to the Mediterranean.

This global nature of the Navy Board models has only served to enrich the dedicated community of historians, model makers, conservators, and curators with an interest in ship models. A directory of Navy Board-style models can be found on pages 230–34.

Peter the Great exhibition, NMM 1998.

Directory of Navy Board Models Held Elsewhere

This directory includes models made in the Navy Board style, or those that have been influenced by the style. It is not comprehensive, as there may be other surviving models which have not been brought to our attention, but it shows the truly global appeal of these rare and important models. It is hoped that this book will stimulate further research into the whereabouts of surviving Navy Board models that can be brought to the attentions of scholars working in this field.

Location	Model	Year	Guns	Rate	Scale
US Naval Academy Museum, Annapolis, USA	*Portland* (No. 33)	1693	50	Fourth Rate	1:48
US Naval Academy Museum, Annwapolis, USA	Possibly *Crown* or *Dover* (No. 50)	*c.*1655	48–56	Fourth Rate	1:36
US Naval Academy Museum, Annapolis, USA	*Grafton* (No. 32)	1679	70	Third Rate	1:48
US Naval Academy Museum, Annapolis, USA	*Britannia* (No. 6)	1682–1701	100	First Rate	1:48
US Naval Academy Museum, Annapolis, USA	*St. George* (No. 1)	1701	90	Second Rate	1:49
US Naval Academy Museum, Annapolis, USA	Unidentified (No. 72)	1715–25	90	Second Rate	1:42.6
US Naval Academy Museum, Annapolis, USA	Unidentified (No. 107)	1650–54	56–58/ 60+	Third Rate	1:48 or 1:36
US Naval Academy Museum, Annapolis, USA	*Nell Gwyn* (proposal) (No. 4)	1676		Yacht	1:32
US Naval Academy Museum, Annapolis, USA	Unidentified (No. 9)	*c.*1695	50	Fourth Rate	1:48
US Naval Academy Museum, Annapolis, USA	Fleet Admiral's Barge (No. 3)	*c.*1695–1705			1:20

US Naval Academy Museum, Annapolis, USA	Advice Boat/Sloop (No. 2)	*c.*1695	10		1:48
US Naval Academy Museum, Annapolis, USA	Possibly *Sussex* (No. 8)	*c.*1693	80	Third Rate	1:48
US Naval Academy Museum, Annapolis, USA	Unidentified (No. 7)	*c.*1705	70	Third Rate	1:56/7
US Naval Academy Museum, Annapolis, USA	Unidentified (No. 5)	*c.*1705	60	Fourth Rate	1:52/3
U.S Naval Academy Museum, Annapolis, USA	*Greenwich* (No. 11)	1699	50	Fourth Rate	1:48
US Naval Academy Museum, Annapolis, USA	Prince *Frederick* (No. 88)	1715	70	Third Rate	1:48
US Naval Academy Museum, Annapolis, USA	Unidentified (No. 34)	*c.*1715	70	Third Rate	1:48
US Naval Academy Museum, Annapolis, USA	Unidentified (No. 21)	*c.*1725	20	Sixth Rate	1:48
US Naval Academy Museum, Annapolis, USA	*Royal William* (No. 39)	1719	100	First Rate	1:48
US Naval Academy Museum, Annapolis, USA	Unidentified (No. 15)	*c.*1690		Yacht	1:32(?)
US Naval Academy Museum, Annapolis, USA	Unidentified (No. 14)	*c.*1689–90	32	Fifth Rate	1:48
US Naval Academy Museum, Annapolis, USA	Unidentified (No. 13)	*c.*1705	24	Sixth Rate	1:44(?)
US Naval Academy Museum, Annapolis, USA	Unidentified (No. 12)	*c.*1705	60	Fourth Rate	1:48
The Kriegstein Collection, USA	*Coronation*	1685	90	Second Rate	1:51
The Kriegstein Collection, USA	*Royal James*	1671	90–94	First Rate	1:48
The Kriegstein Collection, USA	*Northumberland*	*c.*1702	70	Third Rate	1:48
The Kriegstein Collection, USA	Unidentified	*c.*1680	34	Fourth or Fifth Rate	1:48
The Kriegstein Collection, USA	*Lion*	1738	60	Fourth Rate	1:60
The Kriegstein Collection, USA	*Adventure*	1691	44	Fifth Rate	1:48

The Kriegstein Collection, USA	Unidentified	*c.*1695	40–44	Fourth Rate	1:48
The Kriegstein Collection, USA	*Marlborough*	1706	90	Second Rate	1:72
The Kriegstein Collection, USA	Unidentified	*c.*1710	62	Fourth Rate	1:64
The Kriegstein Collection, USA	Queen Anne Royal Barge	*c.*1702–14			1:24
The Kriegstein Collection, USA	Admiral's Barge	*c.*1710			1:20
The Kriegstein Collection, USA	Admiral's Barge	*c.*1720			1:24
The Kriegstein Collection, USA	Ship's Long Boat	*c.*1750			1:48
The Kriegstein Collection, USA	*Diamond*	1708	44–50	Fourth Rate	1:48
Science Museum, London, UK	*Prince* (Inv. 1895–56)	1670	100	First Rate	1:48
Science Museum, London, UK	Unidentified (Inv. 1869–66)	*c.*1700	60	Fourth Rate	
Science Museum, London, UK	Unidentified (Inv. 1881–51)	1719–33	20	Sixth Rate	1:48
Science Museum, London, UK	Unidentified (Inv. 1931–19)	*c.*1706–30	90	Second Rate	1:70
Science Museum, London, UK	*Captain* (Inv. 1917–2)	1708	70	Third Rate	1:60
Science Museum, London, UK	Unidentified	1712–14	70	Third Rate	
Science Museum, London, UK	Unidentified (Inv. 1938–630)	*c.*1707	40	Fifth Rate	1:72
Science Museum, London, UK	Unidentified (Inv. 1939–248)	1702–04	60	Fourth Rate	
Science Museum, London, UK	Unidentified (Inv. 1905–161)	*c.*1719	80	Third Rate	1:60
Maritime Museum of Russia, St Petersburg	Unidentified	*c.*1687–92	50	Fourth Rate	1:48
Maritime Museum of Russia, St Petersburg	*Svyataya Anna*	1719	18		
Maritime Museum of Russia, St Petersburg	*Rossia*	1728	32		
Maritime Museum of Russia, St Petersburg	*Royal George*	1715	100	First Rate	
Maritime Museum of Russia, St Petersburg	Possibly *Seymour/Solebay*	Late 17th century	26	Sixth Rate	
Maritime Museum of Russia, St Petersburg	Possibly *Deptford* or *Sedgemoor*	1687	48–50	Fourth Rate	

Maritime Museum of Russia, St Petersburg	*Royal Sovereign*	1701	100	First Rate	1:48
Maritime Museum of Russia, St Petersburg	18-gun Russian ship	1698	18		
Maritime Museum of Russia, St Petersburg	*Sviatoy Andrey*	*c.*1720	88		
Trinity House, Hull, UK	Unidentified	*c.*1702–14		Yacht	
Trinity House, London, UK	*Prince Royal* (20th century)	1610			
Trinity House, London, UK	*Charles*	*c.*1668–70	96	First Rate	1:36
Trinity House, London, UK	*St Albans*	1687	56	Fourth Rate	1:48
Art Gallery of Ontario, Toronto, Canada	Unidentified	*c.*1692	70	Third Rate	1:48
Art Gallery of Ontario, Toronto, Canada	*Nightingale*	1702	20–24	Sixth Rate	1:48
Art Gallery of Ontario, Toronto, Canada	Unidentified	*c.*1703–10	50–54	Fourth Rate	1:48
Pitt-Rivers Museum, Oxford, UK	*Lizard* (Ac. No. 1886.1.1666)	1697	24	Sixth Rate	1:48
Pitt-Rivers Museum, Oxford, UK	*Charles Galley* – Frigate (Ac. No. 1886.1.1667)	1693–1702	32–40	Fifth Rate	1:64/65
Pitt-Rivers Museum, Oxford, UK	Unidentified (Acc. No. 1886.1.1665)	1706	70	Third Rate	1:48
National Museums Liverpool, UK	*St George*	1701	90	First Rate	1:48
National Museums Liverpool, UK	Unidentified	*c.*1677	90	Second Rate	1:48
Statens Sjöhistoriska Museum, Stockholm, Sweden	Possibly *Riks–Applet*	*c.*1650–61	84–86		1:48
Statens Sjöhistoriska Museum, Stockholm, Sweden	*Victoria*	1683	70		
Orlogsmuseet, Copenhagen, Denmark	*Elefanten*	1687	24	Danish Royal Yacht	
Orlogsmuseet, Copenhagen, Denmark	*Tre Löver*	1689	70		
Museo Naval, Madrid, Spain	Unidentified	*c.*1764	76		1:24

Museo Naval, Madrid, Spain	Unidentified	*c.*1767	26		1:16
Mapperton House, Dorset, UK	*Queen*	1693	100	First Rate	1:72
Mapperton House, Dorset, UK	Unidentified	*c.*1710	70	Third Rate	1:48
Dover Museum, Kent, UK	Unidentified (half-model)	*c.*1715–20	50	Fourth Rate	1:48
Cawdor Castle, Nairnshire, UK	*Victory*	1737	100	First Rate	1:48
Smithsonian Institution, Washington, USA	Unidentified	*c.*1730	60–64	Fourth Rate	1:48
Heeresgeschichtliches Museum, Vienna, Austria	*Hope*	1678	70	Third Rate	1:48
Private collection	Unidentified	*c.*1720	8		1:48
New York Yacht Club, New York, USA	Possibly *London*	*c.*1670–79	96	First Rate	1:54
Private collection, formerly at the Institute of Chicago, USA	*Royal Anne*	1704	96–100	First Rate	1:48
Musée National de la Marine, Paris, France	Unidentified	*c.*1694		Royal Yacht	
Maritime Museum, Bergen, Norway	Unidentified	*c.*1706	*c.* 100	First Rate	
Private collection, formerly in the collection of Lord Sandwich, UK	*Fubbs* (possibly a proposal)	*c.*1682–94		Royal Yacht	1:32
Museum of Fine Arts, Boston, USA	*Royal George*	1715	100	First Rate	1:64
Riverside Museum, Glasgow, UK	*Oxford*	*c.*1727	54	Fourth Rate	1:48
Christie's South Kensington Sale now Private Collection,	Unidentified	*c.*1710–20	44–54	Fourth Rate	1:48
Private Collection	Unidentified	*c.*1705	100	First Rate	1:48
Portland Collection	*Henrietta*	*c.*1679		Royal Yacht	1:32
Private Collection	Possibly *Rouby*	1687		Fourth Rate	
Edinburgh Castle, UK	Possibly *Rippon* (20th century)	1712	60	Third Rate	
Wilton House, Wiltshire, UK	*Essex*	1679–92	70	Third Rate	1:48

Glossary

Board of Admiralty (often simply 'the Admiralty'): The administrative body with responsibility to enact the government's naval policy and oversee the Navy Board.

Aft: A directional term relating to the stern or after part of a vessel.

Amidships (sometimes 'midships'): The middle section of a vessel.

Apron: A timber found behind the lower stem and above the foremost end of the keel.

Athwartships: Across a ship sideways, perpendicular to the line of the keel.

Balusters: Ornamental pillars or pilasters of the balcony or galleries on the stern of a ship.

Baroque: European artistic style, late sixteenth to early eighteenth centuries, which was characterised by movement in form and ostentatious decoration.

Beakhead: The projection or platform immediately forward of the forecastle.

Beam: (1) The transverse measurement of a ship at the widest point, i.e. its breadth. (2) transverse structural timber supporting the deck.

Belfry: The structure which holds a ship's bell.

Bilge: Internally, the space either side of the ship's keel – the lowest point within a ship. Externally, it refers to the point at which at which the sides of the hull curved through the 45-degree angle between horizontal and vertical.

Bilge Pumps: A hand-powered machine for removing unwanted water from the lowest part of the hold either side of the keel amidships.

Bitts: Set of large vertical timbers fixed in the hull and used for securing cables, hawsers or ropes.

Block: A type of pulley, made up of a wooden case surrounded by a strop, into which a sheave is fitted.

Block Model: A ship model made out of layers of solid wood as an accurate but simple and robust representation of a ship's hull design.

Bow: The foremost portion of a vessel, opposite of the stern.

Bowsprit: A spar running out from a ship's bow.

Breadth: The width of the ship at its widest point, either measured to exclude the planking, known as 'moulded breadth', or to include the planking as 'extreme breadth'. As the Navy Board models do not include planking below the wales, the dimension given in this book is 'moulded breadth', usually taken just below the main wale.

Breast Hook: A large horizontal knee situated at in the bow of a vessel to provide structural reinforcement at the junction between the sides of the hull and the stem post.

Bulkhead: A vertical partition dividing a ship's hull into compartments.

Bulwark: The sides of a vessel above the upper deck.

Cant Frames: Angled frames at the bow and stern of a vessel.

Capstan: A vertical cylindrical machine mounted and used for moving heavy loads, such as raising anchor or lifting yards. It was operated by manpower pushing on bars inserted into the body, or later into square holes, known as pigeon holes, on the drumhead of the capstan.

Carling: Timbers situated perpendicularly between the deck beams to support the deck planking.

Caryatid: A sculpted figure, usually female, which served as a column to support an entablature, or in the case of ship models, usually supporting a bulkhead or rail.

Cathead: A heavy timber projecting at an angle from the bow of a ship, onto which the anchor is secured in a process known as 'catting the anchor'.

Chainplate: Iron straps or bands, bolted to the ship's side, used to anchor the lower ends of the deadeyes for the shrouds.

Channel: A shortening of 'chainwale', literally the 'wale' that takes the 'chains' which hold the deadeyes.

Chase Port: A gun port at the bow or stern of a ship, used to fire directly ahead when in pursuit of the enemy, or astern, when being pursued by the enemy.

Chinoiserie: A stylistic term denoting a European style in the arts which reflected and mimicked Chinese art and design.

Coach: The forward part of the cabin under the poop deck.

Cuirass: A piece of armour covering the human chest and back.

Cutwater: The forward part of a ship's stem.

Deadeye: A circular piece of wood, through which three holes are pierced. They are used in pairs, rigged with rope lanyards between, to secure the shroud to the chainplate.

Deadwood: Solid timbering found just above the keel where the hull narrows at the bow and stern.

Deck: Horizontal platform, made up of planking supported by beams, which form the ship's floors on which people can stand.

Deck Pillar: Vertical timber used to support the deck from below the beams.

Depth of Hold: The height of the inside of the hull in midships from the top of the keel to the lower edge of the deck beam of the lower deck.

Draught: (1) See Ship Plan (2) The depth a ship draws in the water.

Draught Marks: A series of numbers, often in the form of Roman numerals, marked on the stem and stern posts, to indicate the level at which the hull of a ship drawing below the waterline.

Drumhead: The top part of a capstan barrel, which is pierced with square holes to take the bars.

Figurehead: An ornamental carved figure mounted on the bow of a ship. In the seventeenth and eighteenth centuries, a carved lion rampant was often used on Royal Navy ships.

Floor Timber: The lowest framing timber, spanning the keel athwartships.

Forecastle (pronounced 'fo'c'sle'): The area below the foredeck; this was normally where the galley stove was housed.

Fore-and-aft: Lengthways on a ship, i.e. parallel to the keel.

Foremast: The forward most mast on a ship, except for the bowsprit.

Frame: A transverse timber, usually consisting of multiple timbers spanning the keel athwartships, the ribs of a ship.

Futtock: A framing timber, or rib, assembled above the floor timber.

Gallery: The structure at the stern of a ship, which includes balconies or windows. Often it forms the officers' accommodation and toilet.

Galley: The area on board ship where food was prepared and cooked, which included the galley stove.

Garboard Strake: The lowest hull plank, adjacent to the keel.

Georgian Model: A style of ship model common from the mid-eighteenth century, characterised by a more realistic finish of fully planked lower hull.

Gratings: A wooden hatch cover made up of cross battens and ledges to provide access, light and fresh air below and between decks.

Gudgeons: The metal socket fixed to the stern post, which together with the pintle forms the hinge that supports and gives free movement to the rudder.

Gun Deck: A deck that carries the guns. On three-decked ships, these are the upper, middle and lower gun decks.

Gunport: An opening in the side of a ship's hull through which guns mounted inside the ship can fire.

Hawse Hole: A round hole in the bow of a ship through which the anchor cable passes.

Hawse Pieces (sometimes 'hawse timbers'): The vertical frames each side at the bow, through which the hawse holes are cut.

Headrails: Curved timber rails that extend round the bow.

High-relief: A style of sculptural carving where the designs are raised to more than half the mass of the figures projecting from the background, giving it a three-dimensional quality.

Inwales: A longitudinal structural piece on the inside the hull.

Jeer Capstan: An extra capstan between the fore and mainmast.

Keel: The main longitudinal timber of a vessel. It forms the backbone of the hull.

Keelson: An internal longitudinal timber fixed on top of the floor timbers along the same line as the keel.

Knee: An angular timber used to reinforce the joint between two timbers.

Larboard: An older term for the port side of a ship, i.e. the left side when facing forward.

Ledges: Timbers situated perpendicularly between the carlings to support the deck planking.

Length of Gun Deck: The distance between the aft-side of the rabbet of the stem post to the fore-side of the rabbet of the stern post. But as John Franklin states 'it is probable that the actual "as built" length given in the ship lists is to the outside of plank'. As a result, this book uses this measurement for the models.

Length of Keel: The length of keel can be measured in a number of ways; the measurement used for the models in this book is the 'touch', which can be defined as the distance from the aft end of the keel to the point where the rabbet of the stem begins to curve up from the keel. The keel length given for ships was often the 'length of keel for tonnage' which could vary but generally was the length of the gun deck minus three-fifths of the breadth. This did not bear a relationship to the actual length of the keel, but could be used to calculate tonnage.

Lower Finishing: A fixture supporting the base of a quarter gallery, and was often decoratively carved.

Mainmast: The principal mast of a ship; on three-masted ships it is the middle mast.

Mizzen Mast: The aft-most mast of a three-masted ship.

Moulding: A light length of wood fitted as a decorative feature.

Navy Board: The administrative body responsible for managing Royal Navy shipbuilding and the Royal Dockyards, subordinate to the more senior Admiralty.

Pawl: A short bar that engages with the toothed pawl ring below or either side of the whelps of a capstan or windlass to stop it recoiling.

Pintle: A bolt or pin fitted to the rudder which slots into the gudgeon to form the hinge that supports and allows free movement of the rudder.

Piss-dales: A type of urinal fitted inboard on the bulwarks.

Planking: The flat pieces of wood, which together form strakes, which are secured onto a ship's framing to create the hull.

Poop Deck: The highest and aft-most deck of a ship.

Port: The left side of a ship if facing forward (also known as larboard).

Putti: Italian for 'boys', the name given to the chubby infants often seen in Baroque art.

Quarter Deck: The raised deck aft of the mainmast; generally, this was from where the captain commanded the ship.

Rabbet: A type of rebate, or recess, cut into a timber to house the edge of planks fitted to it. The upper edges of the keel are rabbeted to receive the edge of the garboard strake, and the stem and stern posts are rabbeted to receive the ends, known as hoods, of the hull planking.

Rate: The six groups into which sailing warships can be divided, based on number of guns carried. Officially introduced to the Royal Navy in the 1750s, it is often used to classify ships before this time.

Roundhouse: Small structures built at the beakhead bulkhead which housed toilets.

Round Tuck: The lower part of the stern which was formed by running the planking in a smooth sweep round the bottom of the stern, as opposed to the square tuck stern which was formed by flat planking either side of the stern post.

Rowle: The rugby-ball-shaped piece of wood mounted on a spindle in the deck, through which the whipstaff passes to connect to the forward end of the tiller. The rowle acts as a pivot, enabling the helmsman to control the tiller via the whipstaff.

Rowlocks: A fixture mounted on the gunwales upon which an oar can pivot during rowing.

Rudder: The large wooden structure fitted centrally to the stern post, used to steer the ship.

Scarph (sometimes 'scarf'): A joint between two pieces of wood, it involves the shaping of the members to create a larger surface area to join.

Scupper: A hole in a ship's side to allow water to escape from the deck.

Shallop: A small boat, usually a light barge with a round and bluff bow, used for transporting people along a river or to convey them to a ship at anchor in a river or estuary.

Ship Plan (also 'draught' or 'lines plan'): The diagram of a ship drawn on paper to show the design, consisting of three views: the sheer plan, showing the longitudinal section; the body plan, showing the vertical cross-sections of a ship; and the half-breadth plan, showing half of the hull in plan-view.

Shrouds: The ropes supporting the masts athwartships and forming part of the standing rigging.

Spar: A wooden pole used to carry a sail.

Square Tuck: The lower part of the stern built flat either side of the stern post, as opposed to the round tuck which was formed by running the planking in a smooth sweep round the bottom of the stern.

Stanchion: A vertical timber, or post, supporting a deck beam or similar structures, such as guardrails and screens.

Starboard: The right of a vessel when facing the bow, opposite to port.

Stays: The fore-and-aft ropes supporting the masts and forming part of the standing rigging.

Stem Post: An upright timber mounted at the forward end of the keel onto which the hull planks are secured. The stem post is a major structural element in any wooden vessel.

Stern Post: An upright timber mounted at the aft end of the keel onto to which the hull planks are secured. The stern post is a major structural element in any wooden vessel.

Strake: A strake consists of a series of planks joined (scarphed) end to end.

Swifter: A rope connecting the ends of the capstan bars, providing further accommodation when weighing anchor – as the swifter itself could be manned in addition to the bars.

Taffrail (sometimes 'tafferel'): The curved timber at the top of the stern of a ship, usually decorated with elaborate carving.

Trailboard: A carved board either side of the stem post to support the figurehead. It was often highly decorated with carved work.

Transom: The timbers across the stern of a ship.

Waist: The area of a ship's upper deck between the forecastle and quarter deck.

Wale: A thicker strake of planking on side of a ship to strengthen the hull.

Waterline: The line around a ship's hull which corresponds to the level of the surface of the water when the ship is afloat.

Whelp: Vertical projections on a capstan drum, they provide extra grip for the rope or cable as the capstan is turned.

Whipstaff: A long vertical pole extending from the forward end of the tiller through the rowle to the deck above. It is used by the helmsman to control the rudder.

Windlass: A small horizontal capstan-like winch, fitted at the forward end of a smaller vessel, used for weighing anchor.

Woolding: A series of rope bands lashed around a made-up mast to strengthen it.

Yard: A wooden pole on a mast from which sails are set.

Notes

Introduction

1 Alistair Roach, 'The Ashmolean Ship Model', *Mariner's Mirror*, vol. 93, iss. 2, 2007
2 L.G. Carr Laughton, 'The Study of Ship Models', *Mariner's Mirror*, 1925
3 Geoffrey Callender, *Catalogue of the Caird Collection of Old Ship Models*, Greenwich, 1930
4 John Franklin, *Navy Board Ship Models 1650–1750*, Conway Maritime Press, 1989

Historical Background

1 Phineas Pett, *The Autobiography of Phineas Pett*, Navy Records Society, 1635, pp.156–7
2 Peter Munday, *The Travels of Peter Munday*, Hakluyt Society VLV, quoted in Franklin, *Navy Board Ship Models 1650–1750*, Conway Maritime Press, 1989, p.179
3 Brian Lavery and Simon Stephens, *Ship Models: Their Purpose and Development from 1650 to the Present*, Zwemmer, 1995
4 British Library, Additional Manuscripts, Letter from Admiralty Committee to Navy Commissioners, 1 April 1649. (Note that during the Commonwealth (1649–1660) the Navy Board became known as the 'Navy Commissioners'.)
5 Samuel Johnson, *A Dictionary of the English Language*, vol. II, 6th edn, London, 1765, p.144
6 Thomas Miller, *The Complete Modellist, Shewing the Exact Way of Raising the Model of Any Ship Or Vessel, Small Or Great, either in proportion, or out of proportion*, London, 1667
7 Brian Lavery and Simon Stephens, *Ship Models: Their Purpose and Development from 1650 to the Present*, Zwemmer, 1995
8 Brian Lavery and Simon Stephens, *Ship Models: Their Purpose and Development from 1650 to the Present*, Zwemmer, 1995, p.14
9 The National Archives (TNA), ADM 106/321/100, 13 March 1677, Navy Board In-Letters, Misc.
10 TNA, ADM 2 1732 f.49, 12th October 1660
11 Christopher Pett (1620–68) was the brother of Peter Pett (1610–72). Robert Latham and William Matthews, *The Diary of Samuel Pepys*, vol. IV, London: G. Bell and Sons Ltd, 1970, 24 December 1663, p.433
12 Coventry was an influential figure in the Restoration of the monarchy in 1660; MP for Great Yarmouth as well as Commissioner of the Navy. Robert Latham and William Matthews, *The Diary of Samuel Pepys*, vol. IV, London: G. Bell and Sons Ltd, 1970, 30 December 1663, p.437
13 Bodleian (BOD) Rawlinson MS. A.189, f.197, *Proposals for rectifying irregularities in Deptford dock-yard, presented to the King by one desirous of being pointed master builder there.*
14 BOD Rawlinson MS. A.172, f.26
15 R.D. Merriman, 'Gilbert Wardlaw's Allegations', *Mariner's Mirror*, xxxviii (1952), p.127
16 NMM, Sergison Papers, Navy Board Minutes, SER 41
17 Navy Records Society, *Queen Anne's Navy*, 12 October 1708, 23 (a)
18 TNA, ADM 106/3551
19 Nick Ball, 'Block Models: Change and Control in Early 18th Century Naval Shipbuilding in Britain', *Proceedings of the International Symposium on Boat and Ship Archaeology, National Maritime Museum of Poland, Gdansk, 21–25 September 2015*, pp.153–9
20 Conte Lorenzo Magalotti, 1637–1712, *Travels of Cosmo the Third, Grand Duke of Tuscany, through England during the Reign of King Charles the Second* (1669), translated from the Italian manuscript in the Laurentian library at Florence. To which is Prefixed, a Memoir of his Life, London, 1821, p.346
21 Peter Thornton, *Seventeenth Century Interior Decoration in England France and Holland*, Yale University Press, 1983, pp.296–7; Liza Picard, *Restoration London*, Phoenix, 1997, p.37
22 Robert Latham and William Matthews, *The Diary of Samuel Pepys*, vol. III, London: G. Bell and Sons Ltd, 1970, 3 August 1662, p.154
23 John Evelyn, William Bray (ed), *The Diary of John Evelyn*, vol. 1, New York and London: M. Walter Dunne, 1901, 10th August 1663, p.369

24 K.P. Guber and A.A. Tron, *The Maritime Museum of Russia*, 2016, p.15

25 N.A.M. Rodger, *The Command of the Ocean: A Naval History of Britain, 1649–1815*, Penguin, 2006, p.96

26 Robert Latham and William Matthews, *The Diary of Samuel Pepys*, vol. III, London: G. Bell and Sons Ltd, 1970, 6 June 1662, p.103

27 J.R. Tanner, *Samuel Pepys's Naval Minutes*, Navy Records Society, 1925, p.246

28 Robert Latham and William Matthews, *The Diary of Samuel Pepys*, vol.VIII, London: G. Bell and Sons Ltd, 1970, 19 June 1667, p.279

29 Robert Latham and William Matthews, *The Diary of Samuel Pepys*, vol.VIII, London: G. Bell and Sons Ltd, 1970, 19 June 1667, p.279

30 TNA, PROB 11/483/275, Will of Fisher Harding, Builder of Deptford, Kent, 12 November 1705

31 J.R. Tanner, *Samuel Pepys's Naval Minutes*, Navy Records Society, 1925, p.374; E.H. Pearce, *Annals of Christ's Hospital*, London: Methuen & Co., 1901, p.123

32 Isle of Wight Record Office, ABY/1035 JER/HBY/104/2

33 'The Sale Room', *The Times*, 18 November 1938

34 Samuel Johnson, *A Dictionary of the English Language*, vol. II, 6th edn, London, 1765, p.144

35 George Savile, 1st Marquess of Halifax, *A Rough Draft of a New Model at Sea* (1694)

36 Robert Latham and William Matthews, *The Diary of Samuel Pepys*, vol. II, London: G. Bell and Sons Ltd, 1970, 5 October 1661, p.193

37 Robert Latham and William Matthews, *The Diary of Samuel Pepys*, vol. III, London: G. Bell and Sons Ltd, 1970, 12 August 1662, p.163

38 Sir Henry Mainwaring, *The Life and Works of Sir Henry Mainwaring*, vol. II, Navy Records Society, pp.85–6

39 Robert Latham and William Matthews, *The Diary of Samuel Pepys*, vol. III, London: G. Bell and Sons Ltd, 1970, 26 July 1662, p.146

40 'The third Parliament of Charles II: First session – begins 6/3/1679', in Chandler, *The History and Proceedings of the House of Commons: Volume 1, 1660-1680* (London, 1742), pp.323–70. British History Online, www.british-history.ac.uk/commons-hist-proceedings/vol1/pp323-370 [accessed 27 July 2017]

41 J.R. Tanner, *Samuel Pepys's Naval Minutes*, Navy Records Society, 1925, p.239

42 J.R. Tanner, *Samuel Pepys's Naval Minutes*, Navy Records Society, 1925, p.239

43 J.R. Tanner, *Samuel Pepys's Naval Minutes*, Navy Records Society, 1925, p.222

44 E. Chappell, *The Tangier Papers of Samuel Pepys*, Navy Records Society, 1935, 25 April 1684, p.324. This Phineas Pett (1628–78) was the grandson of shipbuilder Phineas Pett (1570–1647) and the nephew of Commissioner Peter Pett (1610–72). Sir Henry Johnson was the owner of the Blackwall Yard where many East Indiamen were built

45 *The Daily Post*, London, 28 March 1724

46 Captain Charles Hatton to Pepys, 28 September 1700 in Lord Braybrooke (ed.), *Memoirs of Samuel Pepys, Esq. F.R.S.*, vol.V, London: H. Colburn, 1828, p.350

47 17 June 1702, 'Bishop Nicolson's Diaries: Part II', *Transactions of the Cumberland and Westmorland Antiquarian & Archaeological Society*, vol. II, W.G. Collingwood (ed.), Kendal: T. Wilson, 1902, p.164

48 Henry B. Wheatley (ed.), *Diary of Samuel Pepys M.A. F.R.S*, London: George Bell & Sons, 1899, Appendix I, Pepys's Will, p.264

49 John Aubrey, *Natural History of Surrey and Antiquities of the County of Surrey*, 1719

50 Grant Walker, *The Rogers Collection of Dockyard Models At the US Naval Academy Museum*, Vol. 1, SeaWatch Books, 2015

51 *Evening Post*, London, 14 March 1709

52 *The Daily Advertiser*, London, 10 February 1778

53 *A New and Compleat Survey of London*, by Citizen, and native of London, 1742, p.716

54 NMM, AGC /13/25, 10 Nov 1747

55 Brian Lavery and Simon Stephens, *Ship Models: Their Purpose and Development from 1650 to the Present*, Zwemmer, 1995, p.78

56 Phineas Pett, *The Autobiography of Phineas Pett*, Navy Records Society, p.14

57 Ashmolean Book of Benefactors, Ashmolean Library,

AMS2, 1683–1766. Reproduced as Microfiche 1 in A. MacGregor, *Tradescant Rarities*, Oxford, 1983

58 Phineas Pett, *The Autobiography of Phineas Pett*, Navy Records Society, p.31

59 Robert Latham and William Matthews, *The Diary of Samuel Pepys*, vol. III, London: G. Bell and Sons Ltd, 1970, 9 August 1662, p.160

60 TNA, ADM 42/1

61 TNA, ADM 106/321/100 Navy Board: Records In-Letters, Misc., 13 March 1677

62 TNA ADM 106/321/255 Navy Board: Records In-Letters, Misc., 16 July 1677

63 TNA, ADM 106/321/100, Navy Board In-Letters, Misc., 13 March 1677

64 R.D. Merriman, 'Gilbert Wardlaw's Allegations', *Mariner's Mirror*, xxxviii (1952), pp.115, 127

65 *London Journal*, Saturday, 27 November 1725; issue CCCXXXI, 17th–18th Century Burney Collection Newspapers

66 National Maritime Museum, POR/A/7 Navy Board Warrants 1721–27, Portsmouth Dockyard

67 Brian Lavery and Simon Stephens, *Ship Models: Their Purpose and Development from 1650 to the Present*, Zwemmer, 1995, p.37

68 T.F. Hoad (ed.), *The Concise Oxford Dictionary of English Etymology*, Oxford University Press, 1996

69 TNA, ADM 106/1021/29

70 TNA, ADM 106/1021/30

71 John Stalker and George Parker, *A Treatise of Japaning and varnishing*, 1688

72 TNA, ADM 106/1007/147. George Elphick was referred to specifically as a 'japanner' in a loan agreement made with his brother-in-law. See Essex Record Office, SAY/1342, 4 Nov 1723

73 TNA, ADM 106/1103/122, 23 June 1752

74 TNA, SP 16/350/70, State Papers Domestic, Charles I, 'His Maties directions for the manner and forme of painting and guilding his great shipp', 23 March 1636

75 Thomas Heywood, *A True Description of His Majesty's Royall Ship, Built in this Yeare 1637, at Woolwich in Kent. To the great glory of our English Nation, and not pareleld in the whole Christian World*, 1637

76 Horace Walpole, *Anecdotes of Painting in England*, 1849, vol. ii, p.551

77 Andrew Peters, *Ship Decoration, 1630–1780*, Seaforth, 2013, p.117

78 Andrew Peters, *Ship Decoration, 1650–1780*, Seaforth, 2013, p.118

79 W.G. Perrin, 'The Ornamentation of Men-of-War, 1703', Documents, *Mariner's Mirror*, vol. III, 1913, p.20

80 James Taylor, *Marine Painting Images of Sail Sea and Shore*, Studio Editions, 1995, p.35

81 'Charles II: January 1674 [New Style]', in *Calendar of State Papers Domestic: Charles II, 1673–5*, ed. F H Blackburne Daniell (London, 1904), pp.90–132. British History Online http://www.british-history.ac.uk/cal-state-papers/domestic/chas2/1673-5/pp90-132 [accessed 6 November 2017]

82 George H. Chettle, *The Queens House, Greenwich*, National Maritime Museum, London, 1937

83 Remmelt Daalder, *Van de Velde & Son, Marine Painters The firm of Willem van de Velde the Elder and Willem van de Velde the Younger, 1640–1707*, translated by Michael Hoyle, Primavera Pers, Leiden, 2016, p.177

84 Bainbrigg Buckeridge, 'An Essay towards the English School of Painters', in Rodger de Piles, *The Art of Painting with the lives and Characters of above 300 of the most eminent Painters*, translated from the French, London, 1706, pp.398–480.

85 Bainbrigg Buckeridge, 'An Essay towards the English School of Painters', in Rodger de Piles, *The Art of Painting with the lives and Characters of above 300 of the most eminent Painters*, translated from the French, London, 1706, p.431

86 John Munday, *E.W. Cooke: A Man of His Time, 1811–1880*, Antiques Collectors' Club, 1996, p.246; Lavery and Stephens, *Ship Models,* Zwemmer, 1995, p.41; Pieter van der Merwe, 'Turner's Ship Models: An Unrecognised Napoleonic Incursion', *Turner Society News*, 124 (Autumn 2015), pp.10–14; Clarkson Stanfield owned a number of models, some of which are accessioned in the NMM collections including a Thames Peter boat (ZBA4129); W.L. Wyllie depicted a number of ship models, including a two-decker Navy Board model

(PAE2347) and another of *Victory* (PAE3413) in the NMM collection.

87 Arnold and Henry Kriegstein, *17th and 18th Century Ship Models from the Kriegstein Collection*, SeaWatch Books, 2010, p.222

88 Celina Fox, 'King George and the Royal Navy', in *The Wisdom of King George III*, Royal Collection Publication, 2005, p.305

Construction and Materials

1 The *Mary Rose*, launched in 1511, sank in the Solent in 1545, and was famously recovered during archaeological excavation in 1982. The *Vasa*, launched in 1628, sank on its maiden voyage in the harbour of Stockholm, and was raised intact in 1961. Each is on display, at Portsmouth and Stockholm respectively.

2 Callender, *Catalogue of the Caird Collection of Old Ship Models*, Greenwich, 1930

3 John Franklin, *Navy Board Ship Models,* 1989

4 John Franklin, *Navy Board Ship Models,* 1989, p.6

5 John Evelyn, *Silva,* London, 1679, pp.66–7

6 Brian Lavery, *Arming and Fitting of English Ships of War 1600–1815*, Conway (1987), p.176

7 W. Patrick Edwards, 'Why Not Period Glue?', *Journal of the Society of American Period Furniture Makers*, November 2001, p.2

8 Brian Lavery and Simon Stephens, *Ship Models: Their Purpose and Development from 1650 to the Present*, Zwemmer, 1995, p.26

9 *The British legacy: or, fountain of knowledge*, London, printed for Thomas Chandler, 1754, p.79

10 John Franklin, *Navy Board Ship Models 1650–1750*, Conway Maritime Press (1989), p.45

11 See illustrations in Franklin, *Navy Board Models,* p.11.

12 Peter Goodwin, *The Construction and Fitting of The Sailing Man-of-War 1650–1850*, p.40

13 W.G. Perrin, 'The Ornamentation of Men-of-War, 1703', Documents, *Mariner's Mirror*, vol. III, 1913, p.20

14 Science Museum, Inv. 1908–46, *Rigging and Sail Plans of the Establishment of 1719, Scale 1:72.* See G.S. Laird Clowes, *Sailing Ships Their History and Development*, part II, p.35

15 James Lees, *Masting and Rigging English Ships of War 1625–1860*, Naval Institute Press, 1984

Catalogue

1 R.C. Anderson to Geoffrey Callender, 9 December 1932, NMM Archives

2 Richard Endsor

3 'The Sale Room', *The Times*, 18 November 1938

4 Brian Lavery, *Ship of the Line*, Conway, 1983, pp.35–7.

5 R.C. Anderson to Geoffrey Callender, 9/12/1932, NMM archives

6 J. McMorrow, internal memorandum, NMM, p.105

7 J. McMorrow, internal memorandum, NMM, p.106

8 J. McMorrow, internal memorandum, NMM, p.106

9 The model was positively identified by naval historian Richard Endsor

10 For a detailed explanation of the *Peregrine Galley*'s potential sail plan, see Ian McLaughlan, *The Sloop of War 1650–1763*, Seaforth, 2014, pp.97–9

11 Tony Dalton, *British Royal Yachts*, Halsgrove, 2002, p.66

12 TNA, ADM 91/2, 9 May 1740

13 José Ignacio González-Aller Hierro, *Modelos de Arsenal del Museo Naval: evolución de la construcción naval española, siglos XVII–XVIII*, Lunwerg Editores, 2004.

14 John Franklin, *Navy Board Ship Models*, Conway, 1989, p.170

Legacy of the Navy Board Models

1 Philip Reed, *Building a Miniature Navy Board Model*, Seaforth, 2009, p.7

2 Arnold and Henry Kriegstein, *17th and 18th Century Ship Models from the Kriegstein Collection*, 2nd edn, SeaWatch Books, 2010

3 K.P. Guber and A. A. Tron, *The Maritime Museum of Russia*, 2016, p.147

Further Reading

Ships and Shipbuilding

Deane, Anthony, and Brian Lavery (ed), *Deane's Doctrine of Naval Architecture 1670*, London, Conway Maritime Press (1986)

Endsor, Richard, *The Restoration Warship*, Conway Maritime Press (2009)

———, *The Anne*, Conway (2017)

Fox, Frank, *Great Ships the Battlefleet of Charles II*, Conway Maritime Press (1980)

Gardiner, Robert, *The Sailing Frigate: A History in Ship Models*, Seaforth (2012)

Goodwin, Peter, *Sailing Man of War*, Conway Maritime Press (1987)

Lavery, Brian, *Arming and Fitting of English Ships of War 1600–1815*, Conway Maritime Press (1987)

———, *The Ship of the Line: A History in Ship Models*, Seaforth (2014)

Lees, James, *The Masting and Rigging of English Ships of War 1625–1860*, Conway Maritime Press (1979)

Lyon, David, *Sailing Navy List*, Conway Maritime Press (1993)

McLaughlan, Ian, *The Sloop of War 1650–1763*, Seaforth (2014)

Winfield, Rif, *The 50-Gun Ship: A Complete History*, Mercury Books (1997)

———, *First Rate*, Seaforth (2010)

———, and David Lyon, *British Warships in the Age of Sail 1603–1714*, Seaforth (2007)

———, and David Lyon, *British Warships in the Age of Sail 1714–1792*, Seaforth (2009)

The Royal Navy

N.A.M. Rodger, *Command of the Ocean: A Naval History of Britain, 1649–1815*, Penguin (2006)

Ship Models

Anderson, R.C., *Catalogue of Ship Models*, HMSO, National Maritime Museum (1952), supplement (1958)

Chatterton, Edward K., *Ship Models*, Herbert & Reiach Ltd (1923)

Culver, H.B., *Contemporary Scale Models of Vessels of the Seventeenth Century*, New York (1926)

Franklin, John, *The Navy Board Ship Models*, Conway Maritime Press (1989)

Kriegstein, Arnold and Henry, *17th and 18th Century Ship Models from the Kriegstein Collection*, SeaWatch Books (2010)

Laird Clowes, G.S., *Sailing Ships: Their History and Development*, Science Museum, HMSO (1936)

Lavery, Brian, and Simon Stephens, *Ship Models: Their Purpose and Development from 1650 to the Present*, Zwemmer (1995)

McArdle, Gilbert, *Building a Navy Board Model of HMS Sussex*, SeaWatch (2010)

McNarry, Donald, *Ship Models in Miniature*, David & Charles (1975)

Morton Nance, R., *Sailing Ship Models* (1924)

Reed, Philip, *Building a Miniature Navy Boat Model*, Seaforth (2009)

Stephens, Simon, *Ship Models: The Thomson Collection at the Art Gallery of Ontario*, Skylet Publishing (2009)

Waite, A.H., *National Maritime Museum Catalogue of Ship Models Part I: Ships of Western Tradition to 1815*, HMSO (1980)

Walker, Grant H., *The Rogers Collection of Dockyard Models at the US Naval Academy Museum*, SeaWatch Books (2015)

Biography

Ollard, Richard, *Man of War: Sir Robert Holmes and the Restoration Navy*, Phoenix Press (2001)

Tomalin, Claire, *Samuel Pepys: The Unequalled Self*, Penguin (2003)

Art

Daalder, Remmelt, *Van de Velde & Son, Marine Painters*, Primavera Pers (2016)

Peters, Andrew, *Ship Decoration 1630–1780*, Seaforth (2013)

Robinson, M.S., *The Paintings of the Willem van de Veldes*, National Maritime Museum, Greenwich (1990)

Taylor, James, *Marine Painting, Images of Sail, Sea and Shore*, Studio Editions (1995)

Index